A GIFT
FOR
YOU . . .

From the
Commission
On Archives
And History,
Missouri Conference

On the Occasion
Of your Ordination
June, 2011

Circuit Riders to Crusades

Circuit Riders to Crusades

Essays in Missouri Methodist History

John O. Gooch

PROVIDENCE HOUSE PUBLISHERS
Franklin, Tennessee

Printed in the United States of America

| 04 | 03 | 02 | 01 | 00 | | 1 | 2 | 3 | 4 | 5 |

Library of Congress Catalog Card Number: 00-102307

ISBN: 1-57736-186-5

Produced for the Commissions on Archives and History of the Missouri East and the Missouri West Annual Conferences 2000.

Cover design by Gary Bozeman

PROVIDENCE HOUSE PUBLISHERS
238 Seaboard Lane • Franklin, Tennessee 37067
800-321-5692
www.providencehouse.com

This book is dedicated to the memory of

William P. Hulse
my great-great-grandfather, pioneer circuit-rider,
founder of First Methodist Church, Independence, Missouri,
who represents the past on which we build,

and to

Kaitlin and Jada Ollivier-Gooch,
my granddaughters, who represent the future
which I will not see, but for which I have great hope,

and, always, to

Beth

CONTENTS

PREFACE

D r. Frank Tucker's ground-breaking history, *The Methodist Church in Missouri, 1798–1939*, appeared in 1966. Like all surveys, it was absolutely essential for the work of the historian, and those of us who follow him will always be in his debt and work in his shadow. But, like all surveys, this work left room for more work. For at least twenty years, the Commissions on Archives and History of the two Missouri Conferences have been saying that we needed to update Dr. Tucker's book, which ended with the events of 1939. But talk was as far as the project went. Finally, in 1997, I made a specific proposal to the Missouri East Commission on Archives and History, which they shared with the Missouri West Commission. That proposal included most of the outline for this present volume. When the two commissions voted to accept the proposal, they asked that a chapter on the years since 1939 be added to the outline. I reluctantly agreed, for recent history is all tied up in memories and emotions, as well as written documents. I am much more comfortable working with the origins of institutions, rather than with their recent past. But, in fact, the chapter they asked to be added grew into two chapters. Those two chapters are the only part of the book that are anything like a survey. In that sense, they are incomplete, for no one can take the history of forty years and boil it down to two chapters without omitting important events and persons. Those two chapters serve the same purpose for the period 1939–1979 that Dr. Tucker's book did for 1798–1939. They only mark out some paths through the history of that period and beg for another historian to explore them in both more breadth and more depth.

The other chapters in this book take a deeper look at some issues and areas that Dr. Tucker was able to touch on only briefly. They are, always, expansions of his pioneering work. And, frankly, they are also areas in which I am personally interested. That is one of the benefits of developing a proposal—one gets to write about the things in which one is most interested.

My junior year in college, I was working in the library, trying to find material for a paper for a course in "History of the South." There I stumbled across a book called *An Unbiased History of the War Between the States—from the Southern Point of View*. That title burned an important lesson into my brain—no history is unbiased, but some histories are more objective than others. With that in mind, it is well to name one's biases and get them out of the way quickly. My roots are deep in the Methodist Episcopal Church, South, and in the St. Louis Annual Conference of the Methodist Church. I served for twenty years in the Missouri East Conference, and am more familiar with the dynamics of its recent history. That familiarity has been both a help and a burden as I tried to write the last two chapters. It was much easier to be objective about events in which I was not involved! As much as possible, I have tried to grow beyond my roots and biases and present a fair picture of the Methodist Church in Missouri. I am sure I did not succeed fully in that endeavor, and ask that as you read you keep in mind both my biases and your own.

This book is an attempt to do serious scholarship in a way that is open and inviting to the general reader. To that end, I have tried to keep notes to a minimum. They appear as endnotes to each chapter, so they are available to those of you who want to explore the sources. Endnotes, almost exclusively, show the sources of direct quotations, not more generalized statements about historical background or happenings in the church. Statistics about the church always come from either the conference minutes or the General Minutes, so I have not noted them.

ACKNOWLEDGMENTS

No book is ever written alone, and I am grateful to many people for their help in gathering materials for this one. Bishop Eugene M. Frank graciously granted time for conversation and shared his own memories and insights into Missouri Methodism. John W. Ward Jr., Gregory K. Poole, and J. C. Montgomery Jr. have shared their memories and insights with me for years. Monk Bryan, Fritz Mutti, and Mrs. Ina Schowengerdt provided materials for the chapter on Missourians who were elected to the episcopacy. James Thogmorton for Central Methodist College, Susan Sonnenday Vogel for St. Paul, David Atkins for the Foundation, and Mel West for Creative Ministries were generous in their sharing of information related to their institutions. Rhymes Moncure and Michele Sue Shumake-Keller read drafts of some of the chapters and their comments helped shape the final form. I am more grateful than words can ever say to my wife, Beth Gooch, who read drafts of each chapter and helped me see where there was too much jargon or too much assumption about what readers might know. Andrew Miller of Providence House Publishers was a gracious and helpful editor and publisher. His work helped us get the book to you in a timely way. David Bell of the Missouri East Commission on Archives and History and Tom Van Zant of the Missouri West Commission were generous in their moral support and encouragement. The two commissions made it possible financially for the research, writing, and publishing to take place. Above all, Joy Dodson, the Reference Librarian at Central Methodist College, provided help in locating resources, and made available the archival collection at the college, along with space to work through many long days. For each of these people, and for many others, I am deeply grateful. As always, the mistakes in the book are my own, not theirs.

Chapter 1

PIONEER CIRCUITS AND CIRCUIT RIDERS 1804–1821

The first Methodist preaching in what is now Missouri was apparently in the summer of 1798, near present-day Herculaneum, when John Clark preached at a spot called Bates Rock. Pious Methodist legend has it that Clark was smuggled across the Mississippi in a canoe and preached at night, in secret. What later became Missouri was then a part of Spanish Louisiana, and Protestant preaching was forbidden in the territory. Frank Tucker points out that this rule was honored more in the breach than in the observance. Clark was a friend of Zenon Trudeau, the Spanish Commandant in St. Louis. Legend says that Trudeau often warned Clark against preaching, but always made sure Clark had returned to Illinois before he sent bailiffs to arrest him. One of the great frustrations for historians of Missouri Methodism is the reality behind the legends about Clark.

John Clark was born in Scotland, in 1758. When he was twenty (during the American Revolution), he joined the British Navy. His naval career was a checkered one, ending by his jumping overboard from a British man-of-war anchored at Charleston, South Carolina. After the war, he settled in Georgia and became a Methodist. On a trip back to England (a risky venture for a deserter from the Navy!) he heard John Wesley preach and was deeply impressed. In 1795, Clark was ordained an elder in the Georgia Conference, and soon departed for Illinois. It was from there he made his clandestine trips across the Mississippi. Tradition says that Clark preached in the home of a Methodist layman named John Patterson, who had come to Missouri from North Carolina in 1800 and settled on Cold Water Creek, in what is now St. Louis County. The question for historians, however, is: did Clark actually organize a Methodist class that had an ongoing existence? There are no clear records of Methodist classes in Missouri before John Travis in 1806. So, while the traditions about John Clark and Cold Water Creek cannot be ignored, there is also not enough evidence to give Clark credit as the founder of Missouri Methodism.

At the conference of 1805, Bishop Asbury appointed Joseph Oglesby to the Illinois Circuit and suggested he explore prospects for Methodism in Missouri. To put this assignment in perspective: in 1804, the United States had taken possession of Louisiana and sent Lewis and Clark to explore this new territory. At conference time in 1805, they were somewhere in the Columbia River valley, still heading west to the Pacific. Oglesby crossed over the Mississippi to St. Charles, and then up the Missouri River as far as the Femme Osage (in present-day St. Charles County). He reported to the conference, "I preached at a number of places, had a good congregation at Mr. Calliway's. . . ." This "Mr. Calliway" was Flanders Callaway, the husband of Jemima Boone and son-in-law of Daniel Boone, to whom Oglesby also talked. From the Calliways', Oglesby crossed to the Murphy Settlement (Farmington) and preached in the home of Sarah Barton Murphy, the founder of the settlement. (Note that not all pioneers and founders were men!) Oglesby reported to the Western Conference in 1806 that there were two hundred likely prospects for Methodist work in Missouri. This may have equaled the entire English-speaking population of Missouri in that year—the circuit riders were always optimistic about their prospects!

Joseph Oglesby was born in Virginia in 1782, and converted in Jefferson County, Kentucky, in 1800. He was admitted on trial into the Western Conference in 1803. The minutes record that he "has been in profession of religion about two years, and has preached as a local preacher, about one year. A man of tolerable gifts, and came well recommended." Oglesby was assigned as junior preacher on the Miami Circuit, Ohio, in 1803, and was appointed to Illinois in 1804. It was as a sideline to his appointment to Illinois that he was asked to explore Methodist prospects in Missouri. W. L. Woodard refers to this expedition in his *Annals* as "pre-historic" in Missouri Methodism. After one year in Illinois/Missouri, Oglesby was appointed to circuits in Indiana, Kentucky, and Tennessee (Nashville) before returning to the Meramec Circuit in Missouri in 1808. This was his last appointment in Missouri, though he continued preaching for many years.

The list of Oglesby's appointments shows one of the reasons Methodism was so successful on the frontier: all the preachers were itinerants. They had no one place or congregation, but traveled circuits of various sizes, depending on the number of settlements. In a new territory like Missouri, the circuits would be very large, and the preacher might take four to six weeks to make the rounds. Wherever there were enough people, he established classes, with a layperson appointed as class leader. These classes were the rudimentary organization of the church, keeping people together while the preacher was making his rounds. The circuit rider preached almost every day, at least once a day, whenever he came upon one of his classes or upon a group of people whom he had not met. He preached in cabins, barns, taverns, and under the trees. Another reason for the circuit rider's success was that he did not look for Methodists to whom to minister; he made Methodists out of the settlers he found, wherever he went. He often arrived before a cabin was finished, or, sometimes, before a settler even unloaded his wagon!

Organized work in Missouri began in 1806 with the appointment of John Travis. About the time of Travis's appointment, Lewis and Clark returned from their epic journey of discovery. During 1806, Zebulon Pike led an expedition to the Rocky Mountains and saw the mountain that was later named for him. In one of the great ironies of exploration, he compared the Great Plains to the deserts of Africa.

During the years 1806–1807, Travis organized two circuits, the "Missourie" and the "Merrimack." The former was north of the Missouri River, the latter south of it and centered on the Meramec River valley. Travis reported to the Western Conference of 1807 that there were fifty-six members in the Missouri Circuit and fifty in the Meramec. This is half of the Methodist prospects that Oglesby had reported the year before. Obviously, more English-speaking people were moving into Upper Louisiana, but Travis had covered only a small geographic area in his work that year. Probably Travis held a camp meeting during that year, with assistance from James Gunn and William McKendree, who was the presiding elder. This was the famous camp meeting in modern St. Charles County, where Methodists held their first Holy Communion in Missouri. They used cornbread and sweetened polkberry juice for the elements. Polkberry juice and iron filings were used for printers' ink, and the juice itself is mildly toxic. Probably not the best choice they could have made! The two pioneer circuits had open boundaries, except where they touched each other. Meramec Circuit included classes on Joachim Creek, on Big River, near Potosi, and somewhere around Manchester. Travis may also have gone as far south as the Murphy Settlement, though this is not clear.

John Travis was born in South Carolina in 1773 and received into the Western Conference in 1806. (The Western Conference was the second Methodist Conference in the United States, and originally embraced all territory belonging to the United States west of the Appalachian Mountains and east of the Mississippi River.) His first appointment was to Missouri, a circuit that existed only in the mind of Bishop Asbury. After his pioneer year in Missouri, Travis was appointed to Mississippi, then to a series of appointments in Tennessee. He married in 1815 and located (discontinued) to a farm in Kentucky. There he studied medicine and became a practicing physician.

Jesse Walker was ordained a deacon at the Western Conference of 1802, and appointed to the Red River Circuit in Tennessee. He was appointed to the Missouri Circuit in 1807. He held two camp meetings in the summer of 1808, one on each side of the Missouri River. Bishop McKendree (who had been elected bishop at the General Conference in May of 1808) attended both of these camp meetings. The two circuits in Missouri reported two hundred members to the Conference in 1808, so the camp meetings must have been successful.

It is necessary to pause and note the sweep of Methodist history. Walker, Travis, and Oglesby were all ordained by Bishop Francis Asbury, and had William McKendree as both a presiding elder and a bishop. Asbury had been commissioned to come to America by John Wesley; ordained deacon and elder and consecrated as a bishop by Thomas Coke, Philip William Otterbein, and Freeborn Garrettson, among others. About twenty years after his own ordination, Asbury was ordaining preachers who would be sent to Missouri. So, as Methodists, we can trace our spiritual heritage back to the hands of John Wesley himself.

Camp meetings were a key part of what is called the "Second Great Awakening" in American history. Revivals began in Kentucky as early as 1798, but the great camp meeting at Cane Ridge, Kentucky is the paradigm of the movement. Camp meetings were vast outdoor revivals where people came from miles around and camped for a week or more. The preaching was intense, and so were the emotional responses. There were outbreaks of speaking in tongues and physical manifestations of the Spirit, including "falling" and "the jerks." Washington Irving described a camp meeting:

> Innumerable rows of carriages, wages, &c, standing round; and the sound of female voices, singing in chorus, struck most pleasantly on his ear. Persons of this sect pay particular attention to their vocal music; and the psalms thus chanted in the open air, by voices of great power and sweetness, had a solemn and a thrilling effect. Some favorite preachers were surrounded by immense congregations, while others drew a smaller number of hearers round them; but many of them would suddenly stoop, and launch into severe anathemas against any unfortunate strangers whose more elegant dress would show them to be mere spectators of the scene. In other parts of the grove, processions would be seen moving slowly and solemnly along—elders of the tribes leading their flocks to this holy place of meeting, and occasionally halting to offer up a short but fervent prayer.[1]

Camp meetings were not only religious events but also a time for socializing, politicking, and building relationships with neighbors near and far. The Disciples of Christ denomination has its origins in the great Cane Ridge revival. Methodists and Baptists both exploded across the frontier as a result of the camp meeting revivals. Their numbers skyrocketed in the years following 1801. While the camp meeting was revitalizing religion on the frontier, Timothy Dwight was leading a great revival at Yale.

Other results of the Second Great Awakening included the formation of the American Board of Commissioners for Foreign Missions, the American Bible Society, and the American Sunday School Union. So Walker and McKendree had not only a powerful tool in the camp meeting, but also were riding a great wave in American history.

The young United States was also riding a wave of excitement. The first successful commercial steamboat traveled up the Hudson from New York City to Albany in 1807. The steamboat would become a key element in the opening of the west, and would make St. Louis and (eventually) Kansas City both great river ports. In 1808, Congress banned the importing of slaves into the United States, a bill which would affect Missouri, but not as much as her sister slave states of the deep South. James Madison was elected President. John Jacob Astor organized the American Fur Company. The western fur trade would enrich merchants and shippers in St. Louis for decades, and draw many hundreds of young men to the west.

Amid all the national excitement, a third circuit appeared in Missouri. The Cold Water Circuit with John Crane as preacher embraced the country between the Missouri and Meramec Rivers, including the present-day St. Louis. The Missouri Circuit was now all north of the Missouri River, and the Meramec Circuit was south of the river from which it took its name. Meramec Circuit would produce the first Missouri preacher, Thomas Wright. John Crane, a native of Tennessee, preached for only six years, 1806–1812, before his death. Only two of those years were spent in Missouri. Abraham Amos was assigned to Missouri Circuit and Joseph Oglesby to Meramec. Abraham Amos was admitted on trial in the Western Conference in 1803, the same year as Joseph Oglesby. The conference journal says that Amos "has been in profession of religion two and a half years, of small gifts, and elliterate [*sic*]; but was useful and much esteemed in his neighborhood." He served only one year in Missouri, and located in 1810.

Thomas Wright was born in South Carolina, but was in Missouri by 1803. He joined the church under the leadership of John Travis, and was licensed to preach in 1807. In 1808, he took the place of Joseph Oglesby on the Meramec Circuit, and, according to Woodard's *Annals*, increased the membership nearly 600 percent. In 1809, he became a member of the Western Conference, and served in Missouri until his death in 1825. He was a revival preacher and zealous for the Lord.

In 1809, Missouri was part of the Indiana District of the Western Conference. There were six circuits in the district—Illinois, Vincennes, and the other four (Missouri, Meramec, Cold Water, and Cape Girardeau) in Missouri.

Cape Girardeau was organized in 1809 under the leadership of Samuel Parker, who was the presiding elder of the Indiana District. The Scripps family were leaders in the class and John Scripps, later to be the secretary of the Conference, came from this church.

John Scripps was born in England, and came to Missouri through Virginia. He entered the conference in 1814, the third preacher from Missouri. His first appointments were in Illinois. His labors in Missouri began in 1816, the same year Missouri became a separate conference. He was secretary of the Conference for twelve years and was elected to the General Conferences of 1820 and 1824. He superannuated in 1824, and then located.

At the Conference in 1811, there were objections brought against an E. W. Bowers "for wearing weapons calculated to inspire terror and for threatening what he would do." He wore two guns, probably not unreasonable on a frontier as wild as Missouri was in 1811. It is not known what he threatened to do with them, but it must have been serious enough to warrant the censure of the Conference. The Conference minutes record the following question and answer about Brother Bowers's behavior: "Do we disapprove his conduct?" "We do."

The religious fervor stirred up by the camp meetings met an apocalyptic event on December 16, 1811. In the early morning hours, a severe earthquake hit the southeast Missouri area, along what is now known as the New Madrid Fault. Smaller shocks continued for several weeks, with another great shock on January 23, 1812, and the most severe on February 7th. Aftershocks continued for nearly a year. The earthquake did the most damage in a stretch one hundred miles long, from west of Cairo, Illinois, to the north to the latitude of Memphis in the south. There were landslides, fissures, sinks, the Mississippi River ran "backward" for a short time, and whole forests were leveled. Island Number 94, near Vicksburg, Mississippi, disappeared. Tremors were felt as far away as upper Canada in the north, and by the Indians near the Mandan towns on the Missouri River. Shocks were felt in New Orleans, Detroit, Washington, and Boston. In over one million square miles, or half the United States, the shocks could be felt without any instruments. One old tradition, which the author heard at Independence Hall in Philadelphia, says that the earthquake even rang the Liberty Bell!

The severity of the earthquake, the thick darkness, odors of sulfur and decay released from decaying vegetation, and huge thunderstorms led some people to fear that the end of the world was at hand. Certainly the damage and trauma were severe enough that people filled with biblical images of judgment could indeed think it was the end of the world.

What effect did the earthquake have on Missouri Methodism? The class at New Madrid had been founded in March 1810, when Jesse Walker and John Scripps blazed a trail across the Great Swamp from Cape Girardeau. The 1811 *General Minutes*, which report the year 1810, show New Madrid with 30 members. In the 1813 *Minutes*, New Madrid is listed with 165 members, 140 white, and 25 colored.

New Madrid was not the only Missouri community to show an increase in membership. Cape Girardeau, the next closest circuit, increased from 76 to 138 members. Meramec, which would have been in the area of strong secondary shocks, increased from 147 to 352 members between 1811 and 1812. Even Cold Water, in north St. Louis County, jumped from 87 to 158. These increases are all large enough to be statistically significant. Something happened to cause this kind of increase. That something very likely was the fear of both natural phenomena and of the end of the world brought about by the earthquake.

Dwight Culmer, a distinguished Missouri historian, has argued that the sudden increase in membership was a panic reaction to the earthquake, and that membership quickly returned to pre-earthquake levels. But reports to the General Conference do not show a drastic drop in membership. New Madrid dropped only from 165 members in 1812 to 136 in 1814. Cape Girardeau declined from 138 to 136, and Cold Water from 158 to 147. Today, many Methodists would rejoice at those figures, because they would be the smallest decline in years! In 1812, all the circuits in Missouri were on the frontier, and mobility was always a dominant characteristic of the frontier. The closer to the frontier, the greater the mobility. So the drop in membership probably reflects a restless people moving west, as well as a movement away from land that had been spoiled by the earthquake rather than a turning away from religion after the panic caused by the earthquake.

The aftershocks were still occurring when the War of 1812 broke out. While Missouri was not directly involved in major battles during the war, the British did stir up the Indians in the area, and many isolated settlers moved to larger settlements for protection. With both natural and political turmoil, it is no wonder the circuits lost members. What is surprising is that they lost so few. The faith had already taken deep roots in Missouri.

In 1812, the name of the territory was changed from Upper Louisiana to Missouri. (Louisiana was admitted to the Union as the eighteenth state, so "Upper Louisiana" was no longer an accurate term.) James Madison was re-elected as President, and the U.S. declared war on Britain. Thomas Wright held the first camp meeting in St. Genevieve County (now part of Madison County) in 1812, soon after the earthquake. He surely would have found an attentive audience! The New Madrid Circuit was officially separated from Cape Girardeau.

Saline Circuit was formed in 1814, along the Saline River in what is now St. Francois County. Jerome C. Berryman would come from this circuit to be a leader in Missouri Methodism, and in the Indian Mission. Saline Circuit included the Murphy Settlement (Farmington), New Tennessee, Cook's Settlement, and Callaway's Settlement. At the close of the 1814–1815 conference year, the circuit reported one hundred and fifty members. In 1815, the name of the Meramec Circuit was changed to Bellevue, and the Booneslick Circuit was formed. The second circuit north of the Missouri River, Booneslick covered most of central Missouri if its boundaries were the same as those of Howard County. It was named for the famous salt licks worked by the Boone family, most notably Nathan Boone, Daniel's youngest son. Joseph Piggott was the first preacher appointed to the circuit. That same year saw the beginning of Methodism in Arkansas, with the opening of the Spring River Circuit.

The year 1815 saw some important events on the world stage. The Battle of Waterloo ended both Napoleon Bonaparte's career and the long period of war in Europe. The war between the United States and Britain also ended, though the Battle of New Orleans, the chief land victory for the U.S., was fought after the peace treaty had actually been signed. Today, people can communicate almost instantaneously with anyone anywhere in the world, so it's hard to comprehend the slowness of communication in the early nineteenth century.

The Western Conference of 1815 sent four newly admitted elders to Missouri. Philip Davis was appointed to Spring River, then served circuits in Missouri until 1822, when he located. William Stevenson was sent to Bellevue, but then went to Arkansas in 1816. He was presiding elder of the Black River (later Arkansas) District in 1818. He was a "wandering man," who founded churches in Texas and Louisiana, and served as a presiding elder in Arkansas and Louisiana. Joseph Piggott served churches in southeast Missouri, until his name disappears from the records in 1820. Almost nothing is known of the fourth preacher, Benjamin Proctor, except his name.

In 1816, James Monroe (of Monroe Doctrine fame) was elected President of the United States. Indiana was admitted as the nineteenth state. The Rocky Mountain fur trade continued to flourish, and more and more families moved westward toward a constantly expanding frontier. And, in 1816, the Missouri Conference was formed. It included Illinois and Arkansas, as well as Missouri. Its western boundary, according to legend, was given as "the farthest cabin toward the setting sun."

Actually, the General Conference defined the northern, eastern, and southern boundaries of the conference, but not the western. This lack of definition apparently gave rise to the legend. The first session of the new conference was held at Shiloh Meetinghouse in Belleville, Illinois. The appointments for Missouri were:

Jesse Walker, Presiding Elder
Missouri Circuit, John Schraeder
Boonslick [sic], Joseph Piggott
Cold Water, John Scripps
Belleview [sic] and Saline, J. C. Harbison and Joseph Reeder
Cape Girardeau and New Madrid, Thomas Wright and Alexander McAlister

There were only eight preachers to cover an entire state, to pastor and nurture those who were already members of the Methodist Church, and to evangelize the

The circuit riders were sent across the frontier to save souls, reform the continent, spread scriptural holiness over the land, and to establish churches.

growing frontier. What was a circuit rider? How did he function in his task? We turn from our survey of growth in Missouri to look for an answer to that question.

Methodism was based on a strategy of itinerant ministry, that is, of sending the preachers where they were needed. Bishops Asbury and McKendree used their preachers the way good generals use their troops: looking for opportunities to advance and flinging the resources at their disposal to meet those needs. Methodism attacked the frontier, where people lived on scattered farms or in small villages. Itinerant ministry provided preaching, the sacraments, and church structure to small communities that would not have been able to attract—or to pay— a minister from one of the more settled denominations. Freeborn Garrettson (who made the dramatic ride summoning the preachers to the Christmas Conference in 1784) said of the frontier in New York that the thousands "in the back settlements, who were not able to give a hundred [pounds] in a year to a minister . . . may now hear a sermon at least once in two weeks; sometimes oftener" because of Methodist circuit riders.

Methodist circuit riders were young, single, men. Most often they came from an agricultural or an artisan background. They may have moved toward the frontier several times before they were converted and heard the call to preach. For example, Francis Asbury had been a blacksmith. John Clark had a career in the British navy. Others were carpenters, shoemakers, millers, schoolteachers, and farmers. Most of the early circuit riders had only a minimal education. Most could read and write, and were poured into a course of study based on the Bible, the hymnal, the *Discipline*, and Wesley's sermons. There was very little difference, in terms of education, between the Methodist circuit rider and his congregation. That difference often was the theological education gained from reading the sermons of Wesley.

Salaries for circuit riders in these early days in Missouri were eighty dollars a year, as fixed by the *Discipline*—and even that amount was often not fully paid. John Travis, for example, received only twenty dollars of his promised eighty dollars during his year in Missouri. Out of this small sum, the preachers had to buy a horse, saddle and bridle, clothes, and so on. They usually relied on the hospitality of settlers for food and shelter. Their journals and memoirs indicate that the food was mostly poor and plain, and shelter was a blanket rolled on the floor or in a shed near the house.

A quick glance at the summaries of a circuit rider's career indicates that he was usually assigned to a different circuit each year. Moving was easy, since everything the preacher owned was already in his saddlebags. A typical circuit was between two hundred and six hundred miles around. The preacher was expected to make the rounds of this circuit every two to six weeks. Where there were two preachers on the circuit, one traveled about one-half the circuit ahead of the other, although sometimes preachers traveled together for short periods and for special reasons. Preaching at any given spot was held about every two to three weeks, but seldom on a Sunday. Preaching appointments were set daily or twice daily. When the preacher arrived in a neighborhood, members of the household were sent out to summon the neighbors for a service early the next morning or later that evening. Services were held as early as 5 A.M. in the summer, so the settlers could get to the fields as soon as possible.

The preachers examined the classes at each appointment. Quarterly meetings (the predecessor of "Quarterly Conferences") were held in a central location, and often included a camp meeting and a special time for baptisms, weddings, and Lord's Supper.

Sermons were practical, moral, and dramatic. Methodist doctrine fit well with the spirit of the frontier. The emphasis on free will and grace, unlike the emphasis on limited grace and predestination preached by the Presbyterians and Baptists, appealed to those independent souls who had moved to the frontier and who felt they were in control of their own destiny. Jesse Greene says more than once in his journal, "I gave them Methodism" or "I gave them Methodism, root and branch." A study of his surviving sermons and notes suggests that he meant by this free grace, sanctification, infant baptism, free will, and other doctrines dear to the heart of Methodism. Even among circuit riders who were not college educated, there was a keen sense of theological difference between themselves and their counterparts in other denominations. The Methodists were quick to both explain and exploit those differences. They preached on the fall of humanity; original sin; the redeeming death of Jesus Christ; universality of salvation, personal responsibility, and free will; regeneration: the idea that the soul can be transformed and renewed; the new birth; and faithful living.

William Warren Sweet points out that the circuit rider was a powerful influence in maintaining law and order. The system of Methodism, with its class meetings, quarterly conferences, and so on, helped imposed order on what were often disorderly frontier communities. The circuit rider insisted on decency and order in worship. Both Peter Cartwright, the great Illinois Methodist, and James B. Findley of Ohio record instances when the Methodist preachers had to physically restrain bands of toughs bent on breaking up a camp meeting. Morality was an important theme of the circuit riders' preaching, and the Methodists led the earliest campaigns for temperance in the American west. Given the rawness of society, any decrease in the consumption of alcohol almost guaranteed an increase in public order.

The circuit riders were also book agents—the Cokesbury book stores of their day. The 1800 General Conference passed a rule that "It shall be the duty of every preacher who has the charge of a circuit to see that his circuit be duly supplied with books, and to take charge of all the books which are sent to him, from time to time, or which may be in his circuit; and he is to account with the presiding elder for the same." The books came from the Methodist Book Concern, and included the works of John Wesley and John Fletcher, but also biography, history, philosophy, and ethics. The preachers were charged with selling these books to their flocks and returning the money to the conference. Then, as now, the money from the Book Concern went for the care of "worn-out preachers."

With the kind of schedule they kept and the poor quality of food they were eating, it is no wonder that so many of the circuit riders' health broke. The short sketches of the early circuit riders in Missouri shows that many of them located after only a few years of service. They were literally "worn out" and broken in health. One example is the author's great-great-grandfather, William P. Hulse. He was admitted to the conference in 1835 and was appointed as the junior preacher on the Lexington Circuit. During that year, he organized the class that became First Methodist Church in Independence. He was discontinued (located) in 1836 because of his health. "Rheumatism," or some form of arthritis, made it too painful for him to be out in all kinds of weather, or to ride a horse for long distances. Brother Hulse lived in Johnson County for another forty-nine years, and served as a local preacher.

Hulse's life is a reminder that all those itinerants who located did not give up their ministry. They served as pastors in local churches, provided leadership and preaching in the absence of the itinerants, and often made it possible for the community to have access to the sacraments, marriage, and Christian burial.

Elmer T. Clark summarized the spirit of the circuit riders in an address to the St. Louis Annual Conference in 1960. Clark said of the circuit riders:

1. They were primarily evangelists, who took seriously Wesley's dictum, "you have nothing to do but save souls."
2. They spoke the definite and concrete language of the people.
3. They disregarded themselves, their physical welfare, and the desires for a normal life.
4. They were to build up holiness.
5. They were careful about instructing children.
6. They insisted on strict morality.[2]

It is not an exaggeration to say that the circuit riders transformed the American frontier, winning people to Christ, and, in the process, making The Methodist Church the largest and strongest denomination in America.

In addition to the circuit riders, the Methodist system of lay, or local, preachers helped the church grow. Lay preachers helped provide leadership for infant churches while the circuit rider was "riding the circuit." They provided preaching on a regular basis, gave pastoral care and leadership, and sought out newcomers to the community. Any young man who showed ability in speaking was urged by the class leader to preach, and when the presiding elder came around for "quarterly conference," to receive an exhorter's license. Exhorters were not strictly preachers, but often functioned as them. In revivals and camp meetings, they spoke after the sermon, exhorting the congregation to heed the word that had been spoken and to respond to it in specific and tangible ways. Some local preachers became members of the conference; some traveling preachers who located became local preachers. Either way, they were a strong source of support and cohesion for the growing church.

Buffalo Circuit was carved out of the Missouri Circuit in 1817. St. Francois Circuit was also formed out of Cape Girardeau, and Joseph Piggott and Rucker Tanner were appointed there. Tanner, as a youth, had gone to New Orleans with an older brother. Both were reckless young men and quickly spent all their money. Rucker was dark-complexioned and his brother talked him into being sold as a slave. This way, they could get some cash back. Rucker could then escape, and they could go home. But the brother took the money and left New Orleans. Rucker finally gained his freedom and started to walk home. On the way home, he worked for a while for a local preacher. During that time, he decided to enter the ministry. Like the Prodigal Son, he finally returned home, to be welcomed as one who had come back from the dead. He announced a preaching time, and the largest congregation in the history of the community gathered! Because of the efforts of Tanner and his fellow circuit riders, Methodist membership in Missouri increased by fifty percent during the year.

LaMine (or LaMoine) Circuit was set off from Booneslick. It was the first circuit in what would later be the Southwest Missouri Conference. More is known about what was happening in the circuits at this time, because the preachers began keeping journals, or wrote articles for the *Christian Advocate* describing their work. John Scripps, who moved from the Booneslick Circuit to LaMoine, wrote:

> My circuit extended on the north of the Missouri River from Cote Sans to Grand River, and on the south side from Jefferson City to near where Lexington now is. On the night of February 18, 1818, I preached in Edmondson's Bottom, in the farthest house on the south side of the river. On the twentieth of July, I preached to twenty or thirty persons in the Petitsau Plains, forty miles higher up the river.[3]

Boonville, a small village, was not on Scripps's plan for the circuit, but he found a preaching place in a private home, and incorporated it into the circuit. The first class in Boonville was organized in September of 1818 by Justinian Williams, a local preacher. By 1840, Boonville was a station, the second in the state.

Economic depression hit the country in 1818–1819. Farm prices dropped as the end of the war in Europe reduced demands for American grain, and other products. It is certain that Missouri farmers felt the pinch, along with their fellows across the country. In spite of the economic pain, the church continued to grow. John Scripps was sent to Cape Girardeau (moving every year!) and John McFarland to St. Francois. They united the two circuits, and both men worked on each. They made their round about every six weeks. Scripps described the circuits as:

> Our field of operations this year was bounded on the east by the Mississippi River, from the Grand Tower to the Big Swamp, four miles south of Cape Girardeau; south, by the Big Swamp to Current River; west, by that river to Vernon's mills, twenty miles north of the road to Batesville; north and west, crossing Black River, then St. Francis at Fredericktown, cross Castor to Apple Creek and Grand Tower.[4]

Woodard says in his *Annals* that, in 1893, there were fifteen pastoral appointments in the area Scripps had described as his circuit.

The first meeting of the Missouri Conference on Missouri soil was held in 1819, at McKendree Chapel. John Scripps says:

> It was this year that McKendree Chapel was built, a good hewed-log house, with a shingle roof, good plank floor, windows, etc. It was the first substantial and finished meetinghouse built for us in Missouri, by the hands of regular workmen, and was commenced and completed this year, with special reference to the first annual Conference ever held on the west side of the Mississippi River. It stands two miles east of Jackson and eight miles west of

Cape Girardeau, in a campground hallowed by the recollections of happy hundreds, who have there been born again to sing redeeming love.[5]

Total membership in Missouri increased by 9 percent from the previous year. Economic hard times must have begun to pinch the church as well, since increases in earlier years had been much greater.

President James Monroe was re-elected in 1820, but his election was ultimately overshadowed by two other events that would shape the future of Missouri, indeed of the entire nation. The first was the Missouri Compromise. Missouri had applied for admission to the Union as a slave state. However, there was no application for a free state to keep the balance in the Senate. Finally, Maine applied. The Missouri Compromise agreed to allow Missouri's entry as a slave state, with Maine as a free state. A second condition for Missouri's entry was that slavery be abolished in the other territories formed from the Louisiana Purchase. At the time, statehood for any other territory must have seemed remote, but this fateful legislation would lead ultimately to border wars between Missouri and Kansas and, ultimately, to secession and civil war in the nation. The second event was the passage of land laws allowing the purchase of eighty acres of Federal land at $1.25 an acre. This opened up the possibility for many more farmers with little ready cash to become landowners—and hastened the flood of immigration to the frontier.

In that same year of 1820, the Cape Girardeau District was organized alongside the Missouri District. Two new circuits, Gasconade and Cedar Creek, appeared in the minutes. Gasconade was taken from Cold Water, and Cedar Creek from Booneslick and Missouri circuits. At the end of the year, as Missouri stood on the brink of statehood, there were two districts and eleven circuits in the state. The bounds of Methodism ran from New Madrid up the Mississippi to Palmyra; west to Brunswick and Sedalia; south by way of Versailles and Rolla to the Meramec; up the Meramec to its source; down the Current River to the Arkansas line, and east to New Madrid. There were probably classes in Cape Girardeau, Boonville, New Madrid, Potosi (near the lead mines), and Franklin (the starting point for western trade with Santa Fe and the Rocky Mountains).

Two momentous events occurred in 1821: Missouri became a state, and Methodism moved into St. Louis. From the beginning of Methodism in Missouri, St. Louis had been ignored. Part of the reason was the Roman Catholicism of many of its Spanish and French citizens. The other was that Methodism shunned the cities. An article in the *St. Louis Christian Advocate* in 1853 summed up Methodism's feeling toward the cities in those early days: "God made the country and there He will acknowledge and bless the people; but the devil made the towns and those who live in them are unapproachable by preaching." That was about to change, as Jesse Walker was sent to St. Louis at the conference of 1820. At this time, St. Louis, even though it was the territorial capital, was still a frontier town. By 1816, the town had begun to move west from the Mississippi, expanding beyond the present Fourth Street to the area where the Old Courthouse now stands. The wealth of the western fur trade flowed into St. Louis, and merchants there did a brisk business outfitting wagon and pack trains heading west to trade for furs. William Clark was Territorial Governor and Indian Agent.

Walker rented a house in St. Louis and began holding meetings, as well as a day school and Sunday school. One of his former pupils remembered that Walker furnished the books and offered instruction free to all who would come. The following Sunday, there were ten boys in attendance. Walker began to teach them reading, gave them a short sermon, sang a hymn, and dismissed them with a prayer.

On the first Sunday of January 1821, Walker organized the first Methodist class in St. Louis (though Scripps and others had preached there as early as 1816). By the session of the Annual Conference of 1822, he had built a meetinghouse, twenty by thirty feet, at the corner of Myrtle and Fourth Streets. He reported eighty-seven members, fifty-seven white and thirty colored. That 1822 session of the conference was held in the new Methodist church in St. Louis. That was an act of audacious faith! The session of the conference was scheduled for St. Louis before there was a building or even any members.

The Missouri Conference of 1821 reported three districts besides Missouri. They were:

	Stations	Members
Indiana	8	508
Illinois	7	1873
Black River	5	536

Black River was Arkansas plus Pecan Point, in Texas. Reports for the Missouri District (for the year 1820) showed ten stations (circuits) with 1,543 members, divided as follows:

	Whites	Colored
Missouri and Buffalo	215	11
Boone's Lick [sic]	246	24
Lamarne [sic] (LaMoine)	140	3
Aboeff (Buffalo)	125	12
Bellevue	119	15
Cold Water	84	28
Saline	86	12
St. Francis [sic]	99	28
Cape Girardeau	206	8
New Madrid	75	7
	1,395	148

Appointments for 1821 in the two districts in Missouri are a kind of honor roll of those who carried the church into the new era marked by statehood, an era in which a sturdy adolescent church moved to full maturity.

Missouri District	S. H. Thompson, Presiding Elder
St. Louis	Isaac N. Piggott
Gasconade	John McCord
Missouri	Wm. L. Hawley
Buffaloe	William Medford
Cedar Creek	James Scott
Boone's Lick [*sic*]	TBS
LaMoine	L. Green
Cape Girardeau District	Thomas Wright, Presiding Elder
Bellevue	John Harris
Saline and St. Francis [*sic*]	Samuel Bassett
Spring River★	Isaac Brookfield
White River★	W. W. Redman
Cape Girardeau	Philip Davis
New Madrid	Jesse Haile

★ in Arkansas.

These early circuit riders faced incredible hardships with a song in their hearts. They were men of great faith in Jesus Christ and in the power of the covenant. They knew, at the deepest level of their being, that the bishop and their brothers in the conference stood with them. They remembered, or had heard the stories of Bishop Asbury giving away his coat to a preacher who had none. They knew, wherever they were, that the bishop and the conference held them in their prayers. They came together at the session of the conference each year, with the vision of the wide frontier still in their eyes, and greeted each other with tears of joy. When they sang Charles Wesley's great hymn, "And are we let alive, and see each other's face?" they knew it was only because of the amazing grace of God in Jesus Christ, and they gave him glory and thanks. Indeed, the words of that hymn sum up both the danger and the blessing of the circuit life:

> Preserved by power divine to full salvation here,
>   again in Jesus' praise we join, and in his sight appear.
> What troubles have we seen, what mighty conflicts passed,
>   Fightings without, and fears within, since we assembled last.
> Yet out of all the Lord hath brought us by his love.
>   And still he doth his help afford, and hides our life above.
> Then let us make our boast of his redeeming power
>   which saves us to the uttermost, till we can sin no more.

Let us take up the cross, till we the crown obtain.
    And gladly reckon all things loss, that we may Jesus gain.

For them, those were not just words sung because they had always done it that way, but words of great hope and power. The Lord had brought them together, and they would sing his praise!

Circuits, 1810

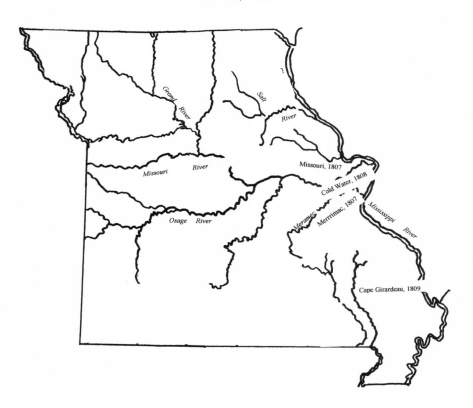

Circuits, 1821

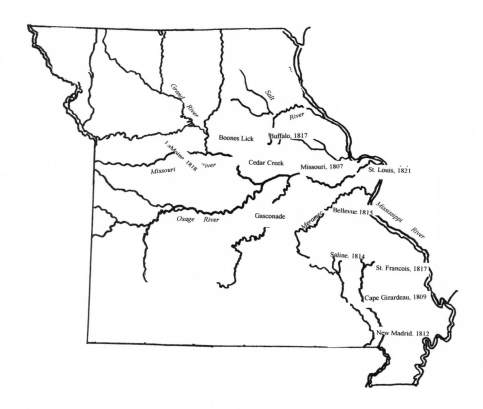

Grand River

Salt River

Boones Lick

Buffalo, 1817

La Mine River

Missouri

Cedar Creek

Missouri, 1807

St. Louis, 1821

Osage River

Gasconade

Meramec

Bellevue, 1815

Mississippi River

Saline, 1814

St. Francois, 1817

Cape Girardeau, 1809

New Madrid, 1812

Chapter 2

OUTREACH AND NURTURE WITH SLAVES AND FREE BLACKS 1807–1844

The first appointment to Missouri after Oglesby's report to the Western Conference was John Travis to the "Missourie" Circuit in 1807. This circuit, of course, did not exist. Travis's task was to find the people, organize classes, begin a preaching schedule, and pastor a flock scattered all over the new territory. The conference minutes of 1808 report statistics from two circuits in Missouri: the Missouri, which included all the settlements north of the Meramec River and along the Missouri, and the "Maramack" [*sic*], which included the settlements along, and south of, the Meramec River. The Missouri Circuit reported fifty-six members; the Meramec forty-four white and six colored members. By 1810, there were four circuits in Missouri, with membership as follows:

Maramack	354
Missouri	102
Cold Water	75
Cape Girardeau	52

There must have been black members in some of the other circuits, since they appear in both 1809 and 1811, but how many is difficult to determine.

Missouri Methodism followed the pattern of the rest of the denomination in being involved with ministry to blacks from the beginning. As early as 1758, John Wesley had baptized the first Negro Methodist. The first Methodist congregation in New York (1766) included a black girl, and a Sunday School organized by Francis Asbury in Maryland that year included both white and black children.

In 1816, the year the Missouri Conference was born, almost one-fourth of the Methodists in the United States were of African origin. Obviously, the majority of these would have been in the South, and plantation missions were strong. The policy of whites and blacks meeting together for worship had been formulated as early as 1780. One of the questions of the Conference for that year was:

> Ought not the assistant to meet with the coloured people himself, and appoint as helpers in his absence proper white persons, and not suffer them to stay late and meet by themselves? (A) Yes.[1]

That question is a reminder of the awful dilemma of the church: how to minister to African slaves without arousing the fears of their owners. In this case, the answer was to provide a ministry, but always under white supervision.

In established congregations, there were often separate galleries for the slaves, but it was still a common practice for both races to worship together. The Southern fear of slave insurrections was probably as much a factor in promoting common meetings as was any sense of fitness about it. But even Southerners were convinced of the need to evangelize the slaves. Bishop James O. Andrew said to the South Carolina Conference in 1832:

> . . . we are fully persuaded that it is not only safe, but highly expedient to society at large, to furnish the slaves as fully as possible with the means of true scriptural instruction and the worship of God. . . .[2]

Much the same attitudes prevailed in Missouri. The evidence is scanty and scattered through the journals of white circuit riders, but clear and unmistakable. Methodists were concerned with taking the gospel to the slaves and with incorporating them into the body of the Methodist Episcopal Church. David Rice McAnally, the great apologist for Southern Methodism in Missouri, in speaking of the years from 1812 to 1814, said:

> Many families (immigrating to Missouri) brought their household servants, or slaves—generally few in number, from two to half a dozen in a family. . . . The newcomer usually had but a single family; and the distinction between master and servant in these families was more in color than in anything else. They lived pretty much on the same plane, and while the master and owner directed and governed the labor, they all worked together for the common good. They were clothed with pretty much the same kind of material, ate of the same kind of food, often slept under the same roof and shared the same toils, amusements, and devotions. They counseled together for the promotion of their mutual interest: the slave expressed his opinion or gave his advice as freely as his master or mistress; nor did he often wait to be solicited. If the family were religious, the slaves followed the example, were

present as part of the family at the morning and evening devotions, and joined in and sometimes led these devotions with an earnestness and fervor truly Christian. The master or mistress would read a portion of the Scriptures, then "line the hymn," that is, read two lines at a time which all joined in singing, and then the master or one of the servants would offer the prayer.

The early preachers understood and appreciated these servants as a valuable factor in their own success; and on the occasion of their visits to the settlements, the Colored people received a large share of their pastoral solicitude and attention. They often called upon some Colored man to lead in prayer at the prayer—and other special meetings, and not infrequently to conclude with prayer the regular exercises on the occasions of preaching. Nearly all of them being good singers, and loving to sing, they joined that part of the public service with great animation, which often imparted a thrilling interest that otherwise would not have been felt; and instances are on record where extensive revivals were carried on among the White settlers by the labors of Colored men.[3]

One suspects that this idyllic state existed only for the brief period before the major emigrations from slave-holding states, and even then existed perhaps as much in fond memory as in reality. There is, however, considerable evidence to substantiate McAnally's comments about the participation of blacks in Methodist services.

John Scripps, who was the secretary of the conference, records that during the conference year 1817–1818, he formed a class at General Ramsey's settlement (across the river from present-day Jefferson City) "where Mrs. Ramsey, her father-in-law, Mrs. Ferguson, and Brother Tom (the name he principally went by), an old Methodist Negro, four in all, joined this year."[4]

In the conference year 1819–1820, Scripps was again on that Booneslick Circuit, working against the Missouri Compromise, and gaining hundreds of signatures to petitions against the proposal to admit Missouri to the Union as a slave state. This was an amazing feat, considering that the Booneslick Circuit was in Howard County, which always had a high percentage of slaves in its population. This leads one to wonder if Scripps were not correct in arguing that slavery would soon have been abolished in Missouri had it not been for the Compromise, and for the work of abolitionists. Scripps preached against slavery at Mr. Ferguson's, and several slaveholders responded by putting in their names for membership in the church! Concerning the black members, Scripps says:

At subsequent meetings several others (slaveholders) joined, and a large class of white and colored was quickly formed, in connection with the four who had joined when I was last here, of whom, by unanimous vote, Brother Tom was made Leader, and an efficient Leader he was; for the Class, at least during the four months I was on the circuit, flourished under him. I once attended one of his night-meetings for prayer. There was a full congregation. I refused his request to conduct the services, but assisted him. At a proper season, he invited mourners. Three Colored people came forward, over whom for a short period he stood, and while tears chased each other down his sable cheeks, delivered (I will not say a most appropriate, only, but) a most eloquent and feeling address on the subject to the Whites, concluding with a solemn appeal to their sensibilities, that, if they had any confidence in the efficacy of old Tom's prayers, to come forward also. All were affected, some came forward. The meeting became more and still more interesting, some were blessed, and I felt it a privilege to be there.[5]

It is not certain how large the "large class" was, but Scripps reported one hundred ninety-five white and eight colored members to the conference at the end of that year. It is more to the point to note that, at least in that class, whites and blacks freely worshiped together, blacks were chosen by vote of both black and white members to positions of leadership, and blacks apparently had some freedom to speak on matters of conscience and the salvation of the soul. It would be interesting to know if Brother Tom was actually a slave or a free black. Since he lived in Howard County, he was most probably a slave. This fact would, indeed, make the meeting "more and more interesting" if a slave assumed responsibility and leadership for those who physically owned him.

A few years later, the Reverend Jacob Lanius began a long and productive career as a Methodist preacher. An early entry in his journal shows a real concern for the black population of Missouri:

I have recently determined to pay more attention to our slave population than I have hitherto done. Great and mighty now are the efforts being made for the salvation of the world—but nothing is being done for the slaves in our circuit. If they attend our regular appointments for the whites, the houses are so small that they are compelled to remain out of doors and receive little or no benefit from the preaching . . . and again if a man preaches in an acceptable style to the whites, the slaves cannot understand him. . . . It really seems to me that if Christ died for them as well as for us they ought to be attended to. I expect that I shall be rewarded when I convert them as well as a "crowd of Europeans". . . . In executing my determination I expect to receive the reproach of the proud and haughty white man, but I want to save souls, as well the black as the white . . . after preaching three hours and a quarter on baptism during the night I preached the funeral of two black men to the Negroes—we had a good time, the crowd was praising God, 3 Negroes joined the church . . . this encouraged me in my resolution.[6]

In addition to the insight into the concerns and motivations of Mr. Lanius, several other points appear in that citation. At least on the Paris Circuit in 1834, where services were held in homes, blacks were forced to remain out-of-doors and not share with the whites. Add to that Lanius's expectation that, if he preached to blacks, he would anger whites. This leads one to believe that the growing national tension over slavery and the relationship between the races was being reflected in the Methodist Church. Note also that Lanius believed that the same sermon could not communicate effectively to both whites and blacks. (At the end of the year, Lanius reported one hundred eighty-nine white and seventeen black members on the circuit, so his commitment apparently bore some fruit. The figures had been seventy-six and one in 1833, so he also apparently did not alienate too many whites.)

In 1836, Lanius was on the Bellwood and Meramec Circuits, continuing to work with slaves, as his journal entries indicate.

> Sunday, Mar. 6th—preached at the Virginia Mines, had a very powerful time. The Christians of every order rejoiced with joy unspeakable and full of glory. I found a class of 4 whites and 8 blacks attended. Six Negro men came forward to receive the prayers of the church. . . . We had a precious session indeed.[7]

Here, at least in the small class meeting, the two races still worshiped freely together.

> March 23—In the morning I rode 12 miles to the little school near what is called three forks of Black River and at 1 P.M. . . . and preached to the blacks as they are numerously called. Some of the people seemed to be very devoted. All seemed to be exceedingly poor in the world's goods. Some as much as they possibly could be, having little less than a little cabin, a few acres of clear land . . . and a few articles of domestic use.[8]

It is not clear whether these blacks to whom Lanius was preaching were slaves or free. However, his description of their economic condition suggests they were, indeed, free.

McAnally's statement about the circuit riders depending on the black population finds support in Lanius's journal entry for July 17, 1836, "there is little religion here except among the Negroes." On the twenty-eighth of the same month, he began a camp meeting along with his coworker on the circuit, a Baptist preacher, and a colored Methodist preacher from the Gasconade Circuit. The appointed pastor for the Gasconade Circuit that year was J. M. Ewing, so the colored preacher must have been a local preacher or exhorter, rather than a member of the conference. However, it is significant that black preachers were free to travel and to share in religious leadership with the white preachers.

With that awareness of the church in mind, examine the statistical record and what actually happened in Missouri in terms of black membership in the church. In the early years, with circuits widely scattered among a tiny population, records were difficult to keep, and reporting was not always as accurate as one could wish. Nevertheless, it is clear that Methodism grew quickly in Missouri, from its humble beginnings in 1807. One of the most valuable documents dating from the period is the membership report for 1821, the year Missouri became a state.

Missouri District	Whites	Colored
Buffalo	106	4
Missouri	140	23
Cedar Creek	125	24
Boonslick [*sic*]	126	20
LaMoine	142	15
Gasconade	135	32
St. Louis	95	32

(St. Louis had been organized that year)

Cape Girardeau District	Whites	Colored
Belle Vue [*sic*]	182	16
Saline	116	16
St. Francis [*sic*]	162	40
Cape Girardeau	260	0
New Madrid	150	24
Spring River	109	12
White River	138	18.[9]

This made a total of 1,976 whites and 247 blacks, or 2,223 Methodists in Missouri. Black members were 11.1 percent of the total.

Table I shows the concentrations of slave population by counties in the period 1820–1840. Emigrants from Southern states settled in the great river valleys (Missouri, Salt, Chariton) and in the city of St. Louis. These are obviously the areas of the greatest concentration of slaves—and of the majority of the circuits identified in Table II.

Northern Missouri was under the influence of Iowa and Illinois settlers, most of whom were anti-slavery. Southern Missouri, with the broken Ozark Mountains and the great swamps of the southeast along the Mississippi, was never suited to large farming operations. The farms here were the kind described by McAnally—the family, with perhaps one or two slaves, working together.

Table II shows the location of Methodist circuits established by or before 1840. In the seventeen counties (and the city of St. Louis) designated as having a high slave population, there were thirty-five churches, of which seven were in the city of St. Louis. There were forty-eight churches in the rest of the state. The first impression is that Missouri Methodism had a strong southern cast, that Methodism was strongest in those counties where the slave population was highest, and it was therefore successful in its mission to the black population.

There are at least two ways to test that impression, given the data at our disposal. Table III shows the relative success of the Methodists in reaching both racial groups in comparison to the total population of each group, by years.

TABLE I
Slave Population

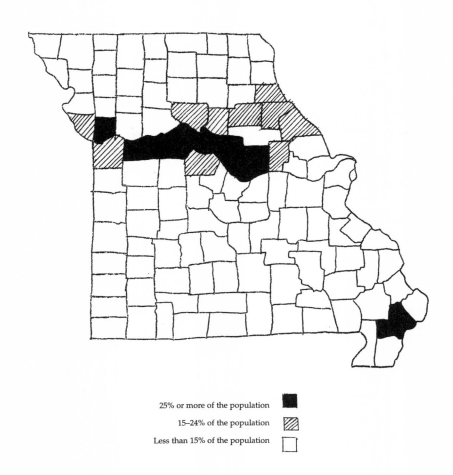

25% or more of the population	■	
15–24% of the population	▨	
Less than 15% of the population	□	

TABLE II
Location of Circuits, 1840

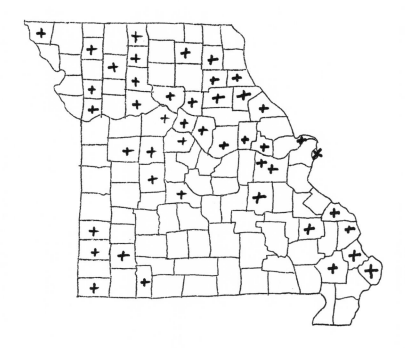

TABLE III

Year	Slave Population	Black Methodists	%	White Population	White Methodists	%
1821	10,222	247	2.41	70,000	1,976	2.82
1830	25,691	379	1.51	115,626	3,369	2.91
1840	58, 240	1,403	2.40	325,462	14,592	4.48

Except in 1821, the percentage of black Methodists to the population is much lower than the percentage of white Methodists. In 1830, the percentage of white members is nearly twice that of blacks, and the same is true in 1840. In real numbers, however, both groups grew at about the same rate, roughly quadrupling between 1830 and 1840. In 1821, blacks were 11.1 percent of the total Methodist membership. That percentage declined only slightly: to 10.1 percent in 1830 and 8.77 percent in 1840. (In 1821, blacks made up 12.7 percent of the total popu-lation, and 15.2 percent in 1840.) Two factors may contribute to the relative

decline of black members in Methodism. First, the decline may reflect the negative feelings of white members (about preaching to blacks) that Jacob Lanius
feared. Second, white settlers from northern states and from Europe began moving
into Missouri in larger numbers during these years, increasing the percentage of
whites in both the population and the Methodist Church.

Table IV looks more closely at specific churches within those seventeen counties where the percentage of slave population was the highest. If the initial
impression of Methodism's success among blacks is correct, then the churches in
these counties should have had a high ratio of black members (at least approaching
that of the slaves in the total population). The figures are for the year 1840, a year
in which the data seem to be reasonably correct.

TABLE IV

Circuit	Whites	Blacks	Total	% Blacks	% Blacks in Population
Columbia (Boone Co.)	333	99	432	22.90	22.22
Callaway Co.	No Church				26.75
Boonville (Cooper Co.)	516	34	550	6.18	20.60
Fayette (Howard Co.)	629	30	659	4.55	28.43
Independence (Jackson Co.)	416	6	422	1.42	17.89
Lexington (Lafayette Co.)	516	36	552	6.52	29.31
Arrow Rock (Saline Co.)	270	20	290	6.90	30.76
St. Louis City	359	300	659	45.52	30.32

In only two churches in these counties with a heavy slave population does
the percentage of black members of the Methodist Church approach that of
blacks in the total population. One of these is Columbia, the other St. Louis,
where the membership was almost equally divided between the two races. But
even in St. Louis, racial feelings were causing problems in the church. The same
conference (1841) to which these statistics were reported appointed two pastors
to a newly formed African Church, which the following year reported the entire
black membership of the church in St. Louis. Separation was overcoming the
pioneering spirit of John Scripps and Jacob Lanius.

By contrast, some Methodist churches in areas with a low slave population were doing quite well in reaching the black population. Table V shows a similar range of statistics for five churches chosen at random from across the state.

TABLE V

Circuit	Whites	Blacks	Total	% Blacks	% Blacks in Population
Bowling Green (Pike Co.)	196	34	230	14.78	15–24
Hannibal (Marion Co.)	376	26	402	6.47	15–24
Richmond (Ray Co.)	362	26	388	7.18	10–14
Cape Girardeau	565	15	580	2.59	5–9
St. Genevieve	240	71	311	22.83	5–9

Two of these churches, Hannibal and Bowling Green, are in the Salt River and Mississippi River flood plains, in precisely those areas most settled by southerners. Two, St. Genevieve and Cape Girardeau, are in southeast Missouri, Cape being on the edge of the great swamp. One, Richmond, is in northwest Missouri. It is interesting to note that, in 1839, 16.99 percent of the membership at Cape Girardeau was black. One wonders, what happened in the intervening year?

Table VI shows those same churches in historical perspective. To a certain extent, the historical data is skewed, since the changes may reflect new circuits being formed from an old one, with consequent drastic changes in membership. However, this change would not be as abrupt at ten-year intervals, unless such a change had occurred just before the decennial period. The dates listed with the circuit are the date of founding.

TABLE VI

Circuit	1821	1830	1840
Columbia (1834)			
White			333
Colored			99
Boonville (1818)★			
White			516
Colored			34

Fayette (1815)★★			
White	126	345	629
Colored	20	6	30
Independence (1834)			
White			416
Colored			6
Lexington (1832)			
White			516
Colored			36
Arrow Rock (1818)★★			
White	142	361	270
Colored	3	16	20
St. Louis (1821)			
White	95	134	359
Colored	32	124	300
Bowling Green (1832)			
White			196
Colored			34
Hannibal (1838)			
White			376
Colored			26
Richmond (1823)★★★			
White		262	362
Colored		16	26
Cape Girardeau (1809)			
White	260	325	565
Colored		33	15
St. Genevieve (1839)			
White			240
Colored			71

★ In 1821 and 1830, Boonville and Arrow Rock were listed together as the Lamoine Circuit.

★★ In 1821 and 1830, Fayette was listed as the Boonslick Circuit.

★★★ In 1830, Richmond was listed as the Fishing River Circuit.

The churches which show the best pattern of reaching black persons are Columbia, St. Louis, Cape Girardeau (when you include the 1839 figures), and St. Genevieve. Two of these churches are in areas with a high percentage of slaves in the population, two are not. These percentages remain fairly constant, with a slight drop everywhere, in the years 1840–44.

From the very beginning, Methodism in Missouri was working with both black and white populations. The early circuit riders felt an urgent call to minister to slaves, and found considerable success in the early period. However, the statistical tables demonstrate rather clearly that Methodism was never as successful with the black population as with whites. From the time of the first census, the ratio of white Methodists to the white population was always higher than the ratio of black Methodists to the black population. With two notable exceptions, churches in the areas where the slave population was the highest never had a black membership anywhere near the percentage of the black population. In other areas across the state, they achieved somewhat better success, but again with the exception of one or two churches, never achieved black membership near the ratio of blacks in the population. It can only be concluded that, despite concentrated efforts, Methodism did much better among the white population than among the black, and even where it did well among the black population (as in St. Louis), separation of the races was beginning to occur by 1840.

So an interesting pattern emerges in these early years. Methodism succeeded fairly well in reaching the black population, though not nearly so well as the white population. There was an initial positive response by blacks to Methodist preaching. There are many examples of blacks and whites worshiping together, and the development of some black leadership in class meetings and in the ranks of local preachers and exhorters. By the 1830s, there was a leveling off of black membership. It would be interesting to know the effects of national events (e.g., Denmark Vesey's revolt in 1822, Nat Turner's rebellion in 1831) on black–white relationships in Missouri. Did white Methodists stop evangelizing—or welcoming—blacks as a response to growing racial fears and tensions? Were blacks in the state fearful of a "white backlash" and therefore stayed away from the church? What about feelings evoked by the Missouri Compromise and Missouri's admission to the Union as a slave state? Was the Underground Railroad affecting black–white relationships? On all these questions, our sources are silent. One can only guess at the possible repercussions of those national events on the church.

By 1840, there was again a large increase in the number of black Methodists, but they had already begun to form separate churches (under pressure from whites?). We would love to know the stories of those separate churches, but, again, the sources for that research do not exist.

Chapter 3

THE INDIAN
MISSION

THE BACKGROUND FOR MISSION

In the early nineteenth century, there was a great wave of enthusiasm for missions in the American churches. The Second Great Awakening gave birth to a host of missionary societies, including the American Home Missionary Society and the American Board of Commissioners for Foreign Missions. The Methodists founded a Missionary Society in 1819, several years later than many other denominations. Part of the reason for this is that Methodism saw itself as a missionary church, and did not feel the need for a separate missionary society. It was interest in missions to American Indians that led to the founding of the Missionary Society.

The first lasting mission to the Indians began with the work of John Stewart in 1815. Stewart, a freeborn mulatto, had been converted at a camp meeting in Ohio, and felt called to preach to the Indians of that area. He began his work among the Wyandots on the Upper Sandusky River in 1816. He quickly made converts and organized a growing congregation. In 1819, the mission was formalized under the guidance of James B. Findley, and a school was organized. In 1820, two Wyandot preachers went to the Ojibway in Canada. Twelve years later, there were ten mission stations, with nearly two thousand adult members, and four hundred youth in eleven schools. Further west, in what would be the Illinois Conference, missions were established among the Potawatomis in 1823 and the Iroquois and Kickapoos in 1830. Missions began among the Oneidas of New York in 1829, and the Sioux, Winnebago, and Western Chippewa in 1834, the same year that Jason Lee began his mission in Oregon.

In the old southeast, the first mission was from the South Carolina conference to the Creek Indians in Georgia and Alabama, begun in 1821. The Tennessee Conference began working among the Cherokees in Alabama in 1822, and the Mississippi Conference among the Choctaws in 1825. These missions were interrupted by the forcible removal of the southern tribes to the west (the "Trail of Tears"). The Missouri Conference picked up the mission to these nations in 1830.[1]

THE SITUATION IN THE WEST

The first Indian groups who migrated west of the Mississippi to escape the whites came voluntarily.[2] A few Delaware and Shawnee from Indiana moved to Spanish Missouri in 1789. They later moved to Kansas and (some of them) to Texas. The first treaty with an emigration clause was made in 1818 with the Delaware Indians of Ohio and Indiana. By 1830, a formal Emigration Policy was in place in Washington, and Indians were moved westward as they ceded their lands in the old Northwest (Ohio, Indiana, Illinois, and Michigan). By 1830, a mix of tribes lived in the river valleys of what would become Kansas. They included the Kansas, Osages, Shawnees, Delawares, Ottowas, Peorias, Kaskaskias, Weas, Piankashaws, Kickapoos, Quapaws, Cherokees, Chippewas, Iowas, Sacs, Foxes, Potawatomies, Miamis, Wyandots, Munsees, and several tribes from New York. Methodists had been working among many of these tribes before their emigration (forced or voluntary) and there is no reason to doubt that the emigrants included some Methodists.

Emigration caused all kinds of problems. The emigrants crowded on the ranges of native tribes at a time when the horse-culture of the plains Indians called for more land, not less. The Osages warred on the emigrant Choctaw in Arkansas Territory, and several U.S. Army posts were built along the Arkansas River in 1826–27 to help keep the peace. Part of the problem was that the emigrants would rather hunt buffalo than plant crops, and they over-crowded the hunting grounds. Raids and skirmishes broke out among the tribes, as far away as the Sioux tribes roaming north of the Missouri River. William Clark (of Lewis and Clark fame) was the Indian Agent in St. Louis, and worked hard to keep the peace and make emigration a smooth transition for all the tribes. He was, however, overwhelmed by the magnitude of the problem and the limited staff and resources at his disposal.

The culture of the emigrants had been affected by contact with whites in the east. They brought with them to the West guns, trade goods, whiskey, and disease. At least some of the warfare between the tribes was cultural. The western tribes wanted to destroy those who threatened their ancestral customs and brought disease to them. This cultural antagonism also helps explain why the western tribes were not as open to Christian missionaries; they saw the missionaries as one more assault on their native culture. There is no doubt that there were many Methodists (and other Christians, as well) among the emigrants, but their experience of the faith may have only hardened the attitudes of the western tribes. A biography of Jesse Greene contains the record of a speech made by Dehedotitimyer, a "principal warrior" of the Big Osage, railing against what happened to those Osages who became Christian:

> Many of our Osages are mad: the Americans have taken away their senses; they neither plant corn in their forefathers' fields, nor hunt for the deer on the mountains, but spend their time in singing, shouting, and weeping. When they pray, they hold up their hands and turn up the whites of their eyes, crying and begging for mercy. Will not the Great Spirit despise them for their weakness? Again, they rise to their feet, clapping their hands and saying Jesus! Glory! . . . They say all this uproar is occasioned by the presence of a good spirit in their assemblies; would a good spirit make people mad? Would he take away the senses of a man? They sing songs of praise, and all the master of our brother Great God, Holy, Wise, Just, and Merciful. Will not the Great Spirit be displeased with their flattery? The Great God can hear the thoughts of their hearts as well as the words of their mouths; will he not be angry at them and turn away his face from their folly?[3]

Dehedotitimyer goes on to complain that there has been no rain for two months, the springs are drying up, the earth is cracking, and the corn is dying. The prayers of their prophets do no good, for the gods have abandoned them. He continues:

> Once we were a powerful nation; our warriors were terrible, our hunters returned loaded with game, and our old men brought us rain at the proper season, but now a strong people have crossed the great waters and oppressed our country.

He decries the loss of Osage land and culture and then asks about the Book of the white men.

> The white people say the book teaches truth, peace, honesty and kindness, but this cannot be the case, or we should not find white men to be such liars and villains as they are.

Clearly he was more impressed by the actions of whites who seized his land and tried to destroy his culture than he was by the words of faith he heard them speak. One of the persistent questions in Missouri Methodist history has always been, "why did we not send missionaries to the Osage? They were here in Missouri. What happened?" Part of the answer, at least, lies in the resentment of the Osage toward the emigrant Indians who crowded in on Osage lands and helped to destroy the Osage culture. Behind the resentment toward the emigrants was the resentment toward the whites who moved them into Osage country. Add to that the apparent hypocrisy of whites who preached peace, love, and truth while taking Osage land at the point of a gun, and you have a strong case why the Methodists were never successful among them. In addition, the Osages seem to have been strong allies of the Chouteaus and other French fur traders from St. Louis. They would likely have been more open to the Catholicism of their allies than the Methodism of people they saw as enemies.

THE BEGINNINGS OF MISSOURI METHODIST MISSIONS

Missouri Methodists began working among the Indians in 1830. In April of that year, Alexander McAlister wrote to Jesse Greene:

> I wish to call your attention to the Caw (Kansas) Indians on your frontier. Col. Daniel Boon, who is the Government's farmer among those Indians, married Mrs. McAlister's sister, which circumstance has led to a correspondence between him and myself, and the Government Agent of those Indians. Boon is among them, perhaps thirty or forty miles from Fort Osage. He promises to do all he can for the support of a school among that tribe. The agent also promises to assist, as far as he can, and informs me that the Caw Indians, according to the provisions of a treaty with the Government, have a considerable sum of money set apart to support schools among themselves, and the Agent advises us to get in there immediately and secure that fund, and improve it to their benefit. I think you might visit them, and know all about it soon, and perhaps get some pious young man to go and commence a school among them before conference.
>
> > In haste, your obedient Servant,
> > A. McAlister[4]

Several points in the letter deserve our attention. First, the "Daniel Boon" mentioned was Daniel Morgan Boone, one of the sons of the great frontiersman, Daniel Boone. Like his sister and brother-in-law, Jemima and Flanders Callaway, Daniel Morgan seems to have been a Methodist. He was related by marriage to a pioneer circuit rider, and interested in the idea of missions. Second, Boone was a "Government Farmer." That is, he had been sent by the federal government to teach the Indians how to farm. This was part of a concerted effort by the government to "convert" free-roaming Indians to a settled agricultural style of life (which would free up thousands of acres for white settlement). Third, treaties with the various tribes included the payment of sums to establish schools, also a part of the process of acculturation. In 1830, the wall of separation between church and state was thin, and both saw mutual advantage in working together. The Indian Agent, George Vashon, wanted the Methodists to get in, get that money, and put it to work.

Jesse Greene, who was the presiding elder of the Missouri District, did go to Kansas apparently, for a letter from George Vashon in July of 1830 refers to a conversation in the latter's office. Vashon reports that the American Board of Foreign Missions was not able to take on the work for another two or three years. He further reports that a Shawnee chief, Fish, was asking for a mission, and for the establishment of a school. Vashon had found both a man and a woman among the Shawnee who spoke English and would make excellent interpreters. He had a potential location for a home and school for the missionaries, and was pushing to get the mission started. He was being transferred to the Cherokee Agency, but his successor was also open to the idea of a mission. The invitations for a mission were almost irresistible.[5]

Methodists seldom ignore an invitation to a field so open to the gospel. At the meeting of the annual conference in the fall of 1830, Greene presented Vashon's letter, and the conference took immediate action. A Conference Missionary Society was organized, and missionaries were assigned. Thomas Johnson was assigned to the Shawnee Mission and his brother William to the Kaw (Kansas) Mission. Remember that in 1830, appointments to Kansas were to a "foreign" mission. Kansas was outside the boundaries of the United States.

Jesse Greene

One of the founders of the Indian mission and a great supporter of its work, Jesse Greene, was born near present-day Knoxville, Tennessee, in 1791, and became an elder in the Tennessee Conference in 1821. In 1823, he transferred to the Missouri Conference, where he served twenty-four years as a presiding elder. In 1830, he was presiding elder of the Missouri District, which included parts of Missouri, Iowa, Indian Territory, and Arkansas, and so was the natural person for George Vashon to call for help in establishing a mission to the Indians. He seems to have taken responsibility for supervising the Indian mission, both in Kansas and in the Arkansas Territory (what is now Oklahoma). His wife, whom he met while she was teaching at Shawnee Mission, later recorded that Greene called Shawnee Mission "home" and often spent his "rest days" there. Anyone who reads Mrs. Greene's biography of her husband, with its long excerpts from his journal, would have to wonder when he ever had a rest day, however.

Mary Todd, later Mrs. Greene, had been appointed a missionary to the Shawnee Mission by the New York Conference in 1838. Her appointment is a reminder that while Missouri spearheaded the mission to the Indians, all of Methodism participated. Mary Todd was a second generation Methodist: her father, before he came to America, had heard John Wesley preach from his father's tombstone at Epworth—another tie between Missouri Methodism and its Wesleyan roots.

ARKANSAS TERRITORY AND WEST

In 1831, Greene was appointed to the Arkansas District, which included almost all of Arkansas plus parts of the Creek and Cherokee Indian territory in modern Oklahoma. During this year, Methodist missions were re-established among those nations, which had been forcibly removed from the old Southeast. A letter from Henry Pengum, a Creek Indian, indicates the need for the mission. There was a Presbyterian minister working among the Creeks, but:

> Myself and my people want to know when the Methodist missionaries will come into our nation. All will be glad to see them. I want you to write to me and tell whether they are preparing and when they will be here. I wish you to tell me when you will come to see us. I think I want to go home with you, and perhaps desire to attend the Methodist Conference with you.[6]

Soon after the letter was written, Methodists appeared as missionaries among the Creeks.

In January 1833, Berville Lee wrote to Greene from the Cherokee Nation. He had been sick with measles, and now with chills and fever, so he was unable to preach or teach. The mission, however, was prospering. The school children were learning to read. Nearly twenty persons had joined the society since conference. When one remembers that conference had been held in late September or early October of 1832, and Lee may have then spent nearly a month returning to his post, this is a remarkable number. Lee reports opposition from the Presbyterians, but also notes that the Methodists added a traveling preacher who had been transferred from Tennessee, and a local preacher, Thomas Elliot, who was working on Red River Circuit.

By March of 1833, Lee was in better health. The recent quarterly meeting had been a great experience:

> The Lord was near to bless us in a very powerful manner. Five joined society, and many Christians were refreshed with the outpouring of God's Holy Spirit. About fourteen have joined since conference, but . . . some have back-slidden, and some have moved away, which leaves us about the same number that we returned at conference.[7]

Lee was planning to be married, an event for which he had waited for two years. The school he planned to open at Fort Smith, Arkansas, was not yet in operation, for there was no building. Lee himself planned to go there and put up a building for the school. These letters tell of both the hardships the missionaries faced, and the enthusiasm with which they went about their task.

On May 21, Lee wrote to Greene from another part of his circuit:

> We are doing pretty well at this mission; we have had considerable increase in the church since conference; upwards of one hundred have joined, and the

most of them appear firm, and declare by their conduct that they desire
nothing so much as the salvation of their souls, and to try to get to Heaven,
where all their sorrows will have an end.[8]

Lee reported thirty-eight children in his school, most of them children of immigrants. He expected that he would soon have fifty. It is important to remember
that many, if not most, of the immigrants had come from sophisticated settings in
the Southeast, where they had schools, churches, newspapers, and a strong local
government. They were interested in education. Many were Christians, including
a good number of Methodists. So Lee and his colleagues had moved into a field
where they were welcomed. Their experience was like that of many other circuit
riders. They were not so much about the task of converting those who had never
known Christ or the church as they were about finding those who were already
Methodists, and bringing them back to the church. From this solid foundation
they were then able to build an outreach to those persons who were not
Christian. Lee continues:

> We have held one quarterly meeting at Schism, on the Canadian, at which
> Mr. Schism, with fourteen of his neighbors, joined the church. Mr. Schism is
> the treasurer of the nation. The council was in session at the same time, near
> his house. The United States give [sic] this nation two thousand dollars annu-
> ally, for the education of their children. Through Mr. Schism's influence, the
> Methodist Church gets use of one thousand. He now wishes the M. E.
> Church to take the matter in hand, and send him good teachers. He says he
> wishes a man and his wife, who are qualified to teach school.[9]

Lee had plans for the future of the mission that he promised to tell Greene at
conference. It is regretable that he did not write them, so everyone could know
what they were. Note the importance of federal money for the work of the
mission. The missionaries were able to use money granted by the government to
the Indian nations for education. The primary use of the funds was for basic
education, but it is certain that the teachers were all carefully chosen for their faith
as well as their teaching skills, and regularly included the Bible as a part of the
curriculum.

A letter from John Hunton, written in June of 1834, offers more insight into
both the work of the mission and the state of the immigrants. Hunton had been
recruited to teach school among the Cherokees:

> I took charge of this station in the nation the 12th of January, where I have a
> large school, and generally a goodly number to hear me exhort. . . . The
> Cherokees are very unsettled, owing to the emigrating part coming in, and
> buying others out. They were much opposed to leaving the land of their
> fathers; have been distressed by the loss of many of their friends, who died on

the way, by cholera and other diseases, with various other circumstances attending emigration. Taking these things into consideration, religion progresses tolerably well among them. . . . I was at a two days' meeting three weeks since; Brother Lee and Brother Harrate attended, with three Cherokee preachers (late emigrants), two Interpreters, and several Exhorters; we had a large congregation and good preaching; sixteen joined society, and many others seemed concerned.[10]

In only a few brief phrases, Hunton captures the pain of the Cherokees who had been forced to leave their homes in North Carolina. They had not come to Oklahoma willingly; they had lost many to death on the way. But, in spite of all the pain, the mission was reaching out to them and re-establishing the church. The three Cherokee preachers who were at the camp meeting are a reminder that there were Methodists among the Cherokee in the Southeast, and they continued among them in their new home. The church was being re-established in a new and sometimes hostile environment.

Learner B. Statler's letter in late 1834 points at a problem arising from the itinerant system, and the necessity for attending a session of the annual conference a long distance from one's appointment. Statler was at the West Creek Nation Mission, on the Arkansas River. It would have taken at least a month, if not longer, for him and his fellow preachers to travel to the seat of the conference from the Arkansas River, and then return home. Statler reports that while the missionaries were gone to conference, the Presbyterian missionary took over the Methodist school. It took Statler some time after he returned from conference to straighten out the situation. There were some one hundred members of the church in this mission, with four schools. (Statler was one of those fascinating itinerants who appears all over the west. After the war, he was appointed superintendent of missions for the South church in Colorado and Montana. He was a member of the Kentucky, Missouri, St. Louis, Indian Mission, Kansas Mission, Western, Denver, and Montana conferences. Not all the restless feet in the old west belonged to fur trappers, scouts, and cowboys!)

The Creek, Choctaw, and Cherokee missions were transferred to the Arkansas Conference when it was organized in 1836.

MISSIONS IN KANSAS

As previously noted, the missions in Kansas began in 1830, with the establishment of the Missouri Conference Missionary Society at the conference session in September. On November 20, Alexander McAlister, the presiding elder, and William Johnson arrived among the Kansas Indians. On December 19, Johnson opened a school there in a room provided by the Indian agent, but had few students that first winter because of extreme cold. In the spring, he built a separate school building, which was also used as a church. The school had ten Indian and seven white children. He wrote to the Missionary Society in June:

> We have preaching every Sabbath, but there are few who understand the English language well enough to be profited by hearing. As to preaching to the Indians at large, I am not at the present prepared to do much, having no suitable interpreter; this circumstance has led me to apply all my convenient time to study of their language. I have formed a vocabulary of about 600 words, and now think 600 or 800 more will enable me to speak with some fluency. . . . This is a large and needy field of labour. There are about 1,500 souls in the Kanzas [sic] tribe; and in addition to these there are large neighboring tribes which speak the same language—making in all about 7,000 who cry aloud for our assistance.[11]

In June, Johnson wrote to the Board that he had two cabins built, twenty acres fenced and planted, and a garden started. The Indians had gone off to hunt buffalo and would return sometime in July. At this point in his ministry, Johnson had to report that he had no converts, partly because of the language barrier. He was learning the language rapidly and hoped soon to be able to preach in the Kansas tongue. In February of 1839, he reported some progress, though he was saddened by the fact that four separate parties were leaving to make war on the Pawnee:

> In conclusion, I want to state a simple fact, and then leave the condition of this people with the church and with God. This people must be rescued from their wretchedness or sunk forever, and no church has undertaken for them but the Methodist Episcopal Church. The government is doing nothing for them but furnishing a farmer and smithery. . . . We ask an interest in the prayers of God's people for this nation.[12]

Thomas and Sarah Johnson arrived in December of 1830 to begin work among the Shawnee. He built a double two-story log building, with two rooms about twenty feet square and fifteen feet apart. The space between the two rooms was enclosed and used as a hallway. The west room was intended for a chapel and schoolroom; the east room for family living quarters. The second story was living and sleeping rooms for employees and guests. They moved in during the spring of 1831. This was a typical frontier mission—build your own buildings, recruit your own congregation and students, and provide the primary support for your own work.

There was actually a fierce competition with the Baptists over who would open the first school among the Shawnee. The band led by Fish, who had had contact with the Methodists in Ohio, accepted the Methodist proposal in November. In December, a committee of Shawnee leaders was appointed to hear Thomas Johnson preach, and then report to the tribe. The committee's report was said to have been that the preacher knew just what they did, only better. This again suggests that many of the Shawnee were already Christians, or had at least been exposed to Christian preaching, before they emigrated.

When the Johnsons returned from conference in the fall of 1832, they found smallpox raging among the tribes and the Indians leaving their villages in an attempt to escape the disease. The school had to be closed because of the epidemic. When the smallpox subsided and the Indians returned home, Thomas Johnson made a commitment to spend the winter moving among the villages, learning the Shawnee language, and preaching the gospel. Children returned to the school, and there were as many as thirty enrolled.

In 1835, Thomas Johnson visited the Kansas and Peoria villages. A member of the Methodist society in the Peoria village had died, and had requested that her people meet at the grave and have preaching when she was buried. Thomas Johnson explained the doctrine of the resurrection to the Indians and he writes: "they all appeared to feel thankful, while they contemplated the happiness of meeting their departed sister where death would never molest them again." He also reported that the Shawnee mission was doing well; both the school and the society were "large and regular in attendance." The Delaware mission was gaining ground, and he also felt hopeful about the future of the Kickapoo mission (where J. C. Berryman was the missionary). He had asked the officers of the dragoons (U.S. Army) stationed in the area to gather information on the tribes between the mission and the Rocky Mountains, clearly with a view of extending his missionary labors to them as well.

In February 1832, William Johnson began a school for the Delawares. In May of that year, General Conference changed the boundaries of the Missouri Conference to include the Indian missions and Arkansas Territory. The Indian missions were formed into a separate district at the meeting of the Missouri Conference in September. In the meantime, the Shawnee nation still living in Ohio ceded their lands to the United States and immigrated to Kansas, with the first arrivals about Christmas time. There was a Methodist society of about forty members among the Shawnee already in Kansas, with Fish as the head of the society.

In 1833, Bishop Soule visited the missions on his way to conference, which was held in Arkansas that year. Jerome Berryman writes:

> Bishop Soule had, on his way to the Conference, visited our Indian Mission among the Shawnees and Delawares, on Kansas River, where Thomas and William Johnson were then laying the foundation for mission work among the several tribes that occupied that part of our western border. The Bishop had spent a few days with the Brothers Johnson, in surveying the ground, with a view of extending the work of missions there, as the result of which he determined to establish two additional stations; one among the Peorias, on the waters of the Osage, and the other among the Kickapoos, just above Fort Leavenworth, on the Missouri.[13]

Berryman was appointed to the Kickapoo Mission that year. He traveled back from conference with Bishop Soule, Jesse Greene, the Johnsons, and Andrew Monroe. Berryman's observations about that trip give a fascinating glimpse into the lives of the circuit riders, particularly among the Indians. The bishop had a large stock of peaches, which he offered to the preachers. Berryman reports that he ate thirty-two, and then a full breakfast! In fact, he says, there was always a contest between himself and Thomas Johnson over who could eat the most. His strong stomach helped him a great deal when eating from a common pot among the Indians, or when dog meat was the delicacy of the evening!

Berryman returned to St. Charles County (in Missouri), bought some necessities for the mission, and set out for Kansas with his wife. The Kickapoos had just been moved from Illinois that summer and did not yet have a permanent settlement. Berryman quickly built a cabin for his family, and a schoolhouse, which soon had ninety pupils. This became the center of the Kickapoo community. In addition to his skills as a preacher and teacher, Berryman was something of an inventor:

> I constructed a machine by which they might at least be aided in learning the alphabet. I took four thin boards about three inches in width and six feet or less in length, and nailing them together so as to form a box I fastened it perpendicularly to the schoolroom wall. Then I took another board that would work up and down in this box and pasted the letters of the alphabet on one side of it at short intervals. I fastened a cord to the top end of this sliding board, and, passing it over a pulley above, I was enabled to take my seat at a convenient distance and by pulling the cord present each letter singly at a small opening made for this purpose in the front side of the box. I then divided my scholars into classes of convenient size, and calling these classes up one at a time caused them to form a half circle in front of my machine, and taught them the alphabet as above indicated. In two days' time I think every one knew any letter at sight. I also taught them to spell words of one syllable in the same way.[14]

The development of the Manual Labor School as a boarding institution apparently helped the missionaries make great strides in helping their pupils learn to read and write in English.

In 1835, Berryman submitted a letter to the *Western Christian Advocate* in which he reported some success in reaching the Kickapoos:

> . . . some of them are truly pious. They are now united with us; and we frequently have very interesting meetings among them. At several of these meetings lately Ke-en-e-kuk, their leader, took the Bible in his hand, after we had preached, and told them that was God's book—that we ought to try to understand it, and that they must look to us for instruction. They seemed

at first to have been afraid that we intended to introduce something new which would be injurious to them; but we trust these fears are giving way to better sentiments.[15]

Ke-en-e-kuk had been preaching to his people for several years in Illinois, before they came west. They referred to him as "the prophet." He was received by the missionaries as a local preacher and put to work as an evangelist. Ke-en-e-kuk practiced flagellation as a form of worship, saying that the punishment from whipping was an atonement and expiation for their sins. The missionaries disavowed Ke-en-e-kuk and his work, and later built up a class of about fifty people who were not under his influence. These included Pes-haw-gun, a Kickapoo, and Eneas, a Kickapoo/Potawatomie. Pes-haw-gun was both an interpreter for Berryman and an evangelist. The two of them visited house to house, either together or singly, and Pes-haw-gun was apparently an effective evangelist among his people. Berryman was preaching to the troops stationed at Fort Leavenworth (at the express request of their commanding officer, Col. Dodge), in addition to his work among the Indians.

Berryman noted in his memoirs some of the delicacies of preaching through an interpreter, and how easy it is to misunderstand another language. He once took for a text, "The Lord is my sun and my shield." His interpreter translated "sun" with the term for "male child," a natural mistake, so that the text became "The Lord is my male child."

Fortunately, Berryman understood enough of the language to catch the mistake; otherwise that would have been an interesting sermon! The Johnsons fared better with interpreters among the Shawnee and Delaware, because they had persons who had studied English in the east, and who were at least favorably disposed toward Christianity.

By 1835, the Commissioner of Indian Affairs reported one hundred twenty-five students and eleven teachers scattered among five tribes in the mission. The Shawnee Methodist Mission Church had a membership of seventy-eight, with another thirty-four on trial. Also in 1835, Thomas Johnson reported to the Missionary Society about the missions. He says about the Kansas Indians:

> They cultivate only a small portion of ground, and this done chiefly by the women, with hoes. They do not plough. They have no fences. Their only dependence for meat is on the chase, and the deer have entirely disappeared from their prairies. They have to go 250 miles, or farther, to find the buffalo, and then are frequently driven back by their enemies; and should they succeed in finding the buffalo, if they bring any of the meat home, it frequently has to be packed by their women, for many of them have no horses to ride; and their means of support are becoming more difficult every year, for the buffalo, like the deer, are fast retiring. . . . We hope to be able, at the next session of our annual conference, to send missionaries among these people.[16]

Johnson was more sanguine about the work among the Peori, Shawnee, Delaware, and Kickapoo tribes. In addition, he reported to the secretary that he would not be able to visit any of the tribes to the west before conference, but that several officers among the dragoons (U.S. Cavalry) were gathering information for him as they met with the Indians between Missouri and the Rocky Mountains. Johnson was clear, at least in his own mind, that the mission to the Indians was not limited by geography!

In May of 1838, Thomas Johnson went to New York to meet with the board of the Missionary Society about establishing a central manual labor training school for the mission. As a result of that trip, the Board of Managers recommended to the Missouri Conference that they establish such a school. The United States government promised funds for constructions of the buildings and for annual support. The resolution also established a committee of three to take charge of setting up the school and reporting to the Conference each year. The number, function, and size of the buildings were spelled out, with some discretion allowed if the cost of construction was too high. It was also on this trip that Johnson challenged Mary Todd (the future wife of Jesse Greene) to come to Kansas to teach. When the Missouri Conference met to establish the school, Thomas Johnson, Jesse Greene, and J. C. Berryman were appointed the committee of three. The site chosen for the school was in present-day Johnson County, Kansas, six miles south of the mouth of the Kansas River and about a half mile from the western boundary of Missouri.

The purpose of the Manual Labor School was to teach students trades, as well as basic education. On one hand, it can be said that the school was an example of the attempt of white society to acculturate the native peoples, and therefore was an instrument for the destruction of native cultures. On the other hand, such schools did help bridge the gap between a hunting culture, which was vanishing with the disappearance of the great herds of game, and a more agrarian culture. It is easy from a modern perspective to judge the work of such schools as instruments of oppression and destruction. But the Conference of 1830 and the missionaries to the Indians do not live in our times. They lived in their own rapidly changing world, and responded to it in the best ways they understood. However triumphalistic modern society might consider their work, it must be remembered that they considered themselves first to be guided by the hand of God in their work, and second to be responding to needs expressed by the native peoples among whom they worked. Certainly the enrollment at the Manual Labor School and the growing membership of the churches suggests that their work was not unwelcome.

In the winter of 1839, Thomas Johnson sent Berryman to Pittsburgh, Pennsylvania, to purchase materials for the school. Berryman went as far as Louisville on horseback, with stops in Missouri, Illinois, and Kentucky to give talks on the mission and raise money. His interpreter, Eneas, went with him as far as Louisville. They raised some five hundred dollars for the mission (a goodly sum in 1839). In Pittsburgh, Berryman stayed with Wesley Browning and his wife. As a result of this visit, Browning requested a transfer to Missouri and was appointed to the Indian Manual Labor School. Berryman wound up chartering a steamboat (serendipitously named the *Shawnee*) to deliver his materials from Pittsburgh to Kansas Landing (now Kansas City).

Thomas Johnson was appointed superintendent of the Indian Mission District, as well as to the Shawnee Mission. Wesley Browning and David Kinnear were assigned to the Manual Labor School, which appeared as a separate appointment for the first time. Mrs. Browning, Mrs. Jesse Greene, and Miss Elizabeth Lee were also assigned to the school. The membership of the Shawnee mission

Thomas Johnson was the founder and leader of the Indian Mission from its inception until the War Between the States.

church was twenty-two white, three colored, and ninety-three Indians. By the early spring of 1840, Johnson was compelled to turn away prospective students from the school until they could provide more buildings. A government grant of $6,250, which arrived in 1840, eased the pressure on the building funds and allowed the school to expand.

Because the boundaries of the land claimed by the school touched on the great migration routes to the west, there were frequent visitors to the mission. These included such notable persons as Jason Lee, the pioneer missionary to Oregon, and Father DeSmet, the "blackrobe" missionary from the Roman Catholic Church to the tribes of the high plains, in addition to the Methodist bishops who called on regular tours of inspection. John C. Fremont stopped by on his expeditions to the west, along with Kit Carson. Dr. Marcus Whitman set out for the Oregon mission from the school.

Thomas Johnson was superannuated by the Conference of 1841, because of ill health. J. C. Berryman was put in charge of the school, and William Johnson made superintendent, as well as missionary to the Kansas tribe.

Thomas Johnson

Thomas Johnson was born in Virginia in 1802, moved to Missouri in 1822, became a member of the Missouri Conference in 1826, and was appointed to the

Indian Mission in 1830. He served that mission from 1830 to 1841 as both missionary and superintendent, and again from 1847 to 1865 as head of the Manual Labor School. His journey to New York to meet with the denominational Missionary Society in 1838 had led to the founding of the school. He was elected to three General Conferences. He became a traveling elder in the Methodist Episcopal Church, South, in 1845, at the time of division. In addition to his career as a minister, he was a delegate to Congress from the Territory of Kansas (though he was not allowed to take his seat). He was also active in the work that led to the formation of Kansas both as a territory and as a state. He was shot by an unknown person in the new year in 1865, and died on January 3rd. The Indian Mission Conference and the Manual Labor School are his monuments.

William Johnson

William Johnson (1805–1842) was born in Nelson County, Virginia, and converted at the age of nineteen. The following year (1825), he moved to Missouri. He was licensed to preach and admitted on trial in the Missouri Conference 1828, and in full connection in 1830. In that same year, he was sent to the Indian mission, where he worked in schools, in churches, and as superintendent for twelve years. He died of pneumonia at the Manual Labor School in April of 1842. Edward R. Ames, who was the Secretary of the Missionary Society, toured the Indian Mission with Bishop Roberts shortly after William Johnson's death. He reported that Johnson was the only missionary "who ever learned an Indian language so as to be able to preach in it: He spoke the Shawnee, so as to be able to converse in it on ordinary subjects. He was probably the only white man that ever learned the Kanzas [sic] language with grammatical accuracy." In a day when language proficiency is the first requirement for a missionary, it seems strange to us that these early missionaries did not learn the languages of the tribes to whom they went. Apparently, William Johnson was the great exception.

Jerome C. Berryman

Also a member of the class of 1828, J. C. Berryman came to Missouri from Kentucky in that year. Shortly after his arrival, he received his license to preach and was appointed to a circuit in Arkansas. In 1833, he was sent to the Kickapoo Mission, as has already been noted. Berryman stayed at the Kickapoo Mission and School until 1847, when he became presiding elder of the Cape Girardeau District. During his long ministry, he was head of Howard High School (Fayette), Arcadia High School, and the founder of Arcadia College. He was the last surviving member of the General Conference of 1844. In the separation, he cheerfully committed himself to the Methodist Episcopal Church, South, but was a staunch Union man during the war.

Life at the Indian Manual Labor School

J. C. Berryman reports that the school had an average attendance of about one hundred, all boarded, lodged, and clothed by the school. There was a "mechanics department" for the boys (which taught crafts such as carpentry and cabinet making), a "domestic department" for the girls (which, among other things, made the clothing for the students), a farm of about six hundred acres, plus a gristmill and a sawmill. The mills did grinding and sawing for the area, which brought in a little extra income. The students worked about five hours a day (except for winter), and were in class about six hours. The school was without cost to parents. The cost per student (above and beyond the goods they produced) was about one hundred dollars. More than once, the school was in debt at the end of the year because the government monies had not arrived. In February of 1843, for example, Edward R. Ames, representing the Missionary Society, pressed the government for the twenty-five hundred dollars due the school, so the school would not lose its credit with the area merchants. The superintendent of the school made a regular report to the Commissioner of Indian Affairs, who in turn reported to the War Department, the cabinet level department charged with Indian affairs. The superintendent also was accountable to the Missouri Conference and the Missionary Society, so he was an agent of both church and state.

The school farm raised all the food for the school, sold enough to pay for tea, coffee, sugar, and so on, and still yielded an annual surplus in both grain and livestock. This obviously lessened the cost of the support for students.

In July of 1843, a choir of about forty students went to a Sunday school celebration at Independence, Missouri.

THE CRISIS OF 1844

The formation of an Indian Mission Conference was approved by the General Conference in 1844, though not without considerable debate. Jerome C. Berryman argued for the formation of a separate conference, on the grounds that preachers would not "flee" from their own conference. Apparently, he thought it was too easy for the missionaries to go back to Missouri and take a circuit, instead of staying with the mission. Berryman also argued that a separate conference would reduce financial dependence on the denomination, because Indian preachers would be raised up in a separate conference and the people would cheerfully support them. Finally, he said, the Manual Labor School (of which Berryman was the superintendent) had broken down barriers between the tribes; a separate conference would help do the same thing. Mr. McFerrin, who also had served in the Indian Mission, argued that the time was not right and that a separate conference would be a failure. The matter was referred to the Committee on Boundaries, which approved the formation of the Indian Mission Conference.

The new conference boundaries were the Missouri River on the north, Missouri and Arkansas on the east, the Red River on the south, and the Rocky Mountains on the west. J. C. Berryman was appointed superintendent of the conference (a common practice in the formation of mission conferences) and E. T. Peery took his place at the Manual Labor School. The first session of the Indian Mission Conference was held in the fall near Tahlequah, the seat of the Cherokee nation. Bishop Morris presided at the session. There were twenty-seven members of the conference, about one-fourth of whom were Indian preachers. The General Conference had already agreed on a Plan of Separation, and the Mission Conference began its existence by dealing with the question of a dividing church. They adopted the following resolutions:

> that they concur in the action of the southern delegates (at General Conference)
> that they elect delegates to the Louisville Convention
> that they deplore the necessity for division and pray for God's blessing on the church

One of the delegates elected to Louisville, William H. Goode (the superintendent of the Fort Coffee Academy in the Choctaw nation), chose not to serve. He was sure that the Indian Mission Conference would "go South," and he was opposed to both the plan of separation and the organization of a separate church. The Mission Conference did, in fact, align with the southern branch of Methodism, which is not surprising given both its geographical location and the fact that nearly all of its ministers had come from southern states.

At the second session of the conference, in 1845, J. C. Berryman and Wesley Browning were elected delegates to the first General Conference of the southern church, which would meet the following year in Petersburg, Virginia.

MISCELLANEOUS

In October of 1848, there was a convocation of the Indian tribes near Fort Leavenworth. The emigrant tribes relit the council fire of the old confederacy of the Northwest. The Wyandots were confirmed as the keeper of the council fire.

In 1848, Thomas Johnson (whose health had recovered so that he could return to the school) began a "Classical Academy" as part of the Manual Labor School. It offered courses in English, literature, Greek, and Latin. Though it had a few Indian students, it was primarily a boarding high school for white students from the States. Rev. Nathan Scarritt was the teacher for the academy. The cost, including board, room, and laundry, was $1.25 per week.

There was agitation in Kansas Territory over the fact that Thomas Johnson was a slaveholder, and that several of the Shawnee chiefs owned slaves who did most of their farm work. The authors of the agitation felt this violated both the letter and the spirit of federal laws banning slavery in the territories.

In 1853, Thomas Johnson was elected a representative from Kansas Territory to the Congress in Washington. He was not allowed to take his seat because of complaints, but he was active for a couple of months in working for the formal organization of Kansas and Nebraska into territories. Johnson held out for the Platte River as the northern boundary of Kansas Territory, but agreed to the fortieth parallel when it became clear that otherwise the bill establishing the territory would be defeated.

In 1854, there were several events important for the future of the mission. A treaty with the Shawnee Indians ceded their territory in Kansas to the United States, except for two hundred thousand acres set aside for homes for their people. The same treaty granted the Missionary Society of the Methodist Episcopal Church, South, three sections of land including the school. Five acres, including the meeting-house and cemetery, were set aside for the Shawnee Methodist church. Johnson had to defend the treaty in the U.S. Senate, where he also defended himself and the other missionaries against the charge of becoming rich at the expense of the government. The General Conference organized the work in Kansas into a separate conference known as the Kansas Mission Conference. It is not clear if this mission included the white settlers, or only the Indian work. The manual labor courses at the school were discontinued, and only literary courses were given in the future.

A reporter for the *New York Tribune* visited the mission in 1855. He called it the "headquarters of the pro-slavery party in Kansas, with Johnson as one of its leaders." Johnson was elected president of the council at the first meeting of the Kansas territorial legislature, which met at the Manual Labor School. Obviously, this missionary preacher and teacher would have a strong influence on the future development of the territory. The annual report of the school showed one hundred twenty-two students, who were taught spelling, reading, writing, arithmetic, English grammar, geography, composition, and declamation (public speaking). The boys continued to work on the farm, and the girls worked at making clothes, managing the dairy, and so on.

In 1856, the Missionary Society of the Methodist Episcopal Church, South, gave Thomas Johnson one of its three sections of land for his services to the society. It granted him a second section, for which he assumed the society's debt to the government of ten thousand dollars. Johnson continued to purchase a slave from time to time, which one writer said was a "strange comment on a Christian church." Johnson was also accused by abolitionists as being "a warm adherent of border-ruffianism." In September, Bishop Pierce convened the first session of the Kansas Mission Conference. The churches had 672 members, of which 482 were white, 2 colored, and 176 Indians. Clearly education had been more successful among the Indians than had evangelism.

The General Conference of 1850 changed the boundaries of the Mission Conference by transferring the missions in present-day Kansas to the St. Louis conference. They then became a part of the Lexington District.

In 1858, the Shawnee Nation and the Missionary Board of the Methodist Episcopal Church, South, voted to recommend that the government not renew its contract at the end of the school year. The reason was that the purpose of the school had not been realized, since the situation among the Shawnees had changed, and they were no longer sending their children to the school. In December of that year, Thomas Johnson and A. S. Johnson, his son, formed a partnership to carry on the Shawnee Manual Labor School and farm. Thomas Johnson then moved to Kansas City and his son remained at the mission. The Shawnees continued to complain about the management of the school, which was why they had withdrawn their children.

Kansas was admitted into the Union in January of 1861. The sixth and last session of the Kansas Mission Conference was held in September under close surveillance by anti-slavery Kansans. In September of 1862, the Shawnee Manual Labor School was suspended, and the contract between the government and the Missionary Society was annulled. Johnson spent the next two years trying to settle the financial affairs of the school with the Department of the Interior. The missionary society still owed two thousand dollars to the government for the land, but the government owed the school some seventy-five hundred dollars. In 1864, a new treaty with the Shawnee declared the contract forfeited on the grounds that the Methodist Episcopal Church, South, was disloyal. The money would be paid if the Secretary of the Interior could certify that the Manual Labor School was being conducted.

The mission that had begun with such high hopes had dwindled away. The focus of Indian missions shifted to the Indian Territory (now Oklahoma) and the Indian Mission Conference moved to an arena independent of the Missouri conferences of the Methodist Episcopal Church, South.

Chapter 4

German
Methodism

EARLY METHODISM: A GERMAN INFLUENCE

John Wesley himself was deeply influenced by German piety. On his voyage to America, he was terrified by the Atlantic storms, sure he was going to die without ever having come into a saving relationship with Jesus Christ. The calm faith of the Moravian Pietists on that ship both attracted and disturbed Wesley, because he knew he did not have the calm assurance they displayed. When Wesley began his first class meeting in Savannah, all the members were Germans. A Moravian missionary, August Gottlieb Spangenberg, helped Wesley see the importance of knowing Christ personally. When he asked if Wesley knew Jesus Christ, Wesley replied, "I know he is the Savior of the world." "Ah," said Spangeberg, "but do you know that he has saved you?" That was the crucial question with which Wesley continued to struggle. Back in England, Peter Bohler, another Moravian, encouraged Wesley to keep preaching faith until he had it. After Aldersgate, Wesley spent several months in Germany, visiting Count Zinzendorf and his community of Pietists at Herrnhut. Although Wesley later broke with the Pietistic tradition, it influenced him at a crucial point in his life. German Pietism helped to shape early Methodism.

Less than thirty years later, Methodists in America were claiming German converts. Robert Strawbridge, the maverick lay founder of Methodism in Maryland, reported success among the German immigrants in his community. Francis Asbury often visited German settlements, but Henry Boehm had to do the preaching, because Asbury spoke no German. Asbury and the Methodists missed a great opportunity when they failed to provide for a mission to the Germans. They felt it would be "inexpedient" to use two languages in the Methodist

Church, and that the Germans should learn English and be assimilated into (English-speaking) American society as quickly as possible. Thus, there would be no need for a special mission to the Germans.

So God created a way to minister to Germans in their own language. Philip William Otterbein was sent to America as a missionary by the German Reformed Church. He began holding meetings not unlike Methodist revivals, and drew many German converts. Otterbein and Asbury were close friends, so much so that Otterbein assisted in Asbury's ordination. But they disagreed so strongly over the question of preaching in German that Otterbein pulled away from Methodism and, together with Martin Boehm, founded the United Brethren Church. Jacob Albright also began preaching in German soon after his conversion. He became a Methodist, believing that this was the denomination whose doctrine fit most closely with his experience. However, when he began gathering Germans into classes and societies whose meetings were held in their own language, the Methodists would not accept the language difference, and Albright called a council of "his" people to organize a new church. So, in 1803 the Evangelical Association came into being. These two groups, which would later unite to become the Evangelical United Brethren, ministered faithfully to German immigrants and their descendants for nearly two hundred years.

GERMAN MIGRATION

What Asbury failed to see was the great migration of German communities to the United States, beginning only a few short years after his death in 1816. In the 1820s about eight thousand emigrants came from Germany to America. Out of this migration came the first great influx of Germans to Missouri. Gottfried Duden came to St. Louis in 1824 and bought a farm in (modern) Warren County. He returned to Germany in 1827 and published a book about how easy life was in the New World. Duden was wealthy enough to hire his American neighbors to clear his fields, plant his crops, and so on, while he explored the countryside, read, and wrote letters home. These circumstances affected his understanding of just how easy life was in Missouri. Unfortunately, the three years he was in Missouri, there were mild winters and lush summers, so his book and his letters promised a life on the frontier that was far easier than the reality would prove in later years.[1] Nevertheless, his book influenced thousands of Germans to come to Missouri.

The times were ripe for German emigration. After the Napoleonic wars, Germany was devastated. Farms and cities were destroyed by nearly three decades of war. So many people had fled from the cities to the rural areas that there was not enough land to provide food for all of them. In addition, the Industrial Revolution of the 1830s and 1840s meant many craftsmen and factory workers were replaced by machines, particularly in the clothing industry. Duden's book—and the reports of other Germans in America—promised cheap land, jobs, low taxes, and political and religious freedom. Germans responded by the hundreds of thousands. In the 1830s, more than 150,000 German immigrants landed in America. Nearly half a million came in the 1840s, driven by hunger and a longing for freedom. The failure of the democratic revolutions of 1848 plus a horrible economy sent another million Germans to America during the 1850s. All told, more than seven million Germans would immigrate to America in the nineteenth century.

Because of letters home by early settlers, many communities in Missouri and elsewhere were settled by emigrants from the same area in Germany. Westphalia, in Osage County, was settled primarily by emigrants from the province of Westphalia. Emigrants from the lower Rhine Valley settled Loose Creek and Bavarians Rich Fountain. Washington, Missouri, was settled by villagers from Osnabruck.

Friedrich Steines, a teacher from Prussia, arrived in St. Louis in July 1834. By the end of the summer, his wife and four children had died in a cholera epidemic. The story of their deaths was repeated again and again in German families: they died of cholera and other diseases, of pneumonia in the cold winters, in ship-wrecks, and storms at sea. Steines moved to Franklin County and began a school for boys, which became a magnet for German families in the St. Louis area for many years. Nearly one hundred fifty years later, there were members of the Steines family still active in Bethel United Methodist Church, in Pond.

German immigrants were skilled craftsmen, tradesmen, doctors, and teachers. They brought desperately needed craft and technical skills to St. Louis and smaller communities around the state. By 1850, Germans made up nearly one third of the population of St. Louis, and filled many smaller towns and villages.

Hermann, Missouri, for example, began with a vision of a community where the German language, values, and traditions would always be carried on. In 1837, the German Settlement Society in Philadelphia purchased a large tract of land where Hermann stands today, and began to send settlers to the west. The first settlers arrived in December of 1837, and struggled to survive the winter. Others spent the winter working in St. Louis and came on to Hermann in the spring. A year later, Hermann had five stores, two hotels, a post office, a brass band, and two shooting clubs. The land was not good for farming, but it was excellent for vine-yards. Wineries, shoemaking, and general commerce made the fortunes of the town, which also became an important shipping point on the Missouri River. The first school was built in 1839. Pupils went to school five hours a day in winter, and a half day in summer, six days a week, with no classes on Wednesday and Saturday afternoons. In 1848, the Missouri Legislature passed a law that said the school in Hermann would "forever remain a German school," with classes taught in German in all grades. This practice continued until well after the First World War.

The first German settlers in Westphalia came in the 1830s to a wild frontier. Dr. Bernhard Bruns had some money and was able to build a large house quickly, but many of the settlers were poor German peasants who had spent everything they had just to get this far. They had to borrow tools from their American neighbors to build rude cabins, and "make do" for almost everything. Having been farmers in Germany, they knew the kind of land they wanted, and chose the best farmland available. In addition to clearing land, planting crops, building homes, splitting rails for fences, caring for livestock, and raising families, they had to adjust to new crops. Corn was the principal crop in their new home, as opposed to the rye or wheat they were used to. Corn bread replaced rye bread as a staple in the diet of those early years. Floods, drought, a blight of squirrels that ate all the corn crop in 1839, loneliness, cholera, and other diseases all combined to make life hard for the settlers. Their dreams of a better life for their children turned sour as they watched those children die. But the survivors did build a better life. Fifteen years after the first settlement, there were sixty-seven hundred people in the county. This same pattern prevailed in other German communities as well. A growing, prosperous population, with schools and community values already planted, was a "field white to the harvest" for the church.

RELIGIOUS DEVELOPMENTS AMONG GERMAN IMMIGRANTS

Many German immigrants were Roman Catholic, and the Catholic Church was already established in St. Louis and ready to provide spiritual leadership for the newcomers. The bishop in St. Louis sent Father Ferdinand Helias, a Jesuit priest, to Westphalia in the spring of 1838. Father Helias had conflicts with the community, particularly with Dr. Bruns, which ended in a lawsuit. Father Helias won the suit, but left the community. He spent the rest of his life ministering to German communities in central and western Missouri.

The Lutheran Church, Missouri Synod, grew out of German settlements. Martin Stephan, a Lutheran pastor in Saxony, was suspended from his position as pastor at St. John's Church in Dresden in 1837. Since he had been the pastor there for twenty-eight years, he had many loyal followers, several hundred of whom helped him form an emigration society to come to Missouri and build a new religious community. Stephan's son, also named Martin, came with him, but his wife and daughters stayed behind in Dresden. (Mrs. Stephan may have had excellent reasons for not wanting to follow her husband to the New World.)

Some six hundred members of the society arrived safely in St. Louis and began desperately looking for work and a place to settle. Finally they bought land in Perry County along the Mississippi River, and the first colonists left St. Louis in April 1839. Soon after, Stephan was charged with adultery, misuse of funds, and other offenses. Several women in the society admitted to sexual relations with their pastor, and he had lived in luxury in St. Louis while the rest of the society lived on the ragged edge of poverty. The colonists voted to remove him from office and gave him the choice of returning to Germany for trial or removing to Illinois. He chose Illinois. The group split up, some staying in St. Louis, some returning to Germany, and the others moving to Perry County. C. F. W. Walther became their spiritual leader.

In spite of their rocky beginning, the colony prospered. In 1839, while they were still struggling out of poverty, the colony opened a college, which offered courses in six languages, religion, geography, history, mathematics, science, music, philosophy, and drawing. Both men and women attended the school, which became known as the Log Cabin Seminary. It lasted only a few years, but was the forerunner of Concordia Seminary in St. Louis, and the rest of the educational enterprise of the Lutheran church. The Evangelical Lutheran Synod of Missouri, Ohio, and Other States was founded in 1847, as a new denomination, with C. F. W. Walther as its first president. Later it would be renamed the Lutheran Church, Missouri Synod and become one of the most influential Protestant bodies in the United States.

Bethel, Missouri, was founded by William Keil as a Christian communal society.[2] Keil had been converted at a German Methodist revival in 1838, but soon left the Methodist Church to become an independent preacher. He was fascinated by the concept of communal living and caught up in the dream of building a religious community based on the New Testament model. In 1844, his community bought thirty-five hundred acres in Shelby County, and some five hundred followers migrated from Pennsylvania and Ohio. They first built a church, then places of business. Within a few years there were more than six hundred settlers in this utopian community. Each family was given a house, and there was a two-story dormitory in the center of town for the single men. The colony consisted of a church, homes, the dormitory, a school, tannery, distillery, mill, glove factory, drugstore, and wagon shop. Gloves made by the colonists were so superior in quality that they won first prize at the New York World's Fair in 1858. The distillery brought in the largest amounts of cash, however. Whiskey was sold by the wagonload in Quincy, Illinois, for fifteen cents a gallon! Bethel had the first steam mill in rural Missouri. Everything used in the colony was made there.

Bethel was a theocracy and Keil's word was final in all matters. Members owned their own homes, but worked together and all the proceeds went to a common treasury. Goods were kept in a storehouse, and anyone could take whatever he or she needed. This did away with a money economy. Bethel thrived for ten years, but Keil was not completely satisfied. He dreamed of a chain of colonies reaching to the West Coast, so in 1855, he planned an expedition to Oregon. Willie Keil was his father's favorite son, and had been promised that he could lead the train to Oregon. Before the expedition left, Willie died. So Keil sent to St. Louis for a metal casket, which he filled with alcohol (perhaps the colony's whiskey?) and put the boy's body into it. The coffin went into a wagon which led the train to Oregon. The emigrant train/funeral procession went to Aurora, Oregon, where the second colony was established. Keil ruled both colonies from his new home in Oregon until his death in 1877, when they dissolved.

THE GENESIS OF GERMAN METHODISM

It has already been demonstrated that Asbury's predictions of the demise of the German language were proved wrong by immigration. By the 1830s, the *Western Christian Advocate* was urging that outreach to the German immigrants be started. The Ohio Conference began this work, when it appointed William Nast (who had come to America in 1828) to work among the Germans in and around Cincinnati. The Board of Missions paid his one hundred dollar salary, the standard for a single preacher in those days. A year later, he was appointed to a three hundred mile circuit centered on Columbus, Ohio. Six years later, this circuit had twenty-two ministers preaching in the German language. Nast began publishing a religious weekly, *Der Christliche Apologete*, in 1839, thus becoming the founder of German Methodist literature, as well as of German Methodism, in America.

A German Missionary to Missouri

In August of 1841, Bishop Morris appointed Ludwig S. Jacoby as "missionary" to the St. Louis area. Jacoby was born in Mecklenburg, Germany, in 1813, the son of pious Jewish parents. He was converted to Christianity as a young man and baptized as a Lutheran. In 1839, he was teaching German in a school in Cincinnati. He says of the German Methodists:

> Of a German Methodist I had never heard. One evening, however, a young man to whom I gave instruction in English asked me if I would not go with him to the German Methodist Church Sabbath evening, as if it was a real theater—a place of much amusement.[3]

Jacoby went, intending to try to make Dr. Nast, the preacher, laugh. Instead, he found himself listening intently. He attended prayer meeting the next Thursday, met with Nast, and borrowed a copy of Fletcher's *Appeal* (a book by the English Methodist, John Fletcher, which had a strong influence on the doctrinal development of Methodism, both in England and in America). Shortly before Christmas, Jacoby joined the church, was licensed to exhort, and began to preach in the German areas of Cincinnati.

When Jacoby and his wife arrived in St. Louis, they rented the use of the Presbyterian Church at Seventh and Biddle Streets. His wife told him that she would probably be the entire congregation for his first service, but Jacoby pulled the church bell so loud and long that a crowd gathered to see what was going on. A Catholic man and his wife who heard Jacoby preach were so impressed that they spread the word about this new preacher, and the church was full the next Sunday. There were many who came to hear the sermon, but others came to cause trouble. They shot off pistols, threw stones through the window, and smeared the church steps with cow manure, making them slick. The German press warned Jacoby not to continue preaching. One evening, the Jacobys returned home to discover that stones had been thrown through their windows into the nursery—one stone was even in the cradle where the baby was sleeping. One can imagine the terror these young parents felt at the sight of that stone in the cradle.

In spite of opposition, by the end of the first year (1842), Jacoby organized the Wash Street Methodist Church (today's Salem-in-Ladue United Methodist Church traces its history back to that German congregation). At the end of the second year (1843), there were one hundred members, and German Methodism had a solid foothold in Missouri. A second German Methodist Church was begun in St. Louis in 1843. German Methodist missions spread from St. Louis up the Missouri River valley, and by 1850, there were circuits in St. Louis, St. Charles, Warren, Gasconade, Osage, Cole, Cooper, Morgan, Benton, Pettis, Platte, Lafayette, Clay, and Buchanan counties. There were also missions in Iowa and Illinois.

Sebastian Barth was an entrepreneur selling German Bibles in Missouri in the early 1840s. In 1843, Jacoby persuaded him to ride the Versailles Mission Circuit. This was a three hundred mile circuit, which Barth rode every three weeks. The preaching places included: (1) Lexington, (2) Brother Meyer's place (either Higginsville or Concordia), (3) Brother Kahr's house on Lake Creek, (4) Gerhard Ringen's, (5) fifteen miles to Conrad Ringen on the prairie (a log church was built there that first year), (6) further on in the forest (one wonders how the circuit riders found that spot!), (7) Brother Gerken's house, (8) Brother Timken's, (9) Schlotzhauer home at Pilot Grove, (10) German settlement twelve miles south of Boonville, (11) Boonville, (12) Keil's (now Jamestown), (13) California, (14) Jefferson City, (15) seven miles west of Jefferson City at Father Zumwald's house. In 1844, Heinrich Nuelsen was assigned as Barth's assistant. He borrowed one hundred dollars from his mother to buy a horse, saddle, saddlebags, and clothing, and went off to preach at a salary of seventy-five dollars a year. By the end of 1845, there were eighty-four full members on this circuit, besides probationers. Barth reported that he often rode to his next appointment at night, after the evening service, because the flies did not bother his horse nearly so much at night.[4]

A German District

The General Conference of 1844 voted to allow the German speaking missions to form separate German districts, each associated with an existing annual conference. This was a makeshift compromise, but it was the best the German missions could get in the way of organization from the General Conference. The original proposal from the German missions had been for a separate conference, but the General Conference was not willing to go that far. Remember that this was the same General Conference that had just made arrangements for the Plan of Separation, and there was a great fear that the Germans also wanted independence rather than union.

One of the three districts set up was the St. Louis German District, with Ludwig Jacoby as the presiding elder. This district was intended to be a part of the Missouri Conference. However, with the Plan of Separation becoming a reality, the Missouri Conference voted to "go South." The German preachers withdrew from the Missouri Conference, and the St. Louis German District became part of the Illinois Conference of the Methodist Episcopal Church. The appointments for 1844–45 were:

Presiding Elder	Ludwig Jacoby
North St. Louis	G. Danker
South St. Louis	C. Yost
Hermann	C. Koeneke
Pinckney	Father Horstmann
Versailles	Sebastian Barth and
	H. Nuelsen
Belleville (IL)	W. Hemminghaus and
	Jospeh Steinhausen
Quincy (IL)	Philipp Barth
Leadmines (Dubuque, IA	
and Galena, IL)	William Schreck
German Creek	
and Walnut Creek (IA)	J. Mann

So far had German Methodism come in the three years since Jacoby arrived in St. Louis!

In the spring of 1845, Jacoby held a quarterly conference in the Lake Creek settlement. They met in the home of Cord Kahrs, with two clergy and nine laity present. The Lake Creek church reported eighty-four full and sixteen preparatory members. Lake Creek is important to the story of German Methodism because of its camp meeting, which continues to this day. Early camp meetings there, like all camp meetings, were times of social gathering, community building, and religious intensity. There were several (long) sermons each day, and emotions were high. Conversion was the important goal of a camp meeting. It is reported that at the camp meeting in 1849, Johann Timken's wife went forward to the mourner's bench. Timken himself was not a Christian and tried to stop her. Hermann Kahrs grabbed Timken by the throat and told him to "sit and be quiet." One suspects that the command was even more impressive in the German language!

Other long-lived camp meetings were established. Steinhagen Charge (about six miles north of Warrenton) began holding camp meetings in 1851, and continued until 1917. The arbor tabernacle burned in 1909, and the meeting struggled after that. Higginsville Camp Ground was established in 1855, near the town of Higginsville. It held the last series of meetings in 1940, and then the property was sold back to the family from whom it had been purchased. Dalton Charge, in Chariton County, also had a campground and held meetings in the early years of the twentieth century. The anonymous statement made about it could serve equally well for any of the campgrounds in the connection: "It served as a blessing and as a means of expanding the Kingdom of God."

A second German district was organized at the 1845 session of the Illinois Conference. Henry Koenecke was named presiding elder of the St. Louis District, which stretched from St. Louis along the Missouri River to Weston and what is now St. Joseph. Heinrich Nuelsen was moved to the new field at Weston, a part of the Platte Purchase, where there were many German settlers but no German church. His territory was about one hundred fifty miles around, with some two hundred German families. The first sermon in German in the St. Joseph area was preached to eight to ten people in a log church owned by the Presbyterians. The German congregation in Weston met in the English Methodist Church. The work continued to expand and, in 1846, after five years of work, there were 22 circuit riders, 8 resident pastors, and 1167 members in the German districts.

The German districts were coming of age in 1847. William Nast paid a visit to the session of the Annual Conference that year and met with the German preachers. What must he have thought, as he heard the reports of their work, and the numbers who were being won to the church! Only a decade before, he had been hoping for one strong congregation of German Methodists. Now there were German churches scattered all over what is today the North Central Jurisdiction, plus Missouri. The German preachers decided to buy catechisms for their congregations, but still felt they could not afford hymnals with notes. Other books were more necessary! As another sign of the coming of age of the German districts, Ludwig Jacoby was elected as a delegate to the 1848 General Conference of the Methodist Episcopal Church.

The Development of German Methodist Literature

Just as there was a need for preaching and pastoral care in the German language, there was a need for literature in German. Bibles were not a problem. The German Bible had been printed for over three hundred years, and copies could be obtained from the homeland. But there were no hymnals, no church paper, and no tracts or other materials.

Even as William Nast was beginning his ministry in 1837, Wesleyan tracts were being printed in the German language. Over the next few years, money was raised to begin a German newspaper, the *Christliche Apologete,* or *Christian Apologist*. It was a German-language equivalent of the *Christian Advocate*'s circulation in the English churches.

In 1845, the Ohio Conference, of which Nast was a member, raised the issue that the Sunday School Union of the Methodist Episcopal Church had no literature in the German language. The German churches asked for an appropriation for the publication of German-language literature. They committed themselves to "endeavor to pay" a quarterly assessment of a penny per pupil toward the support of the Sunday School Union. German Methodists were speaking up for their needs—and taking on heavy responsibilities in return.

By 1848, the German preachers had founded their own tract society, and were having materials they needed printed in German. In 1850, they contributed two hundred dollars for Wesleyan tracts for Germany, where Jacoby had gone as a missionary the year before.

The St. Louis District Launches a Mission to Germany

Nast and Jacoby asked the General Conference (Methodist Episcopal) of 1848 for a missionary to Germany. It was time that German Methodists took the Wesleyan message back to their homeland. General Conference gave permission and in June of 1849, Ludwig S. Jacoby was appointed as a missionary to Germany. He and his wife sailed from New York on October 20, with five dollars worth of literature and a few New Testaments.

They landed in Bremen, where Jacoby intended to begin his work. He was shocked, as a good Methodist would be, by the loose morality he found in Germany. Particularly he was appalled by the disregard for the Sabbath. This had also been an issue in St. Louis, where the city officials, in the name of honoring the Sabbath, had forcibly closed German *Turnvereinen* (social halls) on Sundays as a part of their campaign of xenophobia. Resentment toward city officials also rebounded on Jacoby, who was in trouble with the German community because of his insistence on honoring the Sabbath.

Remember that 1849 was only a year removed from the crushing of democratic uprisings in the various German states. Many of the leading democratic reformers, including men like Carl Schurz (later a Senator from Missouri and a Secretary of the Interior), had fled to the United States. Popular resentment was still high, and the political and economic situation was highly volatile. The unofficially "established" religion was secularism. Rationalism was the dominant theme in theology and in the German intellectual community. Ferdinand Christian Baur had published his critical study of the Gospels in 1847. David Strauss' *Life of Jesus*, which appeared in 1835, denied the historical basis of all the miracles in the Gospels. The works of Immanuel Kant, Friedrich Schleiermacher, and George Frederick Hegel dominated the philosophical scene. None of their work was invalid or heretical. But they helped to set the tone for a highly intellectual approach to religion, one that often tends to submerge the work of the Spirit. It was in such an unfriendly environment that Jacoby began his work.

Jacoby's experience in St. Louis had taught him he could not just begin preaching and expect much in the way of results. He had to have a careful plan if he wanted any permanent results. He met with some of the *Herrnhutern*, those

German Pietists who had influenced Wesley nearly a century before. Then he found a hall in Bremen where he could hold services. The word was spread through the community that a new preacher had arrived, and nearly four hundred people attended his first sermon. Soon the congregation was too large for the hall. Jacoby opened his home for prayer meetings. He found a larger hall, one that would seat eight hundred people. Soon conversions began. In January of 1850, Jacoby added a second preaching point in a lower-class suburb of Bremen, then a third in Baden, where the congregation met in a schoolhouse. In April, he formed a class of twenty-one members, and received them "on trial" at Easter. The first Methodist Communion in Germany was celebrated the same day, followed by a love feast on Easter Monday.

On May 25, the first issue of *The Evangelist*, Germany's own *Christian Advocate*, appeared. There were two hundred copies of that first edition. A Methodist song-book sold out one thousand copies in just over two years. With the work on the paper, Jacoby's schedule was so full he could not accept all the invitations he had for Methodist preaching, even though he preached every night of the week. But help was on the way.

Karl Doering and Ludwig Nippert arrived from the States on June 7, 1850, and plunged into the work. The first Methodist Sunday school was opened in Bremen in June. The success of the Methodist Sunday school in reaching children and youth forced the Lutheran Church to adopt it as well, and Sunday schools quickly spread over Germany.

Still the work continued to grow. The bishop appointed Jacoby Superintendent of the Mission, the equivalent of a "missionary bishop." By the end of 1850, there were already two districts in Germany. With other preachers, probably helped by local preachers and exhorters, Jacoby was able to travel and respond to invitations for Methodist preaching. He went to Wurttemberg and then, in February 1851, to Saxony. These were the provinces where Luther had lived and worked, and where German Protestantism had its beginnings. Jacoby met with opposition in Saxony, but the work went on. By July of 1851, missions were opened in Hamburg and Frankfurt-am-Main, and then in Hesse-Darmstadt.

Jacoby was back in the United States to attend the General Conference of 1856. He asked for permission to organize a mission conference in Germany. This was granted, and the first session was held in September. He also tried to get a book concern for Europe. General Conference would not grant that request, but did authorize one thousand dollars a year for educational materials. Two years later, the mission conference was divided into four districts. In 1868, the status of the conference was changed from "Mission Conference" to "Annual Conference." In July 1874, the conference celebrated the twenty-fifth anniversary of Methodism in Germany. They reported 7,022 members, 1,899 members on trial, and 11,662 pupils in 262 Sunday schools. As the conference was adjourning, they received word of the death of Ludwig Jacoby in St. Louis.

MEANWHILE, BACK ON THE FRONTIER

Railroads were built, or at least begun, across Missouri in the 1850s. The Hannibal and St. Joseph Railroad was granted a charter in 1847, but did not actually begin work until 1853. The completion of the railroad in 1859 was a major economic boost to north Missouri. It connected to the Burlington, which meant shippers in the west had a more direct route to the markets in Chicago. The Pacific Railroad (later the Missouri Pacific) actually broke ground first, in 1851, but moved more slowly. It reached Jefferson City in 1855 and by 1861 had only reached to Sedalia. Many of the workers who built these railroads were German immigrants, and German communities were begun, or experienced growth, because of the railroad.

William Fiegenbaum began visiting German homes in Glasgow, Brunswick, and Carrollton in March of 1847. By autumn of 1848, sixty-five persons had joined churches in those communities, and church buildings were erected in Glasgow and near Carrollton. German Methodist churches were also built in Boonville in 1851, St. Joseph in 1852, and Lexington in 1854.

German Methodists were always deeply opposed to slavery. The passage of the Kansas-Nebraska Bill (which allowed citizens in those two territories to vote on whether or not slavery would be allowed) in 1854 stirred up a hornet's nest along the frontier. Both northern and southern sympathizers organized "colonization" societies to encourage those who agreed with their position to move to Kansas in preparation for the vote. In the Methodist connections, Andrew Monroe was active in urging southern Methodists to move to Kansas. German Methodists were among the northerners exhorted to join the Free-Soil movement and save Kansas from the scourge of slavery. Some Germans moved to Kansas, but many were concerned about the safety of themselves and their families in the volatility of the Kansas frontier and stayed where they were. But enough moved so that the German Methodists were able to organize the Kansas-Nebraska Mission in 1855, with headquarters at Leavenworth, Kansas. The first German Methodist church in Kansas was dedicated at Leavenworth in 1858. A year later, the appointments were Nebraska City and Leavenworth, Wyandotte, Omaha, Columbus Mission, Fort Riley, LeCompton, and Lawrence.

Membership rolls in the St. Louis German District totaled 17,109 in 1857, along with 250 preachers. The outbreak of war and the border conflicts between Missouri and Kansas, followed by the turmoil of civil war, slowed growth among German Methodists, as it did among other branches of the church. The Jayhawkers of Kansas and guerillas in Missouri disrupted the entire area on both sides of the state line, and made "bleeding Kansas" and "Order No. 11" symbols of the horrors of war, magnified when neighbor fought neighbor. In August 1863, a German Methodist camp meeting came to an abrupt end when word came that Quantrill's guerillas were on their way to the meeting place. This meeting must have been right along the border, because the following morning, Quantrill and his men burned Lawrence, Kansas.

THE BIRTH OF GERMAN CONFERENCES

The Methodist Episcopal General Conference of 1864, no longer concerned that German churches wanted to separate from the denomination, organized three German conferences. These were essentially language-specific conferences, whose geographical boundaries overlapped many existing English-speaking conferences. The Central German, Northwest German, and Southwest German ultimately grew into ten conferences in the United States, plus three overseas. The St. Louis District became part of the Southwest German Conference, which had six districts: St. Louis, Belleville, Quincy, Burlington (Iowa), St. Joseph, and Kansas. The first session of the annual conference was held in September of 1864 at Washington Street Church, St. Louis. The city was under martial law because Gen. Sterling Price was raiding in southeast Missouri (a raid which ended in the Battle of Pilot Knob). The first page of the journal includes this statement: "The Provost Marshal came in and each member of the Conference and the delegates took the oath of allegiance to the government of the United States; which was heartily done."

The conference grew steadily, in many cases because of the work of the laity. The westward movement meant that settlement sometimes outstripped the growth of the church. German Methodists appealed to presiding elders in their former homes to send them a preacher. Local preachers, class leaders, Sunday school superintendents, and other strong laity began the churches, and kept them together in the absence of circuit riders. One fascinating story from this period: soon after the Dalton church was dedicated, there was a bad storm, which moved the church from its foundation, but did not otherwise damage it. The congregation left the building where it was, and built a new foundation under it! Here is the fascinating part of the story. The church had been built on a northwest to southeast angle to avoid storm damage. After the storm (and in its permanent location) it was aligned north-south.

With churches in Colorado and Nebraska, as well as Kansas, Missouri, and Iowa, the Southwest German Conference was too large geographically to be effective. The St. Joseph and Kansas districts (which included Colorado) particularly asked for a division of the conference. The General Conference of 1876 passed enabling legislation allowing for a division into two separate conferences. In 1878, the conference was divided. The new West German Conference included Kansas, Nebraska, Colorado, and parts of extreme western Missouri and Iowa. The St. Louis German Conference included the rest of Missouri.

At the time of the division, there were 11,365 members in the Southwest German Conference. Of those members, 8,244 went to the St. Louis German

Conference and 2,811 to the West. The St. Louis German Conference, which is our concern here, reached its membership peak in 1908, when it reported 11,543 members and 19,918 pupils in Sunday School. The Missouri churches in the West German Conference reached their peak in 1917, with 1,855 members. From the early twentieth century, German Methodism declined due to a number of factors which are discussed below.

Central Wesleyan College and Central Wesleyan Orphan Home

German Methodists wanted to train preachers for ministry in their church, and they wanted to continue the teaching of the German language, German values, and traditions. So, in 1852, a group of ministers met in Winchester, Illinois, to organize a German-American college. In 1854, in cooperation with English-speaking Methodists, they formed the "German and English College" in Quincy, Illinois. The school struggled for nine years, always with the German pastors nursing the secret hope they would be able to found their own institution. The English department of the school was dropped in 1863, and, in 1864, the German Methodists met in Quincy, Illinois, to decide whether or not to establish an independent, self-supporting institution.

There was a concern, not only for education, but also for the plight of the many children who had been left orphans by the war still raging between the states. The German Methodists determined their first need was for an orphan's home, and the second for an institute of higher education. They chose Warrenton, Missouri, for the site of the *Doppel-Anstalt*, or "Double Institution." The property they bought was held by an independent corporation, which in turn, transferred its rights to the property to the Southwest German Conference as soon as it was organized. The Missouri Legislature chartered the "Western Orphan Asylum and Education Institute," to receive all students of good moral character. The first curriculum included the Classics, General Culture, "Normal Courses" (elementary education), and Commercial courses. The enrollment was one hundred seventy-nine, including orphan children.

In the 1870s, the school expanded, and new buildings were built. In addition to the building efforts, laypersons such as Louis Kessler and William Schrader gave substantial funds for an endowment for the school. So were established the Schrader Chair of Theology and the Kessler Chair of German Language and Literature.

By 1884, it seemed clear that the orphanage and the school should become separate entities. The daughter institutions were chartered as the Central Wesleyan College and Central Wesleyan Orphan Home.

Tornadoes and fires destroyed buildings over the years, but they were replaced with newer and finer ones. The endowment grew, thanks to the generosity of persons like F. G. and W. F. Niedringhaus, who gave generously and challenged others to give as well. Their endowment made possible a Chair of

Practical and Historical Theology. Teaching at the college was a commitment, since professors could have made larger salaries elsewhere. In 1895, for example, Professor Sauer was paid four hundred dollars and Professor Frick four hundred ninety-five dollars.

In 1908, the German College at Mt. Pleasant, Iowa, also an institution of the St. Louis German Conference, merged with Central Wesleyan to become Central Wesleyan College and German Theological Seminary. In 1905, the cost for a theological student was $27.50 a term; this included room, light, heat, and laundry of bedding and towels. Tuition was $3.75, books $15.00, or a total $46.25 for the term. There were four terms a year, so the year's cost was $185. Note that these costs did not include meals, or one's personal laundry. In 1910, Central Wesleyan became a member of the Missouri College Union and was ranked as a "Class A" school by the University Senate of the Methodist Episcopal Church. After 1912, Central Wesleyan graduates received life teaching certificates without examination by the state. That was a clear recognition of the quality education at Central Wesleyan.

The orphanage was founded to care for those children orphaned by the Civil War. Between 1864, when the orphanage was founded, and 1925, when German Methodism merged with English-speaking conferences, seven hundred children had been cared for by the orphanage. In 1925, the Home owned three hundred acres of land, of which one hundred sixty was woods and pasture, and one hundred forty under cultivation. There were thirty head of cattle, three horses, three mules, hogs and chickens, a large apple orchard, and a large strawberry patch. The bakery turned four hundred pounds of flour into bread every week. To a large extent, the Home was self-supporting for food, and had a substantial endowment. After the merger with the Missouri Conference, the Home struggled. Money for the expenses of the home was hard to raise, and the Missouri Conference wanted to unite Central Wesleyan with the Children's Home in St. Louis. This happened in 1939.

The Women's Foreign Missionary Society

The only records of the Women's Foreign Missionary Society before 1883 are of financial contributions, a total of $338.96 from 1873 to 1878. Beginning in 1884, Miss Margaret Dreyer, the first Superintendent of the German Work of the Women's Foreign Missionary Society, visited German churches in St. Louis, trying to raise interest in the work of missions. In 1890, Miss Mary Kaeser was appointed as the first secretary and treasurer for the Society in the St. Louis German Conference. After this time, the work of the Society in the conference was more aggressive. In 1912, the first missionary from the conference was sent overseas. Miss Cornelia Gruenewald went to Khandwa, India, where she served only three years because of poor health. In 1918 (at the close of World War I, with all the attendant suspicion of German-Americans), the Society had thirty-seven auxiliaries and a membership of 1,184 women, and fourteen societies with 376 members among younger women. In addition, there were 354 children enrolled in 15 societies. These women supported ten Bible women, ten scholarships, two assistants, and five hospital beds, all on special gifts from the societies.

ANTI-GERMAN FEELING THROUGH WORLD WAR I

Xenophobia (fear and hatred of strangers and foreigners, or of anything strange or foreign) has always been a part of the American psyche. Strange though this sounds to a modern ear, the main targets of xenophobia in the nineteenth century were not Hispanic and Asian immigrants (though that was also true), but the Germans and Irish. In Missouri, that xenophobia was heightened by the staunch opposition to slavery expressed by the Germans, and by the fact that both Germans and Irish enlisted in the Union Army in large numbers. It is unfortunate, perhaps, that so many of the Union troops that patrolled the western part of Missouri during the war were German immigrants. This made already strong feelings even stronger. In Clay County, for example, Southern partisans threatened to shoot "all the Dutchmen on the prairie" unless the German Methodist preachers stopped having services and camp meetings. The preaching stopped, but "Uncle" Peter Hartel, a lay-class leader, continued to have Sunday school and class meetings.

The worst expressions of xenophobia, however, occurred during the First World War. Every German, and every German church, had to prove its patriotism over and over. German Methodism provided five thousand soldiers for the United States Army (seven hundred fifty from the St. Louis German Conference). That does not seem like a large number compared to the full size of the American Expeditionary Force, but it was one member out of every twelve in the church. In addition, the St. Louis German Conference reported in 1918 that the churches had bought $653,800 in Liberty Bonds and $90,837 in war stamps.

The use of the German language was a sore point for many xenophobes. It was also an issue for many German emigrants. The author's great-grandfather had come to the United States from Bavaria in the 1850s, and served in the Union Army in the War Between the States. When word came of the German invasion of Belgium in 1914, he slammed his fist down on the table and said, "There will be no more German spoken in this house." The author's grandmother remembered that as a protest against what Germany was doing in Europe. Many in the family remember that incident with regret because it made the family become monolingual rather than bilingual.

In northern Missouri, the Etna German Methodist Church was conducting morning services in German, and evening services in English. The Ku Klux Klan decided to test the patriotism of the church, and, if they found services in German, they were "going to do something." So, a week later, dressed in robes and hoods, the Klansmen filed into the evening service! Since the service was in

English, they went home satisfied. Now, whether they knew the schedule and went to an evening service to save face, or whether they really didn't have a clue, Methodists of German descent in that community were still chuckling over that episode sixty years later.

In an interesting footnote, at the 1918 session of the St. Louis German Conference, the laity called for more democracy in the church—and a greater role for women. They also asked that laity have representation in the cabinet meeting and advise on appointments. The specific request was that one layman become a member of the Cabinet for each superintendent. This was an idea that was far ahead of its time.

MERGER WITH ENGLISH-SPEAKING CONFERENCES

The General Conference (Methodist Episcopal Church) of 1924, gave permission for German conferences to merge with English conferences whenever they felt it was appropriate, but urged them to continue as long as there was a need for special language ministry.

Assimilation into the dominant culture had begun long before. German-speaking merchants and tradesmen of necessity had to learn English in order to make a living in a majority English-speaking culture. Second- and third-generation German children spoke English more easily than they did German. With the change in language came changes in cultural and social patterns. In the church, the first step away from the German language was in children's and youth ministries. Then the Sunday evening service was conducted in English (as in the Etna church, mentioned above). The next step was to keep the Sunday morning service in German, but all other services and ministries were conducted in English. Finally, all the services would be in English, with the possible exception of a German Sunday school class.

Emigration fell off sharply in the twentieth century, which reduced the need for a specific language ministry and separate church. Conference statistics show that the German conferences reached their peak in 1917, with 60,544 members (only 468 more than in 1908). Younger preachers requested transfers to the English conferences: between 1910 and 1922, sixty-four were transferred. German Methodism was rapidly becoming an old people's church. Of their 410 effective ministers, 56 percent were over the age of 50. Part of the reason for the transfers was the low salaries for ministers in German Methodism. In 1922, for example, the average salary in the St. Louis German Conference was five hundred seventeen dollars. In addition, German and English parishes overlapped, and there was considerable duplication and competition.

The German Methodists had ten conferences in America, with 544 preaching points and 58,240 members (1922). There were 574 Sunday schools, with a combined enrollment of 71,139.

The Reverend Theodore Wolff, 1909–1999.
Historian and the last remaining pastor of the
former German Methodist Church.

With permission from the General Conference, the St. Louis German Conference was the second of the language conferences to merge. The conference had memorialized the General Conference for permission to merge with English conferences. In August 1924, the St. Louis German Conference created a commission to plan all the steps for a merger, and to report to the next session of the annual conference. The declaration of merger presented to the conference was adopted by a vote of 53 to 2, and then made unanimous. The unanimous vote did not mean everyone was excited about the merger. There was general agreement that the merger was necessary, though there was concern over questions such as German identity, pensions, salaries, the fate of conference institutions, and so on.

F. W. Wahl of the St. Louis German Conference summed up the realities of the situation in the church when he said:

> The real purpose of German Methodism was to bring the gospel message in the German language to the German immigrants and the German people in our country. . . . That work has been largely accomplished. It has never been the purpose nor the policy nor the program of Methodism that one English-speaking Conference should overlap or cover the same territory that seven other English-speaking Conferences cover.[5]

Methodism had ministered to German immigrants and founded a strong German ministry. With the decline of the use of the German language, German and English churches became more and more alike, and good stewardship called for a merger to avoid competition.

Chapter 5

DIVISION
1844–1860

The United States had always been deeply divided on the question of slavery, even as every part of the nation participated in, and profited from, the institution. In the debates on slavery leading to the Declaration of Independence, northern delegates to the Continental Congress condemned slavery, and southern delegates pointed out that it was northern ships that carried slaves to the plantation owners of the South. Slavery was then written into the Constitution, but always remained a bone of contention.

The Missouri Compromise of 1820 set clear geographical boundaries for the institution of slavery, boundaries which were ignored by extremists in both the North and South. In New England, the abolitionist movement inspired men and women to work actively against slavery and its spread. Southern extremists wanted to push the institution through Missouri to Kansas, and on to the Pacific Coast. Economic and social issues were also involved in the controversy over slavery. The industrialization of the North and the influx of immigrants from northern Europe to work in the factories meant that slavery was not economically viable there. On the other hand, the invention of the cotton gin in 1793 meant the South would become more heavily agricultural, with an emphasis on a crop (cotton) that was highly labor-intensive. In the South, slavery was economically viable, at least in some cases.

The two parts of the nation moved in two different directions socially, economically, and in terms of their attitudes toward "the peculiar institution." Each felt its direction was the right one for its own section and wanted to be left alone to pursue its own direction. In the case of extremists on both sides, the direction of its section was felt to be the only one—for the nation—and had to be both defended by every means possible and expanded into as much new territory as possible. As the extremists on both sides pushed their cases, their voices became more and more shrill, and their "lines in the sand" were drawn ever clearer and deeper. The inevitable tragic result was disunion and civil war.

The same tensions and divisions over slavery wracked the Methodist Episcopal Church. The first General Conference of 1784 adopted a rule that within a year, every slave-holding member had to sign a legal document agreeing to free his slaves. This provision was so unpopular that it was never enforced in the South, and was suspended in June 1785. In 1796, a new rule provided that official members had to agree to free their slaves, and sellers of slaves would be expelled from the church. Important for the future was the provision in the rule that preachers were to give up their positions if they refused to free their slaves where emancipation was legal. Note that there were two elements to the provision. First, preachers who owned slaves had to give up their positions if they refused to free the slaves. Second, this rule applied only where emancipation was legal. Both parts of the provision would be critical to the debates in the General Conference of 1844. There is some evidence that many slaves were indeed freed under this provision, but it became more and more difficult to enforce as Southern states passed legislation forbidding emancipation. Under the leadership of Southern delegates, assisted by those who wanted to preserve the church at all costs, the General Conference of 1840 reaffirmed the right of ministers to hold slaves in states where emancipation was illegal. The New England Conference was censured for continued agitation—abolition was seen as a greater threat to the unity of the church than was slavery!

Methodist leaders both north and south worked hard to avoid any split in their ranks. Southern Methodists tried to disassociate themselves (for the most part) from the political turmoil surrounding slavery and the development of new territories. (This was true of Southern leaders; it was not always true of the rank and file.) Northern Methodists tried to keep the abolitionists on a tight rein within the denomination. In fact, a considerable number of anti-slavery Methodists did secede from the denomination. On May 31, 1843, a convention of anti-slavery Methodists met at Utica, New York, and organized the Wesleyan Methodist Connection of America. By the end of 1844, this new denomination reported fifteen thousand members. For a time, Methodist leaders hoped this would drain off some of the strongest feelings about slavery and buy more time in which to resolve the issue. However, this was not to be.

Both Northerners and Southerners came to the General Conference of 1844 with a strong desire to avoid any discussion on slavery (as had the General Conference of 1840), for fear it would split the church. Two separate issues made that an impossible dream.

THE GENERAL CONFERENCE, 1844

The General Conference of 1844 met at Greene Street Church in New York City, and struggled for six weeks to resolve issues that threatened a division in the church.

The first issue before the General Conference was the appeal of Francis A. Harding, a member of the Baltimore Conference. (Remember that, in the nineteenth century, all members of the annual conference were clergy.) Harding had married a woman who owned slaves, and according to the laws of that day, the slaves became his property.

Because he had not freed these slaves, he had been suspended from his ministerial duties by the conference. He appealed that suspension to the General Conference. In 1844, there was no Judicial Council, and the General Conference was the seat of judicial review and final appeal, as well as of legislation for the denomination. The General Conference discussed Harding's appeal for four days. Full verbatims of the discussion are found in the Journal of the conference. They show: 1) the legal situation in the state of Maryland; 2) the legal situation in the Methodist Episcopal Church; and 3) the strong feelings of both abolitionists and slaveholders in the church. Legally, in Maryland, Harding could have freed his slaves. However, the resolution in the Annual Conference that suspended him was probably illegal (it required him to free three of the five slaves he owned) and should have been thrown out. The mood of the General Conference, however, was so strong that technical legal issues could not be considered dispassionately.

The debates went something like this: Harding was accused of being dishonorable because he tried to beg off the question on the ground that it was his wife who actually owned the slaves. Counsel for Harding argued he could not be removed from his post on moral grounds, since slave holding was not immoral. He then attacked abolitionism in strong terms. Finally, he argued on the grounds of the *Discipline* that, while slavery is a great evil, it is "not necessarily a sin." It becomes a sin only when slaves are abused. It is interesting to note that even Harding's most avid defenders deplored slavery in the abstract, even while they defended it on legal grounds.[1]

In the end, the decision of the Baltimore Conference was affirmed by a vote of 117 to 56. A reading of the record suggests that on legal and disciplinary grounds, the decision should probably have been overturned. As is so often the case, the moral issues were different from the legal ones. But the General Conference seems not to have taken any moral high ground. Rather, the vote was sectional and partisan. For the first time, the moderates were voting with the abolitionists, rather than with the slaveholders. Southern delegates saw the affirmation of the Baltimore Conference as an infringement of the constitution of the church, and an omen of the coming doom of both their section and the Methodist Episcopal Church itself. Northern delegates, on the other hand, seem to have been amazed at the size of the majority.

The case of Bishop Andrew was the final blow to harmony. Bishop James O. Andrew wrote a letter to the episcopacy committee explaining that he did own slaves, but had either inherited them or acquired them by marriage. The laws of the state of Georgia, where the bishop lived, did not allow manumission. Later, in an address to the Conference, Bishop Andrew answered the objection that his wife should have willed the slaves to her children, and saved the bishop from embarrassment. Bishop Andrew said that he feared for the well-being of the slaves if they were given to the children, so that he was, in fact, a slaveholder "for conscience's sake."

Shortly before the General Conference, Bishop Andrew met with the Southern delegates and offered to resign his office, since he thought this would help settle the issue and preserve the peace in the church. The caucus urged him not to resign, since this would almost certainly lead to the South walking out of the conference—and the church. With that assurance, the bishop promised not to resign.

The report of the episcopacy committee said that a bishop embarrassed by a connection with slavery could not serve acceptably in all parts of the church, and requested that Bishop Andrew resign. This report caused a storm of protests. Among the protesters was J. C. Berryman of the Missouri Conference, who argued that the conference could not take such action. (He spoke, even though the unspoken rule of the conference was that younger men did not participate in the debates.) Berryman took his stand on the *Discipline*, arguing that the conference had no power under church law to depose a bishop. Berryman said that he had owned slaves, but decided as a matter of conscience that he had to free them. So his vote in the conference would actually be against his own conscience. J. B. Findley then moved a substitute, asking that Bishop Andrew not exercise the episcopal office as long as he had any connection with slavery. Southern delegates appealed to the Resolutions of 1800, which required preachers who obtained slaves to either give up their orders or free the slaves, *if it be practicable . . . agreeably to the laws of the state wherein they live.* In 1808, each annual conference was given permission to make its own regulations concerning slavery. The General Conference of 1816 wrung its collective hands over slavery, deploring it, but seeing little way to end it. The final statement from that conference was largely a return to the position of 1800: "No slaveholder shall be eligible to any official station in our Church hereafter where the laws of the state in which he lives will admit of emancipation, and permit the liberated slave to enjoy freedom."[2] Armed with this statement, the Southern delegates took their stand on the *Discipline*. They argued that the General Conference could not ask for Bishop Andrew's resignation, because he could not legally free his slaves, nor could he expect them to be able to "enjoy freedom" in the state of Georgia.

Remember that while slavery was the presenting and, certainly, an important issue in the debate, it was not the only one. There were serious constitutional questions about the power of the General Conference as well. The underlying constitutional question was this: were the General Conference and the bishops equal and coordinate, or were the bishops subordinate to the authority of the General Conference? Bishop Andrew's situation was dealt with in the light of this constitutional issue, as well as the more restricted legal issue of slavery.

A second constitutional issue was almost as time-consuming as the question of Bishop Andrew's status: could the General Conference limit the power of bishops to appoint presiding elders? The 1792 *Discipline* had limited the terms of

presiding elders to four consecutive years. The 1844 conference adopted an addition to the earlier provision; after that four year term, a presiding elder could not
be appointed to the same district for six years. In the debate on this question, the
proponents were all from the north and east; the opponents from the south and
west. The question was the center of authority in the church: was all authority
unilaterally in the General Conference, or was authority shared between the
General Conference and the bishops? Or, put another way, could the General
Conference limit the authority of the bishop to appoint? Division on the question was largely along regional lines, though some westerners from states north of
the Mason-Dixon Line (most notably Peter Cartwright of Illinois) sided with the
Southerners. So, on the question of the authority of the General Conference and
the bishops, the conference was also divided along sectional lines.

   Another constitutional question was the guaranteed right of any clergy to a
trial. Southern delegates argued that the Findley resolution, asking Bishop Andrew
not to exercise his office, was, in fact, deposing him without a trial, and therefore
unconstitutional. Bishop Joshua Soule, who was the principal author of the
constitution of the church, argued that this was, indeed, the case. (Note that
bishops were allowed more voice in debates than is the case today.) He said, in an
impassioned speech:

> I say that the resolution on which we are just about to act goes to sustain the
> doctrine that the General Conference has the power and right to depose one
> of the bishops of the Methodist Episcopal Church without the form of
> trial—that you are under no obligation from the constitution or the laws of
> the Church to show cause even. . . . I pray you hold to principles—to
> principles.[3]

Bishop Soule was arguing that the resolution meant a basic change in polity. The
basic nature of the episcopacy, and of the relationship between the episcopacy and
the General Conference, would be destroyed by the resolution. To deny a trial was
a violation of the constitution, and therefore threatened the constitution itself.
Some Southerners even said they would have agreed with the will of the majority
if Bishop Andrew had been "suspended according to law," that is, after a trial. But
they would not agree to deposition without trial. This formed the basis of all the
arguments about the actions of the General Conference being "extra-judicial."

   In the debate, fears were voiced about the effects on the church. The southern
delegates felt that, in the current situation, they could no longer depend on the
Discipline. Both Northerners and Southerners were "in a bind" because of the strong
views of their regional constituents. Both argued (in terms that sound familiar
today) that unless their position prevailed, the church would lose huge numbers of
members. There was a clear "cultural captivity" in both the Northern and Southern
parts of the church. Each was sure that its position was correct. Each was sure that
if the other's position prevailed, the church would cease to exist. At more than one

point in the debate, delegates echoed the words of one who said, "If we push our principles so far as to break up the Connection, this may be the last time we meet."[4] But there were extremists on both sides who were more than willing to push their principles that far. The debate extended the meeting of the conference to six weeks, making it the longest General Conference in the history of the denomination.

Finally, the Findley resolution (asking the bishop to not exercise his office while he held slaves) came to a vote. It was adopted, 111–69. The practical result was a suspension of Bishop Andrew from the episcopal office, though the Conference ordered that his name be printed in the Hymnal, along with the other bishops, and that he continue to receive his salary. Whatever its intent, the resolution guaranteed a separation in the church. The Missouri delegation—W. W. Redman, William Patton, Jerome C. Berryman, and J. M. Jameson—all voted against the resolution, all at least partly on constitutional grounds.

A Southern caucus then met and passed a resolution that the action of the General Conference on abolition and especially on the "extrajudicial proceedings against Bishop Andrew . . . must produce a state of things in the South which renders a continuance of the jurisdiction of that General Conference over these conferences inconsistent with the success of the ministry in the slaveholding states."[5] Again, all four members of the Missouri delegation signed this resolution.

The resolution was turned over to a committee of nine. Dr. William Capers of South Carolina presented a set of resolutions which would set up two general conferences, the dividing line to be the boundary between free and slave states. The two conferences would be equal and coordinate. Northerners on the committee of nine thought it would be impossible to get the votes in the annual conferences to authorize this kind of change in the *Discipline*, so the proposal fell through the cracks. In the end, the committee produced the Plan of Separation, "should the Annual Conferences in the slaveholding states find it necessary to unite in a distinct ecclesiastical connection." It provided that:

1. Northern preachers would not interfere in societies, stations, and conferences that voted to go south, and vice versa, and the two branches of the church would not attempt to establish churches in each other's territory.
2. Clergy were free to choose, without blame, with which branch of the church they would unite.
3. The Annual Conferences were urged to adopt a change in the sixth restrictive rule, so that the capital, property, stock, and so on, of the Book Concern could be divided equitably between the two branches. A committee was appointed to work out the equitable division. This provision was important for the pensions of the preachers, since the profits of the Book Concern were designated for the pension fund.
4. The property of the Methodist Episcopal Church within the territory of the southern branch would belong to that branch and be "for ever free" from any claim by the Methodist Episcopal Church.[6]

All of these provisions (which are summarized here) would very soon become serious bones of contention between the two branches of Methodism, and would ultimately have to be resolved by the Supreme Court of the United States. All were passed by overwhelming majorities. Norwood suggests the Plan of Separation was enacted "in a fit of Christian generosity during the dying hours of the General Conference." The Plan certainly was not greeted with a "fit" of Christian generosity in the annual conferences, as shall be seen later.

In one of the ironic footnotes to history, Dr. Charles Elliott, who would later move to St. Louis and become editor of the *Central Christian Advocate* (and denounce the southern church as secessionist), was the first to move adoption of the plan, on the grounds that separation was necessary for mutual convenience and prosperity.

Before leaving New York, a southern caucus met and proposed that a special convention, made up of members elected by the annual conferences, should meet in Louisville, Kentucky, on May 1, 1845, to determine what the conferences wanted to do about separation.

The constitutional questions had been raised in General Conferences as far back as 1820, long before slavery became an issue that threatened to divide the church. It is probably true that, except for some abolitionist conferences in New England, the northern delegates were not willing to divide the church over slavery. It is probably equally true that, except for a few "fire-eaters" in the southern conferences, those delegates were also not willing to divide the church over slavery. What they were willing to fight for—and divide the church over— was the constitutional question of the authority of the General Conference vis-a-vis the power of the bishops. The two issues—authority and slavery—came together in the person of Bishop Andrew. Tragically, they also drove the church apart, in spite of all the best efforts of those who struggled to hold it together.

THE MISSOURI CONFERENCE, 1844

Missouri churches reacted quickly to the news from the General Conference. In August, the quarterly conference of the Danville Circuit (where the author was born) passed a resolution approving the call for the Louisville convention and the organization of a separate church. So did the Liberty Circuit, whose resolutions appeared in the *Western Christian Advocate* shortly before the annual conference met in late September 1844. Bishop Morris presented the proposed Plan of Separation to the delegates. A special committee on division reported:

1. We look on the results of the slavery/abolition agitation with sorrow and regret.
2. We concede to the northerners purity of intention, but "pronounce the proceedings of the late General Conference against Bishop Andrew extra-judicial and oppressive."

3. We still hope for reconciliation and recommend that the societies be consulted on the subject.

4. We approve the Louisville Conference.

5. We instruct our delegates to oppose division, unless it be found unavoidable; if division happens, it should not be regarded as a secession, but as a coordinate branch of the church, acting under a separate jurisdiction. Beyond this, we do not favor any change in the *Discipline*.

6. If the Louisville Conference proceeds to a separate organization, it shall be deemed a regular General Conference.

7. We regret the violence of some southerners against the bishops and invite "to pulpits and firesides" all bishops and the northern brethren.

8. We favor taking a collection for the expenses of the delegates to Louisville.[7]

Leaders of both proponents and opponents of separation were on the committee. Andrew Monroe was clearly in favor of separation, for example; Thomas Chandler, clearly opposed. Both signed the resolutions when they came to the floor of the conference. It seems clear that Missouri was reluctant to divide the church.

Many churches and circuits quickly concurred. Weston Station thought any division would be disastrous to Methodism. Other circuits opposed to division included New Madrid, Selma, Wesley Chapel, Fredericktown, and Cape Girardeau. In a letter to the *Southwestern Christian Advocate*, James L. Holliday wrote:

> It is not the wish or desire of any true Methodist in Missouri, that the church should divide; but it is the sentiment of the membership generally . . . that if no reparation be made by the North for the injury already inflicted on our esteemed bishop, and the Church South . . . then divide according to the plan of the General Conference.[8]

The Warsaw church adopted a set of resolutions saying that a division in the church was called for by the unauthorized actions of the General Conference of 1844. They said that slavery was an evil, but that abolitionism was a greater evil, one that disturbed the peace of both church and state. They thought that as persons who lived in a slave-holding state, they understood what slavery meant far better than their brothers in the North.

There was a great deal of debate within the church about the status of the Southern churches should they divide. James M. Jameson, a presiding elder, argued in a letter to the *Christian Advocate* that no matter how loudly the annual conference proclaimed the Southern churches would not be in secession, that position was exactly what the Committee of Nine at General Conference had said was impossible, and that separation would be secession. Note that this would later be a major bone of contention between the Northern and Southern branches of the church.

In response, Andrew Monroe wrote of his conviction that the church in Missouri could not stay with the North, because the strength of abolitionism would hinder the work of the church. He felt certain that circumstances were forcing Missouri Methodists to choose between Northern and Southern branches of the church.

All this suggests the Missouri Methodists reflected the feelings of the members of the annual conference. That is, they were against division and hoped the church could work out the differences. But they did direct the delegates to Louisville to go with the South in case of division.

In this atmosphere, Missouri chose its delegates to the Louisville convention. Andrew Monroe headed the delegation with Jesse Greene, John Glanville, Wesley Browning, William Patton, John H. Linn, J. H. Fielding, and Joseph Boyle in the delegation. Some sources have Thomas Johnson in place of Fielding. Since Johnson attended the convention as a member of the Missouri Conference, he may have been a substitute for Fielding. Of the delegation, at least Monroe, Patton, Green, and Glanville were sympathetic to separation. Edward T. Peery and David B. Cummings represented the Indian Mission Conference, which also voted for separation.

THE LOUISVILLE CONVENTION, 1845

Delegates from the conferences in the slave-holding states met in Louisville, Kentucky, in May of 1845. Fifteen conferences from across the South were represented. Dr. Lovick Pierce, of the Georgia Conference, was elected president *pro tem* of the conference, since no one was sure which bishops might be there and what their role in the conference might be. Bishop Joshua Soule, who had been the primary author of the Constitution of the Methodist Episcopal Church, and Bishop James O. Andrew agreed to serve as presiding officers of the convention.

Then to important business. A committee of two persons from each annual conference was appointed to consider if there should be a separate Southern church, and, if so, how that church should be organized. Andrew Monroe and William Patton represented the Missouri Conference on the committee. A couple of days later, on May 5, the convention voted to instruct the committee that if they saw no hope that the Northern conferences would change their minds, they should report in favor of separation.

Delegates from the border states, such as Missouri, were in some turmoil. They were in general agreement with the South, but there were all those mixed feelings back home. If, as slave-holding communities, they stayed with the northern church, would they be outsiders and pariahs? On the other hand, they hated the thought of division. Monroe said to the conference that if Missouri would stay with the north, they would lose their identity as a conference. "If we cannot otherwise control the Missouri conference, it will be competent for the General Conference to disband our conference and connect us with Illinois and Iowa. We have no security but with the South. Missouri will go with the South both from principle and expediency."

The committee read its report to the convention on May 15. It was a formal declaration of independence, saying that the jurisdiction of the General Conference over the South was dissolved. However, the *Discipline* was adopted in full, except where some changes were required by the separation. The debate on the resolution was apparently long and tedious, for both William Patton and Andrew Monroe spoke on a resolution to end debate. One suspects they were tired of hearing the same thing said over and over at great length.

On the resolution to create a separate church, known as the Methodist Episcopal Church, South, the final vote was 94–3 in favor. All members of the Missouri delegation voted in favor of the resolution. Then the conference voted unanimously for a resolution expressing their openness to reunion.

On May 17, Andrew Monroe wrote a letter to Jacob Lanius, in which he expressed his personal feelings about the result of the convention:

> You will be pleased to learn that the Missouri delleigation[*sic*] are perfectly unanimous and the only negative is in Kentucky. 3 nays on the question of separation—in every other resolution thus far the convention are unanimous. Was the like ever known!!! . . . in this intire [*sic*] organization there is perfect agreement except 3 in one resolution—does it not augur well for *our cause*? . . . We have determined on a General Conference in Peters Burgh [*sic*] May 46. This seemed absolutely necessary for the Interests of the South and the ratio at one for 14 this will be a large Dellegation [*sic*] for us and a heavy expense, but it appears indispensible. So dollars and cents should not govern in this matter. . . . Yet I hope all will become right but our brother Chandler has been here all the time and after all you perceive from his communications in Dr. Elliott's papers he is unconverted and determined to make us trouble in Missouri—what will be the result I cannot tell. I am quite satisfied with our doing this far and I hope all will result to the glory of God and you will soon have our proceedings. . . .
>
> > Pray for me and believe me yours truly,
> > A. Monroe [9]

"Our brother Chandler" is a reference to Thomas Chandler, the presiding elder of the Weston district, who was one of the strong opponents of separation. "Dr. Elliott's papers" is a reference to the *Central Christian Advocate*, of which Charles Elliott was the editor. Elliott had been one of the strongest spokesmen for the Northern position in the General Conference of 1844, but had also been one of the first to move adoption of the Plan of Separation. He became a vocal, indeed rabid, opponent of the southern church almost as soon as it was formed.

This brings up a key question: were the actions of the Southern churches a separation or a secession? There is no doubt that many Southerners considered themselves as much a part of the Methodist Church after 1845 as they did before.

But, did they secede from the Methodist Episcopal Church, or did they separate from the jurisdiction of the General Conference and set up an coordinate branch of Methodism? The Plan of Separation certainly seemed to imply the setting up of a coordinate branch of the church. Bishop Morris, who presided over the 1844 session of the Missouri Conference, did not consider the Southern church a secession. When the bishops of the Methodist Episcopal Church (now the northern church) met in July 1845, they passed a resolution resigning their oversight of the Southern conferences, since they regarded the Plan of Separation as binding. But the northern church would soon retract its support of the Plan.

In fact, the Methodist Episcopal Church argued that Southerners had already violated the 1844 agreement by organizing a separate church before the annual conferences could vote on the division. This assumed the meeting of Southern delegates at the close of General Conference was an organizational meeting of a new church. This act alone, northerners argued, made the whole Plan of Separation invalid.

THE MISSOURI CONFERENCE, 1845

The Missouri Conference met in Columbia on October 1. No bishop was present the first day and, as was so often the case, Andrew Monroe was elected president *pro tem*. Bishop Joshua Soule arrived on the second day and began by defending himself against the charge that he had left the Methodist Episcopal Church. This was primarily a restatement of what he had already said to the General Conference in Petersburg, Virginia, in which he contended that he stood "on Methodism." His argument was that the Southern church was not the result of secession, but a body coordinate and co-equal with the Northern church, both of them together making up the Methodist Episcopal Church in America.

Following the bishop's speech, William Patton offered a set of resolutions for the consideration of the conference. The critical resolution was the third one:

> Resolved, That as a conference claiming all the rights, powers, and privileges of an Annual Conference of the Methodist Episcopal Church, we adhere to the Methodist Episcopal Church, South, and that all our proceedings, journals, and records of every kind, hereafter, be in the name, and style of The Methodist Episcopal Church, South.[10]

Note, first, the resolution makes clear that the Southern church considered itself a part of the Methodist Episcopal Church: they were claiming the "rights, powers, and privileges" of an annual conference in that body. It was on that point that the debate centered. James M. Jameson, who had been a part of the General Conference in 1844 and voted against the censure of Bishop Andrew, argued that there was no reason for division. He and his colleagues, Wilson McMurry,

Nathaniel Westerman, and Thomas W. Chandler, denied that the Southern church was the Methodist Episcopal Church, but was really a secession. Andrew Monroe was right: Chandler had been "unconverted" (to the Southern cause) and was determined to "cause trouble." Arguing for separation were Andrew Monroe, Thomas Ashby, William Patton, Wesley Browning, Joseph Boyle, and Jesse Greene. Most of these had been members of the Louisville Convention. Boyle's speech to the conference was reported by the *Missouri Statesman* to be "particularly most eloquent, able, and to our mind conclusive." Boyle's argument was that abolitionism was so strong in the northern church (though the whole church was not abolitionist) that the division was necessary.

On the morning of October 4, Bishop Soule called the roll of the conference, and instructed the members to answer either "north" or "south" when their names were called. Jameson opposed that ruling, so the bishop said each delegate could answer in any way he chose, so long as his position was clear. Anthony Bewley answered, "The Methodist Episcopal Church of the United States of America," which the bishop clearly understood as meaning "north." The roll call vote was 86 in favor of the resolution, 14 against. The *Western Christian Advocate* said the vote was 84–14, but the result was the same. Only a handful of preachers voted to stay with the Northern church. But what would that handful now do? Thomas Chandler consulted with them and reported that they had thought it inadvisable to try to form a Missouri Conference of the Methodist Episcopal Church.

THE DUST SETTLES?

It is important to take a look at the preachers and churches who voted to "go north." It has already been seen that the German Methodist preachers continued to preach in their Missouri circuits, but as members of the Illinois Conference. Other preachers who "went north" also became members of the Illinois or other conferences. A handful, led by the brash Anthony Bewley, met at Spring River, Missouri, on Christmas day, 1845, and organized their own little church structure. Bewley presided and appointed George Sly, David Thompson, Joseph Doughty, Thomas Norwood, J. K. West, James Hanen, Anthony Bewley, and Mark Robertson to circuits in southwest Missouri and northwest Arkansas. This action was a violation of both the spirit and the letter of the Plan of Separation, which had said that Northern churches would not organize in conferences that "went south," and vice versa. Churches on the border with free states had an option which was exercised by, among others, Cape Girardeau, Jackson, and McKendree Chapel. Gary McDowell has shown conclusively that these congregations voted to remain a part of the Methodist Episcopal Church, and stood firm in that conviction all through the years. Since they were on the border of the conference, one which touched a Northern Methodist conference, these congregations were free to exercise their option. Congregations in the southwestern part of the state did not have that option, under the Plan of Separation.

Both the Northern and Southern Methodists began immediately to compete for the border conferences. Dr. Charles Elliott moved to St. Louis and established the *Central Christian Advocate* as a northern voice in the state. It is interesting to note that Dr. Elliott and Dr. David R. McAnally, editor of the *St. Louis Christian Advocate*, had offices in the same building. So far as the record shows, they never spoke to each other, a condition that lasted until McAnally was arrested shortly after the beginning of the war. Acrimony seemed to be the order of the day. Andrew Monroe says in his *Recollections* that:

> This year (1845) we had some good meetings, but the ministry and the membership were more or less anxious about the results of the division. It was a new condition of the church, controversies arose in the papers, the writer and his old special friend, J. M. Jameson (for we had been as David and Jonathan) came in collision in the *Western Advocate*, and the contention was sharp. . . .[11]

With all the sharp contention, it was still the Northern church that suffered the most. The 1845 session of the Missouri Conference reported 23,781 white and 2,529 black members. A year later, the Missouri and St. Louis Conferences of the Methodist Episcopal Church, South, reported 22,408 white and 2,329 black members. The Northern church reported 1,578 members, which is probably fairly close to the real number. It is not until 1852 that reliable statistics are again available for the Missouri Conference of the Northern church. In that year, the Missouri and Arkansas Conference reported a total of 5,064 members. The German Mission Districts, located in Missouri, but part of the Illinois Conference, added another 1,500 to the Northern total. That same year (1852) the Southern branch of the church reported 11,821 white and 1,226 black members in the Missouri Conference, and 11,927 white, 1,002 black, and 237 Indian members in the St. Louis Conference, for a total of 26,213. Whatever the sentiment for union may have been in 1845, it's clear that the Southern church was predominant in the state in the period before the war.

The 1846 General Conference of the Methodist Episcopal Church, South, created the St. Louis Conference from the Missouri Conference. The Missouri Conference was that portion of the state north of the Missouri River; the St. Louis Conference was the state south of the Missouri River.

The Northern annual conferences did not accept the Plan of Separation worked out by the 1844 General Conference. In fact, they rejected the constitutional amendments necessary to make the Plan work. They were insistent that the new church be called one of secession, rather than one of separation. This would create huge problems for the relationship between the two branches of Methodism for years to come, problems that would cause an echo as late as the debates of reunion in 1938.

David Rice McAnally. Editor, St. Louis Christian Advocate. *Methodist Episcopal Church, South.*

The constitutional crisis also meant a lot of new faces at the General Conference in 1848. Moderate delegates to the 1844 General Conference were repudiated by their annual conferences (largely because of their support for the Plan of Separation) and more hard-line delegates elected in their places. Their position toward the Southern church was more intransigent than that of their predecessors, as one episode illustrates. Dr. Lovick Pierce of Georgia had been selected by the Southern church as a fraternal delegate to the M. E. General Conference of 1848. The conference was willing to welcome him personally, but refused to accept him as a fraternal delegate. Dr. Pierce refused to accept this distinction and went home, saying that the next move toward better relations would have to come from the Northern church. It would take decades, and many deaths, for that move to be made.

Based on the actions of the annual conferences, the General Conference of 1848 (M. E.) repudiated the Plan of Separation, and declared that the property which was to have been divided belonged to the Northern church. Northern leaders said they were under no obligation to divide the church property, or the Book Fund, since the southern church was secessionist. The conference had a strict legal right to do this, but it was a denial of the charity exhibited in 1844. As J. N. Norwood says:

> The plan was a wonderful exhibition of Christian charity, manifested in a situation as baffling as any that ever confronted a great religious assembly. . . . When removed from the mellowing influences of that trying session, the North took a more cold-blooded view of the issue; Northern Methodists concluded that their delegates had gone too far. . . . Then in 1848, when the partner most vitally interested in the Plan was unrepresented, the other half of the supposedly dissolved partnership, assuming to act as judge in its own case, declared the act of sanctioning dissolution unconstitutional, null and void from the start.[12]

The Southern church immediately took legal action to protect its own interests. Two suits brought in federal court, one in New York, and one in Cincinnati, finally resolved the issue. The Cincinnati case reached the Supreme Court of the United States in 1854. Ultimately the Supreme Court declared the Plan of Separation to be legally binding. The main points of that Supreme Court decision were:

The Methodist Episcopal Church was divided.
The division was not a secession.
Neither division lost its interest in the common property [a major sticking point!].
The 1844 General Conference had the power to divide the Church.
The sixth Restrictive Rule (on the use of the Book Fund) did not deprive the General Conference of the authority to divide the Church.
The proposed change in the sixth Restrictive Rule was not a condition of separation, but a tool for the General Conference to carry out its purpose.
The separation was legal, and the division of the joint property should be carried out.

So the Southern churches were able to hold on to the colleges, church buildings, printing plants, and the proceeds of the Book Fund promised them in the Plan of Separation. Later, court rulings on ownership of church property were based on the principles laid down in this decision.

DIVISION HEATS UP

The Missouri Conference (M. E.) was re-organized by Bishop Janes in 1848. A year later, the preachers reported a total of 3,591 members, a number which would more than double to 7,764 in 1860. But life was not easy for the Northern preachers. Dr. Elliott's *Southwestern Methodism* reports many stories of violence and persecution against them. At least three were murdered, and several others barely escaped with their lives. Anthony Bewley was hung by a mob in Texas, apparently on charges of inciting slaves to escape. At this date, it is impossible to know if that was the case or not. It is known that several accounts of the murders of Southern preachers during the war were said to be in retaliation for what happened to Bewley.

Gold was discovered in California in 1849 and gold-seekers streamed west by the thousands. With them went both the Northern and Southern branches of Methodism. There was a strong appeal from Bishop Pierce to send more Southern preachers to California. This was seen by the Northern church as a pro-slavery plot to create new slave states. That may indeed have been a part of the motive. In fact, there is a letter from Andrew Monroe that suggests he was urging Southerners to move to California for just that reason. But the bishop's letter sounds much more like a plea for leaders for the mission, not a plot to increase the number of slave states. Elliott says, in *Southwestern Methodism*, "a pro-slavery Church in a free State is a monstrosity." One wonders what that would make an anti-slavery church in a slave state? When human beings fight, they tend to lose sight of reason and justice, and make only the points that fit their own personal cause.

In fact, that is a major lesson for the church from this period. Neither Northern nor Southern Methodism has much to be proud of in its behavior toward the other. Both sides misused the Bible, quoting passages out of context, instead of looking at the central message of Scripture (as Wesley had taught). Southern preachers most often focused on texts such as "Slaves, obey your masters." Northern preachers demanded the abolition of slavery, and seized on whatever texts they could find to make their case. This misuse of Scripture was not confined to the Methodists. It was a regional phenomenon, reaching across denominational lines in both North and South. Like many other debates in the church that focus on a single issue, sermons and writings became shriller in tone and more illegitimate in their use of proof texts. Preachers on both sides often confused the political situation with the religious one and were "carried away" in their comments about each other, and each other's positions. It is a valuable reminder that when factions in the church exclude and demonize each other, disaster is the inevitable result. At this remove, no one is going to argue for slavery as an institution, or make any attempt to defend the misguided (from a modern perspective) attempts of southern preachers to defend the institution. Nor would one make a case for radical abolitionism, which fanned the flames of discord just as surely. Both sides were in grievous error and sin, as is inevitable when churchmen take opposing positions and deny even basic goodwill to their opponents.

Other national events impinged on Missouri Methodism. In 1857, the United States Supreme Court ruled on the Dred Scott case and said that Africans were not citizens. Scott and his family were not made free by being in Illinois. The slaveowner's right to property had been upheld. One interesting result of this decision was an increased opposition to the Methodist Episcopal Church (North) in southwest Missouri, with some spillover into Kansas, Arkansas, and the Indian territory.

The passing of the Kansas-Nebraska Act of 1854, which repealed the Missouri Compromise of 1820, opened Kansas to both pro- and anti-slavery settlers. The ideal was that the citizens of the territory would make the decision about entering the Union as a slave or free state. The reality was a huge rush of settlers from both parts of the country, along with Missourians crossing over to vote in Kansas, and guerilla warfare between the opposing sides. Even with an elected territorial government, Kansas was in a state of anarchy. Abram Still, a northern Methodist preacher from Missouri, became one of the leaders of the free-soil faction, just as Thomas Johnson at the Indian Mission helped promote both the Southern Methodist Church, and the cause of slavery.

John Brown, a rabid abolitionist who was involved in guerilla warfare in Kansas, seized the U.S. Army arsenal at Harper's Ferry, Virginia, in 1859, in an attempt to begin a slave insurrection. His eventual capture and hanging made him a martyr to abolitionists and a demon to slave-owners. His actions fanned the flames both north and south, in the churches as well as in political speeches and newspaper editorials.

In Missouri, the Methodist Episcopal Church was offered, in 1854, buildings and land, for the purpose of starting a school. The offer was accepted, teachers were hired, and a school begun. The trustees then applied to the state legislature for a charter. Their application was rejected by the House, 60–36, on the grounds that the Methodist Episcopal Church was an abolition church, opposed to slavery, and working for its destruction. The same result would happen in 1858 when the denomination applied for a charter for a university in Jefferson City.

On the eve of the war, the Methodist Episcopal Church had 7,869 members in the Missouri Conference. The Methodist Episcopal Church, South, reported 19,723 in the Missouri Conference and 21,022 in the St. Louis Conference, for a total of 40,725.

Chapter 6

WAR, RECONSTRUCTION, AND THE PALMYRA CONFERENCE 1861–1870

A s Southern states began withdrawing from the Union following the election of 1860, Missouri found itself in an uncertain position. The newly-elected Governor Jackson called for a state convention to decide whether or not Missouri would stay with the Union. Missouri was in a vulnerable position. Legally, she was a slave state, but there were strong Free Soil elements, particularly among the German population. What would Arkansas, Kentucky, and Tennessee do? Would the Confederacy be able to offer any protection to Missouri, which was nearly surrounded by Illinois, Iowa, and the Kansas/Nebraska Territories? The State Convention proposed Missouri stay in the Union, and urged the ratification of a proposed constitutional amendment guaranteeing slavery.

After the fall of Ft. Sumter, Governor Jackson ordered the state militia into training camps, with the ultimate purpose of taking the Federal Arsenal in St. Louis. Federal troops under Nathaniel Lyon arrested and disarmed the militia, a fight broke out in the streets of St. Louis, shots were fired, and the war in Missouri began. Even many pro-Union sympathizers felt Lyon's action called for a defense of the state against federal action, and joined the Governor and Sterling Price, the commander of the state militia. The first battle of the war in Missouri was at Wilson's Creek, near Springfield. The Confederate troops defeated Lyon's little army, which retreated to Rolla. Sterling Price then marched the Missouri Guard north and won another battle at Lexington. Missouri's elected government then entered into an alliance with the Confederacy and became the "twelfth Confederate state." The Union army forced Price and his State Guard out of Missouri early in 1862, and the state was under federal control for the duration of the war.

Federal control meant at least two things for the state. First, Governor Gamble set up a pro-Union state government. He wanted to establish a new militia to keep order in the state. General John C. Fremont, the Federal commander in St. Louis, saw this as a threat to his own authority. So the Lincoln administration worked out a compromise. The federal government would pay the Missouri militia if it could be directed by the Union commander in St. Louis. (It helped the compromise that Fremont was soon removed as commander.) Some fifty thousand to seventy-five thousand Missourians enrolled in the militia, freeing that many federal troops for action elsewhere. The second was martial law, first declared in August 1861, and renewed through a series of decrees by Union commanders. Martial law meant that no one could travel without a military pass. Trade was restricted; newspapers deemed hostile to the war effort could be shut down. Among other papers to be shut down was the *St. Louis Christian Advocate*, the official newspaper of the Methodist Episcopal Church, South. A system of provost marshals was set up over the state. They had almost unlimited power of arrest and imprisonment, with no ordinary legal restrictions on their activities. Prisons were set up at Myrtle Street and Gratiot Street in St. Louis for prisoners charged with serious crimes. Political prisoners could be set free on heavy bond or sent to some northern state for the duration of the war. Saboteurs or guerillas could be executed or incarcerated in the new federal prison in Alton, Illinois.

General Henry Halleck, who succeeded Fremont in St. Louis, imposed a "test oath." Persons were required to swear allegiance to the Union by mid-December 1861. Those who did not were considered disloyal and were fined or had their property confiscated to help pay the costs of the war. The test oath, and other oaths like it, would cause major problems for southern Methodist preachers all through the war and reconstruction periods.

Missouri suffered greatly during the war because of guerilla activity. Both Southern guerillas and Northern militia roamed the countryside, often terrorizing civilians, looting and burning property, and killing those who opposed them. Guerilla warfare was also an excuse for individuals to pay off grudges held against neighbors from long before the war. Guerillas were basically of two types: Confederate raiders, such as Colonel Joseph Porter, and bushwhackers, like William C. Quantrill.

Quantrill originally organized his raiders to protect pro-Southern citizens in western Missouri from Union troops in Kansas. These troops looted western Missouri towns and farms. When the Union commander in St. Louis said he could not control the troops in Kansas, Quantrill took matters into his own hands. He was supported by the local population, who looked to him as a kind of guardian angel of Southerners. J. E. Godbey tells of being junior preacher on the Independence Circuit at about this time. He and his senior, W. M. Leftwich, were in the church when they saw the Kansas militia ("Jayhawkers") coming in. Stores were broken into and looted of goods. Houses were burned, and the preachers had to come down out of the steeple where they were hiding when the

Jayhawkers threatened to burn the church. The leader of the Jayhawkers took the names of all the men and said he'd be back in a week and burn out every one who refused to enlist. When the week was almost up, a young man walked into the office of the militia captain and asked to see the list. When he had the list in his hand, he drew a gun and calmly walked out of the office. The names were lost, and so no one could be forced to enlist in the Union militia. The young man was Jesse James, one of Quantrill's lieutenants. Godbey reports that Southerners in the Independence area were grateful to Quantrill for protecting them from the Jayhawkers.[1]

The situation on the border grew worse, until finally, in 1863, General Tom Ewing rounded up all the women known to be associated with Quantrill and his men. He put them in a makeshift prison, which collapsed and killed five of the women. Retaliation was swift. On August 21, Quantrill and his men raided Lawrence, Kansas, killing over one hundred fifty men and burning the town. It is also said that the "Centralia Massacre" led by "Bloody Bill Anderson" in 1864 was an act of revenge for Ewing's acts. One of Anderson's sisters had been killed in the collapse of the prison and another badly hurt. So hatred and revenge fed on each other, and innocent people continued to suffer.

General Ewing's response to the burning of Lawrence was the infamous "Order No. 11," which led to a forced evacuation of Jackson, Cass, Bates, and the northern half of Vernon Counties. Kansas troops were called in to enforce the order, which made things worse. This border area was in ruins within two weeks and was known for years as the "Burnt District." The hatred of Missouri and Kansas citizens for each other did not die with the war. Even today, the football coach at the University of Missouri can have a losing season, but still hold his job if he beats Kansas (those hated "Jayhawks"). A trivial matter, but an indication of how deeply feelings ran over the war.

In the midst of the war, the Radical Union party was founded, and it swept the election of 1864. These Radicals would dominate the convention that would write the new constitution for Missouri after the war.

METHODISM AND THE WAR

What happened to the Methodist Church in Missouri during the war? The records clearly illustrate the point that there is no "objective history." Depending on whether one reads Charles Elliott or W. M. Leftwich, one gets an entirely different picture of the war. Elliott was one of the architects of the Plan of Separation who later hardened his position and insisted that the Southern church was in secession. He became editor of the *Central Christian Advocate*, a northern newspaper in St. Louis, and wrote *Southwestern Methodism: A History of the M. E. Church in the South-West from 1844 to 1864*. His theme was that the Southerners, who had no right to a separate church, were persecuting the Northern preachers in Missouri, Arkansas, and Texas. W. M. Leftwich was a leader in the southern church who wrote a two-volume work, *Martyrdom in Missouri*. His theme was the suffering of the Southerners during the war and in the early years of reconstruction. Both writers were triumphalists about their own cause, and more than capable of imputing to the other side the basest of motives. One example from each writing will both illustrate the problem of the historian and the reality of relationships between the two Missouri branches of the church.

Dr. Elliott, in the context of the capture of Camp Jackson, again raises the charge of secession against the Southern church (forgetting his own contributions to the Plan of Separation). He accuses Southern Methodists of fomenting secession by their "foul apostasy" against the "true" church. In another column, he writes an impassioned paragraph about the increasing moral defense of slavery. "Thus," he says, "step by step was taken in the moral descent till it was practically conceded to be right to murder Bewley and others, and to drive citizens from Texas, Arkansas, and Missouri because they were members of the Methodist Episcopal Church." He later wrote to Simon Cameron, Lincoln's Secretary of War, that members of the Methodist Episcopal Church in Missouri will be "persecuted unto death, confiscation, or banishment" if Missouri were to leave the Union. It is certainly true there was action by mobs and others against the Methodist Episcopal Church. In May 1861, the church in Jefferson City was attacked by a mob and seriously damaged. The mob charged that the Methodist Episcopal Church had no right to be in Missouri, that the Northern Methodists were abolitionists and Negro-thieves, and that they should be either banished or deprived of the rights of citizenship until they left. Certainly, Northern Methodist preachers were in danger. Isaac Martin of the Shelbyville Circuit was warned not to preach under penalty of being tarred and feathered and then set on fire. He continued to preach, but only in Shelbyville, where Union citizens protected him. S. Ing went to a quarterly meeting in Salem in January of 1861 (long before the first signs of secession on the political scene). He was warned to leave, being charged with meddling with slaves. If he disobeyed, he would be tarred, hung, or something similar. One Methodist Episcopal preacher in Platte County was regularly threatened with tar and feathers if he continued to preach. Another was taken by a group of eighteen men to the courthouse, accused of preaching abolitionism, and given seven days to leave the state. Elliott says there would have been no persecution at all without the agitation of Southern Methodist preachers. Elliott, like Leftwich, allows his own personal feelings to dictate his choice of words and examples. There is no doubt that there were persecutions—even murders—of Northern Methodists. There is little doubt that, in some cases, Southern Methodist preachers were involved. To say there would have been no mob violence without the urging of Southern preachers, however, strains credulity.

W. M. Leftwich compiled a huge file of stories of persecutions of Southern preachers. His prose is not as elegant as Elliott's, but it is every bit as impassioned. For example, he says, in the context of the border war in the west:

In Southwest Missouri several of the ministers of the M. E. Church, South, were robbed and otherwise maltreated, amongst them Rev. W. H. Mobley, now gone to rest, and Rev. John Monroe, one of the oldest ministers of any Church in Missouri. These occurrences began to attract attention by their frequency and atrocity, and it was soon discovered that a systematic effort was being made to so annoy, and harass, and persecute the Southern Methodist ministers that they would have to abandon the State, and leave their churches and flocks to be seized and absorbed by others.[2]

In fact, there were leaders in the M. E. Church whose goal was to "seize and absorb," as shall be seen shortly. Leftwich accuses Elliott and the *Central Christian Advocate* of trying to persuade the federal authorities that there would be no rebellion in Missouri if it were not for the Southern Methodists.

One specific example of persecution concerns Rev. Andrew Monroe, an acknowledged leader in the Missouri Conference, and a proponent of the separation of the church:

In 1864 Mr. Monroe was living on a farm about eight miles from Glasgow, in Howard County. . . . Mr. Monroe was out in a field on his little farm, and all his family away from home except a servant, when a company of Kansas soldiers passing along the road halted, entered the house, and robbed it of everything of value they could find. The house was literally pillaged. Mr. Monroe's watch, a fine cloth coat, several pairs of bed-blankets, quilts, comforts, and, indeed, everything of any value they could find. While thus engaged they saw a young man who lived near approaching the house, all unconscious of what was going on. He was arrested and relieved of all his money, $75. One rough-looking Dutch soldier rode out to the field and accosted the venerable man (Monroe) with an imperative demand for his money. When he found that he had but two dollars in the world, he would not take it, but rode back in disgust.[3]

Note the bias expressed toward both Kansas troops and Germans, who were the backbone of the Missouri militia as well, and the bane of Southern sympathizers. At that, Monroe was fortunate. Many of his colleagues suffered worse than he did.

For example, David R. McAnally, editor of the *St. Louis Christian Advocate*, spent considerable time in prison on the charge that he was a Southern Methodist preacher. Marcus Arrington, of the St. Louis Conference, was exiled beyond the Union lines to Tennessee, and did not return after the war because he refused to take the Test Oaths. Rev. Green Woods, a presiding elder in southeast Missouri, was taken from a field where he was planting corn and shot, with the only reason given that he was a Southern Methodist preacher, and therefore disloyal. It was commonly assumed that being a preacher in the Methodist Episcopal Church, South, automatically meant one was a traitor to the United States. There are many stories in Leftwich's volumes about federal officers requiring Southern Methodist preachers to take an oath of loyalty, give bond to ensure their loyalty, or to preach "under the flag," that is, with a United States flag either on the pulpit, or on a pole outside the door. Arguing against such rules on the basis of separation of church and state was to no avail.

There were humorous moments as well. The Missouri Conference of the Methodist Episcopal Church, South, met in September 1861, at Arrow Rock, but quickly moved to Waverly, fleeing the threat of a Federal gunboat on the river or Federal reinforcements marching to Lexington, depending on the source. J. E. Godbey, who was admitted on trial at that conference, was amused by the preachers riding for their lives, scattering hymnals, Bibles, and papers, and was inspired to write a bit of doggerel:

> September twenty-fifth, in sixty-one
> The St. Louis Conference was held on the run.
> Prousman's motion to adjourn
> At first excited but little concern.
>
> But soon the approach of a Federal boat
> Assisted the brethren to cast the vote;
> So friends of Arrow Rock, to you
> The Conference bade a hasty adieu.
>
> Tolbert, who first opposed the plan,
> Now in retreat was found in the van,
> While other brethren, less subject to fear,
> Covered the flight and brought up the rear
>
> Dr. Kavanaugh led the flight
> Until the approaching shades of night;
> He stopped at a farm house by the way,
> And there awaited the approach of day.
>
> He found no rest upon his bed;
> Visions of Federals filled his head.
> At early dawn he seized his saddle,
> Mounted his steed and began to skedaddle.
>
> Kind friends of Arrow Rock to you
> Our warmest thanks are ever due,
> And much do we regret, indeed,
> That your Conference was a grand stampede.[4]

Not the most politic thing for a young preacher to write about the elders who were to vote on his admission to the conference! But it is nice to have a light moment in the dark years of the war.

After cutting through the rhetoric, there is still more than enough pain and suffering to go around. On both sides, preachers were murdered, threatened, or driven out of their communities. Their wives and families suffered hardship and loss. Once martial law was declared in the state, Southern Methodist preachers were put in prison (David R. McAnally, the editor of the *St. Louis Christian Advocate*, spent several years in Gratiot Street Prison, for example), or exiled to Northern states.

Statistically, neither branch of the church fared well during the war. In 1861, the Missouri and Arkansas Conference of the Methodist Episcopal Church had 6,245 members. In 1865, there were 5,018 members in the Missouri Conference. The two conferences of the Methodist Episcopal Church, South, had 40,593 members in 1861. By the end of the war, the church structure was so badly broken that there were no statistics available.

The "Test Oath" Controversies

A "test oath" was an oath of loyalty to the federal government, and/or to the state government of Missouri. The person taking the oath swore he was loyal to the federal government, not in rebellion against it. One had to take the oath in order to vote, serve as an officer or trustee of a public institution, function as a lawyer or minister, serve as a juror, or even be a witness in a trial. In many cases, the person taking the oath also had to post a heavy bond for the performance of the oath. This could include posting a deed of trust or mortgaging property in order to post the bond. One can imagine the potential for fraud among unprincipled or greedy sheriffs, or commanders of smaller military districts. They had only to claim a failure to keep the oath in order to seize the bond or confiscate the property of the person swearing it. This system allowed not only for fraud, but for revenge on one's neighbors, against whom one held a grudge. If a person wanted to get even, one could say that his/her neighbor had failed to keep the oath. A refusal to take the oath was considered evidence of treason. Since county officials, or even captains of militia companies, could require additional oaths, there were so many oaths that sometimes people did not even remember to which ones they had sworn. Leftwich quotes an "old man Ricketts," a hotel keeper in Fayette, as saying that whenever he saw a blue coat with shoulder straps coming, he took off his hat and raised his right hand, so he could swear whatever oath they demanded.

The humor expressed by "old man Ricketts" is a testimony to the resiliency of the human spirit, even in the most trying of times. But there is no doubt that the test oaths worked a great hardship on both clergy and laity in the church. Leftwich mentions several oaths including the "Halleck oath," an oath demanded by Congress in 1861; an oath required by the General Assembly in 1863; the "Rosecranz oath" of 1864; and the "Test Oath" demanded under the new Missouri Constitution of 1865. These were effective statewide. Never at a loss for historical comparisons that will support his feelings, Leftwich compared the test oaths to King Darius ordering Daniel not to pray, the Sanhedrin forbidding Peter and John to preach, the persecutions under Nero and Domitian, and the Spanish Inquisition.

Here is an examination of the so-called "Rosecranz Oath," or General Order No. 61. This order required that no religious bodies (such as an annual conference) could meet, since they might be disloyal. In order for any such group to meet, its members had to give evidence to their loyalty to the United States government. The oath read:

> I, _____, of _____County, State of _____, do hereby solemnly swear that I will bear true allegiance to the United States, and support and sustain the Constitution and laws thereof; that I will maintain the National sovereignty paramount to that of all State, County, or Confederate powers; that I will discourage, discountenance and forever oppose secession, rebellion, and the disintegration of the Federal Union; that I disclaim and denounce all faith and fellowship with the so-called Confederate armies, and pledge my honor, my property, and my life to the sacred performance of this my solemn oath of allegiance to the Government of the United States of America.[5]

When the St. Louis Conference of the Methodist Episcopal Church, South, met March 23, 1864, they appointed a committee to meet with General Rosecranz. The committee informed the general that the members of the conference were all citizens of Missouri, they had taken an earlier loyalty oath, they were all ministers, and they were meeting for church business. They therefore asked to be excused from taking the oath. General Rosecranz was surprised by what they told him. In fact, though the order had been issued in his name, he had not seen it, and he told the conference that if they would send him a certificate stating they had taken an earlier oath, that would be all that was required. The Missouri Conference, meeting two weeks later in Mexico, faced the same difficulties with the Provost-Marshal in that city. They also appealed to General Rosecranz, who issued an order that the conference was to be allowed to meet without further interference. These may have been the most humane dealings with test oaths during the entire war.

General Rosecranz' compassion aside, many Southern Methodist preachers suffered loss of property, jail, or expulsion from the state because they refused to take the test oaths.

Clergy in the Methodist Episcopal Church and in the German Conferences gladly swore to the oaths, since they felt the oaths were designed only to punish "secess" and traitors.

The Stanton-Ames Order of 1863

One of the bones of contention between Northern and Southern Methodists was church property. The Plan of Separation had spelled out the rights of the Southern church to the property within its borders, and to a *pro rata* share of the Book Fund. It has previously been noted how the Northern annual conferences refused to ratify the changes in the constitution this division required, and how this refusal led to the repudiation of the Plan of Separation by the Methodist Episcopal General Conference in 1848. Even though a series of lawsuits, leading to a ruling by the Supreme Court of the United States, secured the property to the Southern church, there were many Northerners who still felt they had been cheated of property that rightfully belonged to their church.

After the Union army occupied Nashville, Tennessee, a chaplain wrote to Bishop Simpson that the Methodist Episcopal Church could recover the empty Southern churches, if the matter were properly put before the federal authorities. Bishop E. R. Ames then went to see Edwin M. Stanton, the Secretary of War, asking for assistance in recovering lost property. The result was an order from the War Department to all commanding generals and officers in the United States Army. It read, in part:

> You are hereby directed to place at the disposal of Rev. Bishop Ames (M. E. Church) all houses of worship belonging to the Methodist Episcopal Church, South, in which a loyal minister, who has been appointed by a loyal Bishop of said Church, does not now officiate.

> It is a matter of great importance to the government, in its efforts to restore tranquility to the community and peace to the nation, that Christian ministers should, by example and precept, support and foster the loyal sentiment of the people. Bishop Ames enjoys the entire confidence of this Department and no doubt is entertained that all ministers appointed by him will be entirely loyal. You are expected to give him all the aid, countenance, and support practicable in the execution of this important mission.[6]

The military was also commanded to "furnish Bishop Ames and his clerk with transportation and subsistence when it can be done without prejudice to the service and . . . afford them courtesy, assistance, and protection."

Behind this order was the assumption that Southern rebellion and Southern Methodism were identical. Beyond that tragic misjudgment, there were other serious flaws in Stanton's order. It was, in effect, an establishment of religion and therefore a violation of the Constitution. It flew in the face of a ruling of the United States Supreme Court and therefore violated the law of the land. But Stanton's view of how to treat a defeated enemy was far different from that of President Lincoln's. Lincoln wanted to end the war, restore the Union, and "bind up the nation's wounds." Stanton wanted to punish those who dared to be in rebellion against the Union. (Stanton also thought he was more capable of being president than Lincoln was, and often acted as if he were president.)

In any event, Bishop Ames set forth with a vengeance, seizing property, including churches, schools, publishing plants, and so on that belonged to the Methodist Episcopal Church, South. When he met with resistance, he called on the army for help, and federal troops obliged by forcibly removing Southern clergy and church members from their buildings. This happened all over the areas in the Mississippi Valley where Union troops were in control, including Missouri. In the minds of many Southerners, this was one more evidence of Northern oppression, and one more reason why they would never agree to work with their Northern counterparts.

Southern Methodists organized to protest this high-handed action. A convention meeting in Louisville in April 1864, appealed to President Lincoln to "restrain and prevent its enforcement," that is, to keep the Union Army from carrying out the order. John Hogan, a Southern Methodist layman, had been friends with Lincoln since they had worked together in the Whig party in the 1830s. He went to Washington, saw Lincoln personally, and got the Stanton-Ames order suspended for Missouri and Kentucky. He was also instrumental in restoring to the Methodist Episcopal Church, South, their publishing house in Nashville, Tennessee. Lincoln pressured Stanton into restricting the order to states still in rebellion. This gave relief to the border states, including Missouri. But the property was still in Northern hands in many cases, and local churches began bombarding the federal government for the return of what was rightfully theirs. In early 1865, Lincoln began the process of restoring the property to the Southern churches.

THE END OF WAR, BUT NOT PEACE

The war ended at Appomattox Courthouse in April of 1865, but that did not bring peace to Missouri. After four years of guerilla warfare, there was widespread devastation and despair in the state. In addition, there were dozens of lawless gangs left over from the border fighting—the James brothers, the Youngers, Dave Pool, and Archie Clement were only the more prominent ones. During the war, at least some of them were legitimate guerilla fighters, but now they became outlaws. When the war ended, Union troops had been hunting down these gangs, but the army was quickly withdrawn, and the chaos of lawlessness increased.

A convention to draft a new constitution met in St. Louis in January 1865. Its first act was to abolish slavery, even before the Thirteenth Amendment. Charles Drake was the dominant figure at the convention. He was a member of the Radical Union party that emerged during the war, and was committed to restoring order to the state. Because of widespread support from rural delegates,

Drake was able to impose his will on the convention, and on the constitution that grew out of it. Drake fought for full civil rights for the newly freed slaves, but the racial prejudices of even the Radical Unionists forced him to back down on this point. The Germans demanded and received voting rights for aliens who declared an intention to become citizens. Drake gave in on that point, but insisted that former Confederates and Confederate sympathizers be barred from voting, holding office, practicing law, serving as teachers or ministers, and from serving as corporation officials or trustees. To enforce this bias, Drake insisted on what was called the "Ironclad Oath." Voters were required to swear they had never engaged in armed hostility to the United States, or given aid to the Confederacy, or any other of eighty-six different acts defining disloyalty. Lawyers, clergy, church officers, and officers of corporations had to swear a slightly different oath before they could vote or carry out the functions of their offices. The same test restrictions had been included in the legislative oath of 1862. Another section of the constitution provided that all judges of the Supreme Court and other state courts, plus circuit attorneys, sheriffs, and country recorders be ousted from office. This ensured that the more conservative judiciary could not overthrow the work of the convention.

Missouri voted, by a narrow margin, to adopt the Constitution. It seemed the best hope to end anarchy in the state and get rid of the outlaw gangs who were still active in the state. With federal troops being withdrawn, there was a sense of helplessness against the outlaws, and security concerns carried the day.

Immediately, the Test Oath was tested in the courts. John Cummings, a Roman Catholic priest from Louisiana, Missouri, refused to take the test oath as a matter of conscience. He was arrested and convicted. When the Missouri Supreme Court upheld the Test Oath, he appealed to the United States Supreme Court. In January 1867, the Supreme Court, in *Cummings vs. Missouri*, reversed the decision of the Missouri court on the grounds that the test oath was an *ex post facto* legislation, and a bill of attainder. The ruling made clear that the test oath was designed to punish something that happened before the law was passed, which is forbidden by the Constitution. This ruling restored freedom of the pulpit in Missouri, though it was not the last lawsuit that had to be filed on behalf of clergy. This ruling allowed Enoch M. Marvin, now a bishop of the Methodist Episcopal Church, South, and dozens more like him, to return home and carry on their ministry in the church.

THE PALMYRA CONFERENCE OF 1865

With the war's end, the Methodist Episcopal Church tried to establish itself throughout the South, assimilating the battered Southern church. The Northern church said, or at least implied, that slavery and the separation of the church had gone together. Now that slavery was no more, there was also no need for the

Southern church, and its members could come home to the "true" church. The Missouri and Arkansas Conference of the M. E. Church, meeting in the spring of 1865, issued an invitation to receive all those who "did truly and earnestly repent of their sins, and were in love and fellowship with the loyal religion and religious loyalty of the Mother Church." Indeed, the future of the Southern church seemed bleak. Some Southern leaders were even investigating the possibility of a union with the Protestant Episcopal Church; others were ready to give up and go back to the Methodist Episcopal Church.

In the midst of despair and lost-ness, Missouri stepped to the front once again. Not that things were well with the Missouri Church: much of the property seized by Bishop Ames

Andrew Monroe, the patriarch of Southern Methodism in Missouri, called the preachers to the Palmyra Conference, which gave new life to the struggling Methodist Episcopal Church, South, at the close of the war.

was still in Northern hands. One of the annual conferences in Missouri had not met for three years, and the other for two years. The church was disorganized, and many preachers were in exile or hiding. There was no conference paper and no easy means of communication. There was no bishop in the state. But, as W. H. Lewis said, as God chose Moses to lead Israel and Martin Luther to lead the Reformation, so God chose Andrew Monroe to save the Southern church. Monroe was "the pioneer and patriarch of Missouri Methodism," perhaps the oldest and surely the longest-serving minister in the Missouri Conference of the Methodist Episcopal Church, South. He had represented the conference at many General Conferences, and had been an active part of the founding of the Southern branch of the church. Many, many, years he had been elected president of the conference and presided until the bishop arrived. During the war, he convened the conference and made the appointments.

Now, in the late spring of 1865, he called for a meeting of the preachers and leading laymen of the Missouri Conference to meet in Palmyra on June 22, 1865, to report on the state of the church, and to decide what would be its future. When the conference met, Monroe was elected president and John D. Vincil secretary. The records available list the names of the preachers who attended, but not the laity. The preachers who were there included: Andrew Monroe, C. I. VandeVenter, F. A. Savage, B. H. Spencer, W. M. Rush, R. G. Loving, James Penn, H. H. Hedgepath, W. M. Newland, W. W. McMurry, John D. Vincil, R. P. Holt, A. P. Linn,

Louis Downing, H. A. Bourland, E. A. Hudson, Jacob McEwin, L. Rush, W. Warren, P. M. Pinckard, S. H. Huffaker, and W. M. Leftwich. W. D. Cox, and W. O. Cross, local preachers, were also in attendance, along with several laity. Remember that at this point, laity still did not have a vote in the annual conference, so it was not considered crucial to record their attendance. However, their presence gave weight and support to the work of the conference.

To determine the state of the church, they called the roll of the conference. Each preacher stood as his name was called and gave an account of the condition of the church in his appointment or as he knew it from neighboring appointments. A committee on the State of the Church was then appointed to take these reports into account and make recommendations for action to the conference. The committee had no light task: what was at stake was no less than the question, "does the Methodist Episcopal Church, South, still have a purpose in the postwar world, or has it outlived its usefulness?"

While the committee was meeting in the home of Thomas E. Thompson, the conference agreed to take no action on the Test Oath. It did not make any formal reply to the invitation from the Missouri and Arkansas Conference of the Methodist Episcopal Church. On the second day of the conference, Bishop Hubbard H. Kavanaugh arrived. His presence both helped the morale of those there and gave specific editorial help to the work of the committee.

The report of the committee, which was adopted without change by the conference, is important enough to merit being printed in full, rather than simply in summary:

> Your committee, in considering "the importance of maintaining our separate and distinct ecclesiastical organization," beg leave to present the following resolution and accompanying paper:
>
> *Resolved,* That we consider the maintenance of our separate and distinct ecclesiastical organization as of paramount importance and our imperative duty.
>
> The reasons are many and obvious. While we have maintained a separate and distinct ecclesiastical organization for twenty years, yet we claim original paternity and co-existence as a Methodist Church with the other branches of the great Methodist family in the country. Facts will not permit us to yield to any other Church of that name priority of age; nor in any other light than as an attempt to deceive the unsuspecting among our people can we regard the specious claims urged to the confidence and patronage of the Methodist public under the name of "Old Church."
>
> In contravention of the Plan of Separation agreed upon by the General Conference of 1844—the legitimacy and binding force of which were

recognized by the Supreme Court of the United States—the Northern wing of the Church has acted in bad faith toward us in many ways.

And since that Church was forced by law to give to our Church her pro rata division of property—which she was too mercenary to do without an appeal to the highest judiciary of the country—she has persisted in an unprovoked and undesired war upon us—a war which has aggravated the questions of difference, widened the breach, and produced an estrangement of feeling and a destruction of fellowship for which she alone is responsible, and which we cannot even seek to remedy without compromising principles and yielding all self-respect.

Those who publish to the world that all differences between us are swept away with the institution of slavery are either ignorant of the facts or are trying to mislead the public. The question upon which the Church divided was not whether the institution of slavery was right or wrong per se, but whether it was a legitimate subject for ecclesiastical legislation. The right or wrong of the institution, its existence or non-existence, could not affect this vital question. It is now abolished by Federal and State legislation, which event we accept as a political measure with which we have nothing to do as a Church. And it remains for us to demonstrate our ability to exist without the institution of slavery, as we have existed with it, which we have already done in California and other places.

Now, if we go into the Methodist Episcopal Church, we will by that act yield the position we have so often taken, admit the charges we have so often refuted, and, by accepting political tests of Church-fellowship, stultify ourselves and compromise the essential principles of the gospel. If we seek an alliance with or permit our Church to be swallowed up by any other ecclesiastical organization, we admit the charge that with the institution of slavery we stand or fall.

The subject of Church reconstruction or consolidation has been widely discussed by the press and the ministry of the Methodist Episcopal Church (North), and reasons, both political and ecclesiastical, are urged with an ill-disguised pertinacity why we should consent to an absorption of our entire ecclesiastical body by that Church.

It cannot be disguised that what they failed to accomplish during the war by military order and authority they now seek to effect by ecclesiastical strategy and diplomacy—that is, to get possession of our Church property, and rather than recognize us now as a Christian Church entitled to their ecclesiastical fellowship and Christian fraternity (which they by formal vote of their

General Conference refused to do in 1848) and in that way, and with a Christian spirit, seek to offer negotiations upon the subject, they prefer to ignore our existence, or, which would suit their purpose better, pronounce us disloyal to the government, and per consequence not entitled to an existence at all; then invade us and by misrepresentations seek to disaffect our people, disintegrate our Church, and inaugurate an ecclesiastical strife that will involve the third and fourth generations.

The only consolidation or reconstruction they would accept would be that we turn over to them our Church property and interests and influence; yield the whole field; confess that we have been in the wrong; indorse [*sic*] the politics of their Church as a condition of membership; and become political hucksters instead of gospel ministers; then even our motives would be suspected, and we looked upon with contempt for our cowardly truckling to party and power.

Again we affirm that our itinerant system has become a great moral agency in elevating the masses of the people, preaching the gospel to the poor and "spreading scriptural holiness over these lands." Under its wide-spread operations we have gathered the people together, planted Churches, organized Sabbath-schools, acquired Church property, built up and endowed institutions of learning, and become a moral and religious element of the country at least equal to any other Protestant Church.

The people have learned to look to our ministry for the gospel, to our Churches and Sunday-schools for religious instruction, and to our influence in restraining vice, encouraging virtue, maintaining law and order, and promoting the well being of society. We cannot, therefore, abandon our Church and people, or betray the interests and trusts committed to us as a Church, without a plan and culpable disregard of duty that would subject us to the contempt and derision of the Christian public.

We are not at liberty to dissolve our ecclesiastical organization or permit our Church to be absorbed by any other, even should we desire to do so, for our people have been consulted as far as practicable, and they are unwilling to seek any other Church connection, but with great unanimity demand at our hands the maintenance of our Church organization intact.

It is, therefore, due the great mass of the people who oppose the prostitution of the pulpit to political purposes, it is due to our large membership who have been converted and gathered into the fold of Christ under our ministry, and who love our Church doctrines and discipline too fondly to seek any other fold now—it is due every principle of self-respect and ecclesiastical propriety that we maintain, with firm reliance upon the help of the Great Head of the Church, our organization without embarrassment or compromise.

While these are some of the many reasons why we should adopt the above resolution, we desire most ardently to cultivate fraternal relations with all the evangelical Churches, and "as much as in us lies live peaceably with all men."

> Wm. M. Leftwich, Chairman
> John D. Vincil
> Wm. M. Newland[7]

Some obvious self-serving remarks aside, the "Palmyra Manifesto" states clearly why the Methodist Episcopal Church, South, should remain in existence. They saw a clear difference between the civil issue of slavery that had split the nation and the ecclesiastical issue of episcopal authority which split the church. They refused to reunite with the northern church as a matter of survival, when the main points of difference had not been decided. They voted to continue the existence of a church which seemed to be in extremis.

As the word spread across the Missouri conference, the Southern Methodists rejoiced. The *St. Louis Christian Advocate* for December 7, 1865, included this letter from a correspondent who had traveled across the state, north of the line of the Hannibal and St. Joseph Railroad:

> Old men, who had clung to the Church through all the storm, lifted up their voices and wept for joy when they read the reports of the Palmyra meeting, and rode over their neighborhoods to scatter the glad tidings that the ship would not be given up. I saw one old man, now over sixty, who walked three miles to obtain a copy of the proceedings, and then wore it out reading it to his neighbors.[8]

That "purple prose" cannot disguise the fact that ordinary men and women were delighted their church was going to continue. Part of the delight, no doubt, was a basic clinging to identity: "Well, we lost the war, but at least we still have our church." Part, no doubt, was due to the lift of the spirits given by those who, when things seemed darkest, were willing to light a candle and proclaim the coming of the dawn.

The response across the South was equally enthusiastic. Bishop Kavanaugh reported that the people of the South drew strength from the power of the Palmyra meeting. They thought that if the Missouri preachers, who had suffered more than in any other state, and who still stood under the oppression of the test oath, could say the Church would stand, then "it shall be maintained, and, with God's help, we will rally to the old standard, reset the old landmarks, and pledge . . . to maintain our ecclesiastical organization at all hazards and to the last extremity."

Enoch M. Marvin reported from Texas that the report of the meeting was like the trumpet calling knights to battle, inspiring new courage and confidence. The *Episcopal Methodist*, of Richmond, Virginia, said the Palmyra Manifesto was like "life from the dead" to the church in Virginia and the Carolinas. In addition, the manifesto had a major influence on the statement issued by the bishops of the church later that year.

The Pastoral Address of 1865

The bishops of the Methodist Episcopal Church, South, met in Columbus, Georgia, in August of 1865. The six bishops, three of whom were in poor health, called Holland McTyeire, former editor of the Nashville *Christian Advocate*, to meet with them and write their Pastoral Address. The words are McTyeire's, the ideas are his and the bishops', and the inspiration came from the Palmyra Manifesto.

The Pastoral Address said clearly that the questions raised in 1844 had not been settled by the war. Indeed, the war had aggravated them. The fact that the northern church was insisting on social dogmas and political tests for church membership meant that church had become too radical. The bishops rejected all suggestions for reunion. The invasion of territory which the Plan of Separation had declared out-of-bounds to the northern church was denounced. There was a call for a General Conference in 1866. (The 1862 General Conference had not been able to meet. It was scheduled for New Orleans, which had fallen into Union hands prior to the time of the conference.)

THE GENERAL CONFERENCE OF 1866

The General Conference of the Methodist Episcopal Church, South, convened in New Orleans in April 1866, with renewed hope for the future. Representing the Missouri Conference were Patrick M. Pinckard, Andrew Monroe, Cornelius I. VandeVenter, Perry Spencer, and W. M. Rush, while David R. McAnally, William M. Prottsman, Francis A. Morris, George M. Winton, and John T. Peery represented the St. Louis Conference. Historians have called this General Conference one of the most significant in the history of American Methodism.

What made it so significant? Change was in the air. The bishops were sensitive both to the pressure for change and to the sentiments of more conservative members of the church. They pointed out in their Episcopal Address that change for its own sake was not necessarily a good thing, but that wisdom might well call for "new applications and developments of fundamental principles." Bishop James O. Andrew called for a spirit of brotherly love, and a hope that proposals for change would not be condemned out of hand. Nor did he want those who proposed changes condemned, since they were "as good friends of the Church as others who oppose them." One of the leaders against any change was Bishop

Pierce, so Bishop Andrew knew well what he was asking of the Conference!

There were seven major proposals before the General Conference. Though all were important, only two of them will be considered here. The first was the inclusion of laity in the Annual and General Conferences. It passed General Conference by a large majority. When it was ratified, laity began taking their places in the Annual Conferences immediately, and the first lay delegates to General Conference were seated in 1870. This brought incredible new energy and talent into the General Conference and strengthened the southern church for the hard times that still lay ahead. On the question of lay representation, McAnally, Morris, Winton, Pinckard, VandeVenter, and Rush voted "yes." Peery, Monroe, and Spencer voted "no."

A second major proposal was a change of name. The word "South" in the name was considered a handicap in the border conferences. The Conference voted overwhelmingly to change the name, and chose "The Methodist Church" by a vote of 111–21. The next day the conference re-considered and "The Episcopal Methodist Church" was the name submitted to the annual conferences. The annual conferences did not approve the change, however. Jerome C. Berryman, a long-time leader of Missouri Methodism, may have summed up the feelings about the name change when he said, "I shall vote against the proposed change of name, for I am no more ashamed of the suffix 'South' in my Church name than of the affix 'Berry' in my surname."[9] A long letter in the *St. Louis Christian Advocate* argued against the name change on the basis of the Plan of Separation and the right of churches to designate their geographical location in their name.

The General Conference also elected four new bishops: W. M. Wightman, Enoch M. Marvin, D. S. Doggett, and Holland McTyeire. Enoch Marvin therefore became the first native Missourian to be elected a bishop in any branch of American Methodism. He was elected on the first ballot, even though he was not a member of the conference, nor even present at the time of his election.

The conference also gave permission for five new annual conferences, including one in Illinois. This first incursion into northern territory came at the request of the Christian Union Church, a group of congregations who had broken with the Northern church during the war. In addition, the Baltimore Conference left the Methodist Episcopal Church and affiliated with the Methodist Episcopal Church, South, at this session of the General Conference.

Finally, the General Conference passed important constitutional reforms. Class meetings were abolished, as were probationary periods for membership, and gender segregation in worship. The maximum length of a pastoral term was extended from two to four years.

Relationships Between Northern and Southern Churches

The Methodist Episcopal Church was still feeling triumphant. The *Central Christian Advocate* said, "The only true theory of Methodist reconstruction is to push on our work." That same editorial said that the Methodist Episcopal Church had to occupy the South, whether there was a Church South or not, and had to restore unity by taking over the former Southern church. The Northern churches invited the Southern churches to return individually, or in small clusters. But the Southern leadership insisted the only reunion could be that of two denominations. They relied on the Plan of Separation to argue that they had separated as a body and could only come back as a body. Each side wanted the other to repent, stop the partisan bickering, and restore church property. Then it would be time to talk about reunion.

In 1869, two Northern bishops met with the Southern bishops to discuss reunion. The Northerners assumed that because slavery had ended, the cause of division in the church was gone. The Southern bishops responded that the North had to stop sending missionaries to the South, return Southern church property that had been seized, and repent of their actions. Furthermore, they said, the main cause of separation had not been removed. The cause of separation had not been slavery, but constitutional issues. Slavery was only the "presenting problem" of separation. Finally in 1876, in a meeting at Cape May, New Jersey, the Northern church recognized that the Southern church was a permanent and legitimate body. After that recognition, the wounds of war could begin to heal, though it would be over sixty years more before the two bodies reunited.

Chapter 7

MISSOURI—THE MOTHER OF CONFERENCES: EVANGELISM AND CHURCH GROWTH IN THE NINETEENTH CENTURY

E vangelism and church growth has always been a priority for American Methodism. Wherever there were people who had not heard the gospel, the circuit riders and then the settled preachers took the good news, organized classes, formed the classes into churches, and bent their energies toward building up the Body of Christ. Missouri Methodism was no exception. Methodism flourished in Missouri because Methodists thought it could. Missouri Methodism flourished because Methodist leaders were intentional about church growth. Missouri Methodism grew because there were specific strategies for growth. And Missouri Methodism became the "mother of many conferences." This is the story of how that growth happened.

Missouri Methodism began, as has been seen, with the pioneering work of Joseph Oglesby. He found two hundred prospects for Methodist work in Missouri in his brief tour—probably all the English-speaking people in the territory. Oglesby's exuberant optimism was typical of Methodism in the nineteenth century. If there were unchurched, English-speaking people, they belonged to the Methodists! The Missouri Circuit was organized in 1806, and reported one hundred and six members at the end of the first year. From that humble beginning, the circuit riders moved out across the state, organizing classes and churches. As. "J. H." said, "They followed the paths of the emigrant, sought him in his first rail-pen tent, or cabin, as the case may have been, and as early as possible preached to him the word of life."[1]

One sign of a healthy, growing church is vocations. In 1815, the first young man raised and converted in Missouri went out to preach. His name was John Scripps and he was to have a long and honorable record in Missouri Methodism.

And he was only the first of hundreds of young men (and, later, women) who heard God's call to preach and responded in faith.

The Missouri Conference was organized in 1816, a reflection of a common pattern in early American Methodism. Conferences were organized on the frontier long before territories became states. That first Missouri Conference included Indiana, Illinois, and Arkansas, as well as Missouri. No western boundary for the conference was set, giving rise to the tradition that the western boundary was "the farthest cabin toward the setting sun." Certainly the Methodist itinerants acted as if that were the case.

Those early pioneers saw the whole world as a mission field. They were always reaching out to new areas, seeking to win souls for Jesus Christ—except in the cities!

> How often had I heard the saying "God made the country and there he will acknowledge and bless the people, but the devil made the towns and those who live in them are unapproachable by preaching": they neglected the towns—circuits were formed and called after some river or creek, while perhaps the principal town . . . could not have even the advantage of preaching. . . . It was probably from this cause, in part, that during the twelve years in which Methodism had been operating and forming circuits in Missouri, that no continuous effort had been made to form a society in St. Louis, the principal town of the state.[2]

It was not until 1820, when Missouri was on the brink of statehood, that Jesse Walker began the Methodist mission in St. Louis. His ministry is another story, but note that when the 1822 conference met in the new church in St. Louis, it had one hundred twenty-seven members. Once the Methodists dared to face the devil in the cities, they were as intentional about evangelism and growth there as anywhere else. In fact, conference had been set to meet in St. Louis in 1822 before there was even a Methodist building in the city.

Riding the circuit meant being intentional about the work. In 1829, John Monroe was on the Monticello Circuit. He "traveled 2,450 miles, preached three hundred times, held class ninety-six times, love feasts eighteen times, administered Lord's Supper sixteen times, held prayer meeting fifteen times, baptized thirty times, added in all eighty-two (new members); this done in three hundred eighteen days." He had only three hundred eighteen days, because he spent nearly a month traveling to and from the session of the conference, and attending the conference itself!

Samuel G. Patterson was appointed to the Bowling Green Circuit in 1834:

> To fill the appointments on this circuit the preacher had to travel about one hundred and seventy-five miles every round. The circuit extended . . . from near Troy on the south, to New London and Salt River on the north, and from Clarksville on the Mississippi to near Middletown in Montgomery

(County). The regular preaching places were Bowling Green, Auburn, Paynesville, Clarksville, Louisiana, Frankfort, and New London—seven towns. Besides these, Buffalo Knob, Wells, Republican meeting house, Ashley, Ingraims, Indian Creek, James', Blankenships', Tom Elys, Jacob Kribaums', Fuquas, Trimbles', Buffalo meeting house, Gregory's Creek, Stradley's Digs, and Wm. Taylor's—sixteen country appointments, twenty-three in all. Besides these I had some side, irregular, appointments; all of these were filled every twenty-eight days.[3]

He preached, as was the custom, twice, or often three times on Sunday, and once every other day of the week. On the circuit there were no Methodist church buildings, and only two of any kind. Preaching was in homes, except at Bowling Green and New London, where services were held in the courthouse. This was a fairly typical circuit. No one told them it couldn't work!

The circuit riders, the true itinerants, were men with the restless pioneer spirit, as surely as Daniel Boone or Jedidiah Smith (who was a Methodist local preacher as well as a famous "mountain man"). They were restless, eager to see what lay beyond the next hills, and always on the move. They were also the exception in Missouri after about 1830. They pioneered the work and moved on. The work of nurture was left to the local pastors and the traveling preachers who had located or were supernumerary. The author's great-great-grandfather, William P. Hulse, served as a traveling preacher for only one year. He was the junior preacher that year on the Lexington Circuit and helped organize the class which later became First United Methodist Church, Independence. After that year, he located—his heart was still in the work, but arthritis would not allow him to spend long hours in the saddle or nights sleeping on the ground. He moved to a farm in Johnson County and helped build up the church there until his death.

EMIGRATION AND EVANGELISM

Missouri Methodism made great gains in the early period simply by gathering into classes and churches those who had migrated from the East and South. They were more intentional about mission in ethnic groups.

The first African Americans in Missouri were slaves, brought first by the French to the lead mines, and then by settlers from the southeast. Jacob Lanius was typical of the circuit riders in his real concern for the African-American population:

> I have recently determined to pay more attention to our slave population than I have hitherto done. Great and mighty are the efforts being made for the salvation of the world—but nothing is being done for the slaves in our circuit. . . . It really seems to me that if Christ died for them as well as for us they ought to be attended to.[4]

Left, Jacob Lanius, pioneer circuit rider, who embodied the passion for souls in nineteenth century Methodism. At right, Rev. Cleo Kottwitz, whose first-person narration of the life of Jacob Lanius continues the tradition.

The passion for souls is reflected in Lanius's words, as is the conviction that the message of salvation took precedence over social and legal conventions. That passion bore fruit. In 1821, the year that Missouri became a state, blacks made up 11 percent of the total membership of the Methodist Church. By 1840, rising social tensions had led to the formation of separate churches for African Americans. The African Church in St. Louis had two hundred members in 1840. By 1843, it had three hundred fifty members and was the largest church in St. Louis. Division of the church in 1844, the pain of civil war and reconstruction, racial hostility, and the organization of the Colored Methodist Episcopal Church (now the Christian Methodist Episcopal Church) after the war led to a decline in black membership in the Methodist Episcopal and Methodist Episcopal, South, churches which lasted through the rest of the nineteenth century.

The great German migrations to America came after the failure of democratic revolutions in Germany in 1830 and again in 1848. By 1860, there were 88,500 Germans living in Missouri alone. They settled in the great river systems which reminded them of their native land. St. Louis early became a kind of distribution point for German immigrants. In 1841, Ludwig S. Jacoby organized Missouri's first German-speaking Methodist church in St. Louis—with forty-one members out of a total population of some fifteen thousand Germans. It grew rapidly and established a second church in 1848. Between 1842 and 1849, German-speaking churches were founded at Hermann, Pinckney, Boonville, Jefferson City,

Brunswick, Carrollton, Lexington, Independence, Weston, St. Joseph, and Canton. In 1849, Jacoby was sent by German Methodists in Missouri to begin a mission in Germany itself. Today's Methodist Church in Germany is the result of his mission.

On October 26, 1852, the *St. Louis Christian Advocate* carried an open letter to Methodists in St. Louis, entitled "Another Church Wanted." It was a letter of concern for immigrants from European countries and called for workers for "the most important missionary field now open before the Methodist Church in our own country." The writer knew what would work among immigrant groups. He held before his readers the model of the German churches and the great good they were doing. Then he cried:

> Who has cared for the Irishman? Oppressed and downtrodden at home, he fled to this country for refuge. The country received him with open arms— but who has opened for him the house of God, and invited his weary feet to turn in thither, where he might find rest for his troubled heart?[5]

The writer reminded his readers of Methodist roots in Ireland and pleaded that the Irish not be left to become Roman Catholics by default, because Methodists would not minister to them. His project had the blessing of the bishop. Land had been promised for a building, and an Irish-born preacher was available. The writer called for a subscription for what he called "the first Irish church in the country—here in St. Louis!" This is the only appeal for funds to build a church in order to organize a congregation that was found in the *Christian Advocate*. Other congregations met in homes, in borrowed quarters, or built a building on their own. The appeal may not be the only reason this Irish congregation was never formed, but it is an interesting coincidence.

Missions were established to a resident ethnic group as early as 1826. In that year, Daniel Morgan Boone, the "government farmer" in western Missouri, urged the establishment of a mission to the Indians of Kansas. His request included the information that the Indians had a considerable sum of federal money which had been designated for building schools. Jesse Greene, the Presiding Elder of the Missouri District, went to Kansas and met with the Indian agent, who gave him a written request for the establishment of a mission. In September 1830, the Missouri Conference voted to "get in there and get that money for a mission to the Kansas Indians"—and also for a mission to the Shawnees. Thomas Johnson was appointed to the Shawnee Mission and William Johnson to the Kansas Mission. By the spring of 1831, there was a two-story log house in Wyandotte County, Kansas, which served as home, church, and school. In spite of a smallpox epidemic in 1831, the mission reported fifty-two members in the Methodist societies in 1832. In 1838, the Missouri Conference established a central manual labor school, and pledged to give up to ten thousand dollars in support. The federal government provided 2,240 acres of land to the mission. The Indian Mission Conference was established in 1844.

CHURCH GROWTH: HOW DID THEY DO IT?

Methodists had a strategy for growth. David Rice McAnally was, for years, editor of the *St. Louis Christian Advocate* and a leading voice in the Methodist Episcopal Church, South. He was also a leading spokesman for church growth. In an editorial titled, "Where is our proper Missionary Field?" he argued for priorities in mission strategy. Money given for missions should be spent where it would do the most good. For McAnally, the most important mission field for Methodists was in this country. The thousands of immigrants coming in every year needed to hear the gospel:

> We should have missions—well-sustained missions—for our foreign born population of every class and of every grade. Besides this, we should see to it that every town, every village, and every neighborhood throughout the country be well supplied with the ministrations of Christianity as held and taught by orthodox Protestants. This is indispensable. And where sections of the country are unable, or only partly able, to support a minister, they should be assisted by the missionary contributions of others.[6]

Note that McAnally had some interesting presuppositions. One was that the great flood of immigrants had never heard the gospel. Considering that most of them had come from Europe, this seems highly unlikely. But the second presupposition also explains the first—they must hear the gospel in its "orthodox Protestant" form. Obviously, Roman Catholics would be prime targets for evangelism in this strategy. So would the Anabaptist groups, who were not "orthodox" Protestants. So there was clearly a great field white to the harvest (in McAnally's mind) among these Christian immigrants.

To meet the demands of his carefully defined mission field, McAnally advocated first enlarging each circuit, adding new preaching places, and reaching out to neighborhoods where people were living in poverty as they struggled to gain a foothold in the new world. On one hand, every preacher should look for new preaching places to add to his circuit, rather than sitting comfortably with the preaching places already established. On the other hand, if preachers really reached out to persons living in poverty, usually in crowded city neighborhoods, there would be open doors for all kinds of mission work, modeled on the precedent set by the Wesleys in their days at Oxford. Preachers could establish schools and medical clinics, and help persons find jobs as well as hope and meaning for their lives. To whatever extent the church is willing to reach out, to that extent there will always be opportunities for mission, service, and growth. McAnally's second mission/outreach strategy was to raise preacher's salaries. Part of the reason preachers did not reach out, he argued, was that they were so poorly paid that they had to spend part of their time working in secular employment in order to feed their families. Give them a decent wage, he argued, and they will have more time to spend reaching out to this huge new mission field.

Trained preachers and teachers were crucial for the work of outreach and mission, and Missouri Methodism did not have enough of them. In an editorial titled, "Our Missionary Field—how is it to be Occupied?" McAnally argued for the founding of a good college to train men for teaching as a profession. In light of the need, he said, it was opportune that the St. Louis and Missouri Conferences "have resolved earnestly to go to work and by their united efforts build up a college proper . . ." However, one might disagree with McAnally's perception of who "needed" the gospel, he did have a clear strategy both for reaching out, and for providing trained leadership to preach and teach.

Growth

The strategies worked. The persistence and enthusiasm with which they were put into effect resulted in growth. It has been said that between 1800 and 1925, American Methodists organized, on the average, more than one congregation a day that continued in existence for at least ten years. Many others that were organized disappeared in less than the ten years. That's an incredible statistic—more than one a day for one hundred twenty-five years! Missouri had her share of those new congregations.

The Methodist Episcopal Church organized a Church Extension Society to build new churches in the trans-Missouri west. The society provided gifts and loans for the building of new churches. C. C. McCabe was the assistant secretary of the society from 1868 to 1884. One day, riding on a train, he saw a newspaper article about a speech Robert G. Ingersoll had given, saying that churches were dying out all over the land. At the next station, McCabe got off the train and sent Ingersoll the following telegram:

> Dear Robert: "All hail the power of Jesus' name"—we are building more than one Methodist Church for every day in the year, and propose to make it two a day! C. C. McCabe.

This telegram sparked a wave of enthusiasm among Methodists, who tended to be a bit jingoistic in the late nineteenth century, and soon they were singing:

> The infidels a motley band, in council met and said:
> "The churches die through all the land, the last will soon be dead."
> When suddenly a message came, it filled them with dismay:
> "All hail the power of Jesus name! We're building two a day."

Between 1865 and 1900, the St. Louis Conference of the Methodist Episcopal Church, South, increased from 8,000 members to 26,500, and from 80 churches to 279—more than triple in both cases. The Missouri Conference of the South church increased from 11,900 members in 138 churches to 44,500 in 476 churches—again more than triple. The net membership gain was 51,000, or 1,457 per year. That averages out to four new members per day—every day for 35 years! The net gain in churches was 537, or an average gain of 15.3 churches per year. Not one a day, but certainly enough to say that Missouri had done its share in giving the denomination a boost.

How did they do it? Four families in a neighborhood began to meet for prayer and Bible study; a group of women in a community decided they needed a church and invited a pastor from a neighboring town to hold a revival. Pastors found a community without a church and started one. They met in schools, in homes, in churches belonging to other denominations, in unfinished stores, in city hall, and in the courthouse. Some of them built a church building the year they were organized, others went for years in borrowed quarters.[7]

How did they do it? They didn't wait on conference programs, or special emphases, or financial aid. They saw a need and met it. An anonymous writer for the *St. Louis Christian Advocate* expressed the feelings of many when he called for a church extension association.

> There are 100,000 inhabitants in St. Louis and only eight southern Methodist churches. Why are there only eight? . . . From Wesley Chapel in the southern part of our city, to Jefferson Barracks, there is not a Methodist church or congregation, we are informed; yet thousands and thousands of immortal souls live between those two places. We have no church above the Mound Methodist Church, but thousands of people live up there, many of whom desire to be members of our church.[7]

There was an awareness of the need for churches to be organized, an awareness of persons who did not have the ministry of the church, and—if we Methodists are forced to tell the whole truth—probably more than a touch of denominational pride.

How did they do it? They did it by adding members to existing churches, even as they reached out to build new ones. Look at what happened to Methodist Episcopal, South, churches in St. Louis in 1855. First Church, with over three hundred members, had a revival. Unfortunately, the results are unknown, since the author was so eager to tell that five members of that church had been members of the first class in St. Louis (organized by Jesse Walker in 1821).

Centenary (Fifth and Pine) had a 25 percent membership increase. Mound doubled its membership. Asbury had one of the most flourishing Sunday schools in the city. Sixteenth Street doubled its membership—it had been a "colony" from Centenary. City Mission organized Christy Chapel. First Boatmen's Church was ministering to the sailors and boatmen who swarmed into St. Louis. People were working hard at reaching out for Christ and the church. On a sad note, Green St. African Church, which had at one time had the largest membership of any church in the city, was dying. The report says this was because of "the destruction of the northerners who are contending for the property." The hard truth is that the church was probably destroyed by the two branches of episcopal Methodism fighting over the property.

It is obvious that the strategies were not necessarily planned and developed at the conference level. There were no "master plans" for the churches to follow. "Master plans" would become important after World War II, but in the nineteenth century, the strategies and actions were more local and grass roots. They sprang from outreach to neighborhoods and communities that needed a church and a ministry.

THE MOTHER OF CONFERENCES

Just as Methodism grew in Missouri, so it grew beyond the state, and the original Missouri Conference of 1816 was to become the "Mother" of many conferences across the west. The states of Illinois and Indiana were districts in that first Missouri Conference. That was one of the accidents of geography and history. The French and Spanish had followed the Mississippi northward and founded settlements in Missouri before the great migrations westward across the Appalachians after the end of the Revolutionary War. The purchase of the Louisiana Territory in 1804, and the expedition of Lewis and Clark focused national attention on St. Louis and the vast territories to which it was the gateway. Settlers "jumped over" Illinois and Indiana, and those territories were only sparsely populated. So Missouri, with the largest population, gave her name to the Conference. But Missouri Methodism was only beginning in 1816.

In 1809, William Stevenson moved to Belleview, Missouri. He was a Methodist local preacher, and was active in organizing new congregations. At Belleview he lived near the Moses Austin family, was a friend of Stephen Austin, and was to be as important to the history of Texas as the Austins would be. In the fall of 1813, Stevenson's brother came to visit from Arkansas. His accounts of life in Arkansas and the hunger of the people for the gospel were a "Macedonian call" to Stevenson. Soon after, he preached the first Methodist sermon in Arkansas. Of that visit, he said:

> the people had made a great many small settlements through the country from five to twenty miles apart. No wagon roads yet laid out, as they had generally moved on pack horses; nothing but horse paths. . . . No ferry boats except on one or two rivers. We had to cross by canoes or rafts or on horseback. . . . They pressed me hard to come, or get some preacher from the Illinois (country) to come and preach to them. I said . . . if I could not get a preacher sent to them, I would return next fall and stay as long as possible with them.[8]

Stevenson returned to Arkansas in 1814 and began Methodist work "from scratch." By 1815, he had organized a circuit with ninety-two members. He was received into full membership in the Missouri Conference that year, even though he did not make the conference session. At the time conference met, he was preaching to a small group of trappers and outlaws at Pecan Point, Texas, becoming not only the first Methodist preacher in Texas, but the first Protestant one!

In 1816, the year the Missouri Conference was organized, Stevenson was appointed to Hot Springs, Arkansas. He took with him to Hot Springs a group of Methodists from Belleview. It was a member of this group who preached the first Protestant sermon in Little Rock. In 1818, Pecan Point became the first Texas town to be listed as an appointment in the Methodist Episcopal Church. It appeared in the official minutes of the Missouri Conference. Missouri Methodism was not only growing within the state—it was reaching out all across the frontier!

But William Stevenson was not through. The Oklahoma State Historical Society credits him with holding the first Protestant service in what is now Oklahoma—somewhere along the Sulphur Fork of the Red River, in 1815.

Stevenson was the founder of Methodism in Arkansas, Texas, and Oklahoma— a worthy career for any circuit rider. But Stevenson was still not finished. In 1825, he reported to Bishop Roberts that he had sufficient ground for a four weeks circuit around Nachitoches, Louisiana. He held a camp meeting in that area and organized a circuit. In 1826, Natchitoches and Stevenson were transferred from the Missouri to the Mississippi Conference.

This book has already noted the pioneering work among Native Americans in what is present-day Kansas and Oklahoma, under the leadership of Missouri Methodism. Under the terms of the popular sovereignty of the Kansas-Nebraska Act, those territories were opened to white settlement in 1854. That same year, W. H. Goode preached the first sermon among white settlers in Kansas, at a cabin north of what is now Baldwin, Kansas. (Remember that the Johnsons and others had been preaching and teaching among the Indians in Kansas since the 1820s.) The Missouri Conference of the Methodist Episcopal Church formed the Kansas-Nebraska Mission District that same year, with Goode as the presiding elder, and seven pastors under his leadership. The Methodist Episcopal General Conference of 1856 authorized the forming of the Kansas-Nebraska Conference as a separate body.

And, in an indirect way, Missouri Methodists helped found the Methodist Church in California. In May of 1849, the bishops of the Methodist Episcopal Church, South, authorized a "foreign" mission to California and put it under the supervision of Bishop Robert Paine. In August of 1849, D. W. Pollock of the St. Louis Conference was appointed to California. Many in the southern church were sure the mission would fail, because California would be a free state. Missouri was enthusiastic. The majority of the overland emigrants to California started from Missouri, and more Missourians went to California than from any other southern state. The Methodist preachers were going to people they knew. Pollock started a church in Sacramento in July of 1850. The General Conference meeting in St. Louis that year authorized the forming of an annual conference. This actually happened in 1852, the first Methodist conference west of the Rocky Mountains.[9]

The 1867 minutes of the Missouri Conference, Methodist Episcopal Church, South, list appointments in the Montana District of the conference. In 1869, that district had six circuits, four of them supplied with preachers. The 1869 minutes also list appointments to the Colorado District.

Missouri—Gateway to the West—Mother of Conferences. Dr. Albea Godbold's study of the "family trees" of the Methodist conferences at the time of union with the Evangelical United Brethren Church indicates the results of Missouri Methodist effort to reach that "remotest cabin."[10] Conference boundaries have changed. Conferences have merged and divided. But a trace through Dr. Godbold's study provides a list of twenty-one present-day conferences which are descended from the Missouri Conference of 1816:

Little Rock	Missouri East
North Arkansas	Missouri West
Rocky Mountain	Nebraska
Northern Illinois	Oklahoma
Central Illinois	Oklahoma Indian Mission
Southern Illinois	Central Texas
Northern Indiana	North Texas
Southern Indiana	Northwest Texas
Kansas East	Southwest Texas
Kansas West	Texas
Louisiana	Yellowstone

Add to that list the Methodist Church in Germany. Missouri Methodism has every right to be proud of the fruits of her labors in evangelism and outreach.

Numbers Do Tell A Story

How important are statistics? On the one hand, there are those who argue that numbers don't tell the whole story; discipleship cannot be measured statistically. That is, in fact, true. But, on the other hand, numbers do tell a story. And every number reported by the local church does represent a human being. So what do the numbers say? What was church growth like in Missouri in the nineteenth and early twentieth centuries?

In the Methodist Episcopal Church, there was great growth. The Missouri Conference grew from 13,019 members in 1873 to 32,553 in 1931, an increase of 150 percent. During the same years, the St. Louis Conference grew from 11,617 to 47,041, over 400 percent! The conferences of the Methodist Episcopal Church, South, grew as well. The St. Louis Conference grew from 9,603 in 1874 to 52,845 in 1931. The Southwest Missouri Conference had 14,064 members in

1874, and is included in the St. Louis Conference statistics for 1931. The increase from 23,667 to 52,845 means the conference more than doubled. (The percentage would be higher if statistics for the Springfield District had been available for 1931.) The Missouri Conference grew from 24,435 in 1874 to 29,106 in 1931. In an interesting historical footnote, those years were chosen because, on the early end, the state of Arkansas was taken from the St. Louis Conference in 1872. On the late end, the two Missouri conferences merged in 1932 (authorization had been given by the 1928 General Conference for a merger any time during the quadrennium). The votes for merger were actually taken in 1931 and were almost unanimous. All that was needed to complete the merger was the signatures of the bishops. But, the quadrennium did not end until the close of General Conference in 1932. If the two conferences remained separate until then, the St. Louis Conference would have six clergy and six lay delegates, and the Missouri Conference three each. The merged conferences would have eight clergy and eight laity. So, for the sake of two additional votes in General Conference, the bishops did not sign the documents for merger until the last thing before the adjournment of General Conference.)

Remember that John Travis reported 106 members at the end of the first year of Methodist preaching in Missouri (1807). There were 889 white and 60 colored members in Missouri when the Missouri conference was organized in 1816. In 1931, there were 161,545 Methodist members of the Methodist Episcopal and Methodist Episcopal, South, conferences. In addition, there were about 2,500 Methodist Protestants, or a grand total of 164,045—a long way from 949 when the first Missouri Conference met.

Part of the growth in church membership was due to the growth in population. For example, the federal census reported 140,455 residents in Missouri in 1830. By 1860, just before the outbreak of the war, the population was 1,182,012. By 1890, the population had more than doubled to 2,679,185. This in spite of the fact that many new settlers in Missouri throughout the century moved on west. It was also in spite of the fact that the War Between the States caused widespread death and destruction in the state. But simple population growth alone does not account for all the growth in the churches. People can move into a community and never become associated with a church—or they can choose to join another church. In spite of the divisions within Methodism and all the pain and anger resulting from the division, the strategies worked—and the churches grew!

ADDENDUM—THE MISSOURI CONFERENCE OF THE METHODIST PROTESTANT CHURCH

As far as available records show, conference was first held in the Missouri District in 1844, at Mount Pisgah Camp Ground, near Springfield.

Unfortunately, those early minutes are lost, and the oldest minutes available date from the year 1847.

B. J. Nowlin is regarded as the father of the Methodist Protestant Church in Missouri. In 1847, the Missouri District had fifteen ministers in a district that covered the entire state. That same year, the Methodist Protestant Church of St. Louis was added to the Missouri District. In 1849, the Conference petitioned the General Conference for a division of the district. A new district, north of the Missouri River, would be known as the Platte District. The division actually happened in 1851. During the war, conference did not meet, and many of the existing churches were dissolved.

In 1865, the Conference was established officially, with churches in Greene, St. Clair, Laclede, Webster, Polk, Johnson, Benton, Dallas, Pettis, Douglas, Hickory, and Jasper counties. In 1866, the Conference received permission to send missionaries to the Indian Territory (now Oklahoma) and to organize churches there.

In those pioneer days, a pastor's salary of fifty dollars was a large sum. The Board of Missions and the General Conference sometimes helped with salaries, but some pastors received as low as fifty cents a year! In 1867, a resolution was adopted that the salary of a single man should be not less than two hundred dollars a year, and a married minister four hundred dollars, with an additional twenty dollars for each child under the age of fifteen. This resolution apparently had little effect for, in 1871, three hundred fifty dollars was the highest salary paid!

The first mention of a woman minister was in 1875, and another woman was ordained in 1876. In 1888, a conference resolution forbade the licensing of women to preach. The General Conference voted to ordain women and elect them as delegates to General Conference in 1895. The Missouri Conference voted in favor of this (after first rejecting it) in 1896. In 1939, there were eight women ministers in the conference.

Conference agencies included a Preachers' Aid Society to provide for widows of ministers and for superannuates. Their money was loaned to the Board of Missions in order to earn interest until it was needed.

The Missionary Society (or Women's Work) was organized in 1866. In 1886, a Women's Foreign Missionary Society was organized. In 1926 Miss Maybelle Shaffer came from the Board of Missions to Missouri to reorganize and strengthen women's missionary work among the churches.

Young People's Work was begun in 1924, with Sunday School and Christian Endeavor programs.

Beginning in 1874, the Missouri Conference instructed that its General Conference delegates go work to bring about a union with other Methodist Churches. In 1884, the conference voted for union with the Cumberland Presbyterians and with the United Brethren and Congregational Churches in 1903. With that background, it is surprising to read that the conference voted against the Plan of Union—twenty-three for and thirty-one against. But delegates were elected to the Uniting Conference with instructions to do everything they could to bring about union.

Membership in the Missouri Conference increased for 426 in 1848 to 3,515 in 1888, and then decreased to 2,922 in 1938.

The last session of the conference was held October 5–6, 1939, in Fordland, with Bishop Broomfield presiding.

Chapter 8

The World Comes to Kansas City: The Uniting Conference of 1938

Many, perhaps most, United Methodists don't remember when we were far more divided than united. Yet it was only sixty years ago that three major branches of American Methodism came together to form "The Methodist Church." Division, which had begun early in the nineteenth century, and worsened with the crisis of 1844, was finally overcome. But the road to reunion was long and full of potholes, some of which threatened to swallow the process forever.

NAMING SOME POTHOLES

The process of healing and reunion was last visited with a look at the Cape May Conference of 1876, where the Northern and Southern branches of episcopal Methodism "buried the hatchet" and agreed to exchange fraternal delegates. This helped the healing process, but there were no formal steps toward union. The same result came from the great celebrations of the Centennial of the founding of American Methodism as a separate body in 1884. There was a closeness growing between the branches of Methodism, but not union.

One thing was clear: union could not come from a return to the status quo of 1844. Too much had happened, and the two episcopal Methodisms had changed too much. Any union would have to be a new thing, a new church formed out of careful deliberations and negotiations between equals. This realization, at least, was a step forward. From 1848 to 1876, Northern Methodists had continued to look at their Southern counterparts as secessionists from the "true church." With that attitude behind them, the two Methodist churches could begin talking seriously about what it would mean to create something new in place of the old. But at the turn of the twentieth century, neither church was willing to pay the price. There was some cooperation in the foreign mission field, with agreements not to evangelize the same areas, and even to combine some work. But in the United States, there was still competition between Northern and Southern Methodism, with churches of both denominations in the same community, sometimes even on the same street. Missouri, a former border state, had always been an arena of competition between Northern and Southern Methodism. Many Missourians can still remember having both northern and southern churches in the same town—or can at least remember where the "old south church" or the "old north church" stood.

The Methodist Protestants were also interested in the question of union, but pulled back early in the process. Their position was that there were so many differences the two episcopal Methodisms had to work out—differences that did not affect the Methodist Protestants—that they would wait until their larger siblings worked out their differences, and then come back into the conversation. This proved to be a wise decision and, in the end, it was the Methodist Protestants who gave the final boost to the process toward reunion.

JOINT COMMISSIONS AND PROPOSALS FOR UNION

Early in the twentieth century, the General Conferences began appointing Joint Commissions on Unification to work out the issues and make proposals for union. Almost from the beginning, there were proposals for a new layer of conference called "Regions." Ultimately, this proposal would prevail, in what is today called the "jurisdictions," but it also was potentially divisive. The proposed constitution worked out by the Joint Commission appointed in 1916 began with "Regions." They proposed six geographic regions, plus one that would include all the Negro members of the churches. Two other proposals included the formation of a Judicial Council and serious financial support of the Christian Methodist Episcopal Church.

The Northern response was negative. They thought regional conferences would be divisive, because they would perpetuate regional pride and regional differences. Bishop William A. Quayle (long associated with Missouri) said they would "ensmall" the church. Whether one shares the bishop's opinion or not, one has to delight in the descriptive phrase he chose to describe the results of regions. The South, on the other hand, said that if the plan were adopted, they would lose two hundred thousand members. There is a long series of precedents for fighting against any change we Methodists don't like by saying we'll lose members over it!

Race also continued to be an issue. One of the Regional Conferences was to be non-geographic and include the historic black churches and annual conferences. This was clearly a perpetuation of segregation. But it did open the door wider for representation at the General Conference from the black conferences. One

Northern delegate said he would never support a General Conference that did not allow blacks to be seated. Since the opposite side of that coin was part of the reason why Southerners thought they would lose so many members, it was a crucial point.

In any event, the proposed constitution was approved in principle by the General Conferences, and a new Joint Commission was appointed to work out the details. (Note: an "approval in principle" means that one likes the idea, but reserves the right to disagree with any of the points. It is a way of voting for something popular with one's constituency, without actually committing to anything. In essence, it says "OK, now we can see if hard work will bring anything out of this.") The new Joint Commission had no limitations put on its work, and proceeded to write a new constitution for a new church. The General Conferences approved the new constitution, and it was carried by a majority of votes in the annual conferences, but not by the three-fourths vote necessary for approval. On one hand, this meant unification was dead in the water. On the other hand, the vote unleashed a flood of popular support for union.

One result of the vote was that the laity demanded more of a voice in the process. They felt strongly that the clergy (who alone had the vote in the annual conferences) had cheated them out of the future they were looking for. So in 1926, the General Conference of the Methodist Episcopal Church, South, voted to have one lay member of the Annual Conference from each pastoral charge. Earlier, the lay representation, voted back in 1866, had been a proportion of the clergy members of the conference. In addition, the youth of both churches were passionate about unification. Youth meetings and student conventions passed petitions asking why their churches persisted in remaining separate. For example, the Methodist Young People's Convention of 1926 called for the unification of "all forces of American Methodism."

Fred Maser, in a survey of the move toward union in *The History of American Methodism,* lists the forces pushing toward union:

1. All three branches of Methodism were built on the same doctrinal standards. They were using the same creeds, the same hymnals, and the same order of worship.

2. Having two or three churches of different branches of Methodism in the same community was an expensive duplication of efforts. In addition, this "altar against altar" mentality caused division and bitterness in communities.

3. Polity differences were gradually disappearing. The Methodist Protestant insistence on lay representation was being met in the episcopal Methodisms. We have seen the move in the southern church for equal lay representation in the annual conference. After 1922, women were given equal rights with lay men. Women had been given full lay rights in the northern church in 1900. There laity were not admitted to the Annual Conference until 1932, but this was not a serious bar to union. The

Methodist Protestant Church began to feel there was something to gain from an episcopal system. In 1920, they made the presidency of the denomination a full-time position. So major differences were being overcome.

4. Feelings of bitterness were disappearing, and Methodists were feeling better about each other.

5. The First World War had taught the churches the need for a united voice, both in ministering to soldiers, and in speaking on national and international issues. How could the church call for world unity and understanding when it was divided within itself?

6. The time was right. People were ready for union.

7. There were strong leaders in all the branches of the church who were committed to union, and willing to continue working for it in spite of setbacks.[1]

All of these forces kept the unification issue on the front burner for the churches, and prodded the denominational leaders to keep working.

The Final Stages

With prodding from the Methodist Protestant Church, the other two branches of Methodism again took up the banner of union. The General Conferences of 1932 (M. E.) and 1934 (M. E. S.) appointed a new Joint Commission on Union. From this group would come the final steps toward unification and a new constitution.

There were seven major ideas in the new plan:

1. The name of the new church would be "The Methodist Church."

2. There would be one General Conference, which would be the highest legislative body. Its work would be limited by the Restrictive Rules.

3. There would be six Jurisdictional Conferences, five geographic and one racial, to include all the Negro Annual Conferences. Bishops would be elected and assigned at the Jurisdictional Conferences, instead of the General Conference.

4. Clergy and laity would have equal representation in General, Jurisdictional, and Annual Conferences.

5. There would be a Judicial Council, which would function as a "Supreme Court" for the church.

6. The new church would keep the episcopacy, and the Methodist Protestant Church was authorized to elect two new bishops.

7. The Articles of Religion would be the historic articles held in common.[2]

The new plan passed all three General Conferences and their annual conferences by huge majorities. The Methodist Protestant and Methodist Episcopal

Churches voted in 1936. The Methodist Episcopal Church voted by annual conferences first, since its General Conference did not meet again until 1938. Again, the vote was overwhelmingly in favor. But there was still vocal opposition. Delegates in all three denominations, but particularly in the Methodist Episcopal Church, considered the plan a step backward in race relations. Aware the new constitution was tragically flawed, the delegates still supported it, because the push for union was so strong.

Opponents of the plan in the Methodist Episcopal Church, South, planned to challenge its legality. So the Council of Bishops of that church asked the Judicial Council to rule on the legality of the action. Judge Martin E. Lawson of Missouri was the president of that Judicial Council. After three days of deliberation, the Judicial Council ruled that both the annual conferences and the General Conference had acted legally in adopting the Plan of Union. The legal argument was that there was no constitutional ground for saying that every annual conference had to approve the Plan of Union. The United States Supreme Court had ruled that in 1844 the Methodist Episcopal Church had been legally divided by the action of the General Conference alone. Therefore, the Plan of Union was authorized.

All three churches had approved the Plan. This is an important distinction. The Uniting Conference of 1939 did *not* meet to vote on union. It met to write a Book of Discipline based on the Plan of Union already acted on by all three churches, and to celebrate the union.

Missouri Resolutions

At the annual conference sessions in 1938, the Missouri Conference of the Methodist Episcopal Church, and the Missouri Conference of the Methodist Episcopal Church, South, voted to present a memorial to the General Conference on conference boundaries.

> Whereas, there are in the State of Missouri, approximately 728 pastoral charges of the three Methodist bodies forming the new Methodist Church, therefore, be it resolved that this Missouri Annual Conference of the Methodist Episcopal Church, in session this 30th day of September 1938, hereby memorializes the Uniting Conference of the Methodist bodies, to form at least three annual Conferences in the State of Missouri, one of which shall be north of the Missouri River, the boundary lines of which shall approximate those of the present Missouri Conference of the Methodist Episcopal Church, South.[3]

The memorial from the Missouri Conference of the south church was briefer, but said the same thing. Two things were important here. First, there needed to be a conference with the name "Missouri." Second, there needed to be a conference north of the Missouri River that would deal directly with the needs and concerns of the churches in that part of the state. North Missouri has always had a different ethos and a different culture from the rest of the state, and these two conferences wanted their people and interests protected in the new denomination.

A second resolution about unification came from the St. Louis Conference and the Missouri Conference of the Methodist Episcopal Church, South. It requested that the churches in Missouri be given the right to "complete the present church year as they are now organized in order to enable more complete reports in the matter of benevolence and other financial obligations." This was not opposition to the Plan of Union, nor any intent to delay. It was simply a concern that the present conferences in the three denominations be allowed to wind up their affairs in an orderly manner. Since the General Conference came almost midway through the (then) fiscal year, it was not an unreasonable request.

THE UNITING CONFERENCE OF 1939

The world came to Kansas City, Missouri, April 26–May 10, 1939, meeting in the Municipal Auditorium. Bishop John M. Moore read the Episcopal Address,

signed by all but one of the existing bishops of the church. Bishop Collins Denny of the Methodist Episcopal Church, South, had opposed union for years, declined to become a bishop of The Methodist Church, and did not sign the address. The president of the General Conference of the Methodist Protestant Church, James H. Straughn, also signed the Episcopal Address.

Early in the conference, the Methodist Protestant delegates met separately to elect two bishops. They chose James H. Straughn and John C. Broomfield. Both had previously served as president of the denomination. The next Sunday they were consecrated as bishops in the united church. Their consecration is significant, because it meant bishops were not a higher order of ministry in the new church. Rather, it was an office which could be held by an ordained elder who was elected to it.

Bishops John M. Moore, Edwin Holt Hughes, and James H. Straughn declare The Act of Union and the formation of The Methodist Church.

Kansas City—Gracious Hosts

To host a General Conference is no easy task. There are all kinds of logistical requirements to be met—hotels, transportation, entertainment, pulpit supply, music, lights and sound, relationships with the media, and on and on. Persons who do all the behind-the-scenes work are sometimes introduced to the conference, but are quickly forgotten. Fortunately, the *Journal of the Annual Conference* has preserved at least the names of the Local Committee on Entertainment. While not all of them may have been from Kansas City proper, they were from that area, and deserve a place in our history. Just to list the names of these people and of the committees they chaired is to remind ourselves of the heavy responsibility involved in hosting a General Conference.

Finance:	R. Carter Tucker
Budget:	T. O. Cunningham
Hotels:	Dr. E. J. Kulp
Ushers:	Dr. E. L. Hobbs
Transportation:	J. W. Miller
Hospitality:	Dr. W. C. Hanson
Women's Activities:	Mrs. Fred A. Lamb
Negro Activities:	Dr. G. F. Tipton
Pulpit Supply:	Dr. S. B. Edmondson
Music:	Mr. Powell Weaver
Broadcasting:	Dr. King D. Beach
Restaurants:	C. M. Hayman
Press:	Frank Tucker
Decorations:	Ed J. Barnes
Information:	George Ryder
Housing:	Dr. Mills Anderson
Telephone:	Mrs. J. W. Showalter
Post Office:	A. A. McCullum
Physical Arrangements:	W. J. Campbell
Director of the Auditorium:	George L. Goldman
Superintendent of the Auditorium:	C. A. Mook
Asst. Superintendent of the Auditorium:	Mr. Abe. W. Conners
Loud Speaking Equipment Engineer:	Ed Roach
Electrician:	Lawrence Riley

In addition, it is known that J. Max Kruwel, the Minister of Music at Boulevard Methodist Church in Kansas City, was the official organist of the Uniting Conference.

These persons spent days and weeks of volunteer time to assure that all the logistical support for the conference was in place, and that nothing that could be cared for would be allowed to detract from the historic significance of the occasion.

Missouri Delegates to the Uniting Conference

Central West Conference, Methodist Episcopal
    B. F. Abbott, St. Louis (Clergy)
    Miss A. M. Williams, St. Louis (Lay)
    Reserves: B. R. Booker, Sedalia, Mo. (Clergy)
                       L. W. Lightner, Denver, Co. (Lay)

Missouri Conference, Methodist Episcopal
    E. J. Kulp, Kansas City (Clergy)
    J. F. King, Springfield (Clergy)
    F. W. Wahl, St. Louis (Clergy)
    Edward Hislop, Kansas City (Lay)
    Grace L. Bragg, St. Louis (Lay)
    C. W. Hanke, St. Louis (Lay)
    R. C. Tucker, Kansas City (Lay)
    Miss A. B. Duhigg, Bingham Canyon, Utah (Lay)

Missouri Conference, Methodist Episcopal, South
    R. C. Holliday, Columbia (Clergy)
    Frank C. Tucker, St. Joseph (Clergy)
    David K. Pegues, Hannibal (Clergy)
    J. D. Randolph, Mexico (Clergy)
    W. M. Alexander, Nashville, Tenn. (Clergy)
    F. F. Stephens, Columbia (Lay)
    J. M. Woods, Hannibal (Lay)
    W. H. Utz Jr., St. Joseph (Lay)
    P. M. Marr, Milan (Lay)

Saint Louis Conference, Methodist Episcopal, South
    C. W. Tadlock, St. Louis (Clergy)
    C. W. Webdell, University City (Clergy)
    E. H. Orear, Malden (Clergy)
    W. W. Parker, Cape Girardeau (Lay)
    Mrs. Jeptha Riggs, Cape Girardeau (Lay)
    F. E. Williams, St. Louis (Lay)

Southwest Missouri Conference, Methodist Episcopal, South
    J. C. Glenn, Raleigh, N.C. (Clergy)
    H. J. Rand, Independence (Clergy)

L. M. Starkey, Sedalia (Clergy)
Mrs. F. A. Lamb, Kansas City (Lay)
R. J. Smith, Springfield (Lay)
W. L. Earp, Nevada (Lay)

Missouri Conference, Methodist Protestant
E. R. Stribling, Monett (Clergy)
Mrs. B. E. Dillon, Rogersville (Lay)

In addition, there was an Iowa-Missouri Conference of the Methodist Protestant Church. Given that the Methodist Protestant churches in north Missouri were small, it seems likely that none of them were represented in the delegation.

Just to read the names of the delegations is to remind ourselves that the Methodist Episcopal Church, South, was the largest of the three churches in Missouri. The Methodist Episcopal Church at the time of union had 92,843 members, and the Methodist Episcopal Church, South, had 136,948 in three conferences. The Methodist Protestant Church had 3,100 members. The total was 232,891.

Committee Memberships and Responsibilities

The task of the General Conference was to write a Discipline for the united church. This work was done in committees, and so the assignments to those committees were important. A listing of committee memberships shows the following Missourians:

Committee	Name	Annual Conference
Conferences	E. J. Hislop	Missouri, ME
	E. H. Orear	St. Louis, MES
	Mrs. Jeptha Riggs	St. Louis, MES
	Frederick Wahl	Missouri, ME
Ministry and Judicial Administration		
	John C. Glenn	SW Missouri, MES
	James F. King	Missouri, ME
	Leslie J. Lyons	Missouri, ME
	E. R. Stribling	Missouri, MP
	Frank C. Tucker	Missouri, MES
	F. E. Williams	St. Louis, MES
	J. M. Woods	Missouri, MES
Membership and Temporal Economy		
	Charles W. Hanke	Missouri, ME
	Robert C. Holliday	Missouri, MES

R. J. Smith	SW Missouri, MES
L. M. Starkey	SW Missouri, MES
F. F. Stephens	Missouri, MES

Missions and Church Extension

Mrs. B. E. Dillon	Missouri, MP
Miss Ada B. Duhigg	Missouri, ME
Mrs. Fred A. Lamb	SW Missouri, MES
David K. Pegues	Missouri, MES

Education

W. M. Alexander	Missouri, MES
Mrs. Grace L. Bragg	Missouri, ME
W. W. Parker	St. Louis, MES

Publishing Interest

W. L. Earp	SW Missouri, MES
Edmund J. Kulp	Missouri, ME
P. M. Marr	Missouri, MES
J. D. Randolph	Missouri, MES

Superannuate Support

C. W. Tadlock	St. Louis, MES
W. H. Utz Jr.	Missouri, MES
C. Wesley Webdell	St. Louis, MES

Rituals and Orders of Worship

H. J. Rand	SW Missouri, MES

Special Standing Committees
Courtesies, Privileges, and Introductions

W. W. Parker	St. Louis, MES

Enabling Acts and Legal Forms

W. M. Alexander	Missouri, MES

Mr. Alexander was the Secretary of the Committee

Judiciary

Frank C. Tucker	Missouri, MES
R. J. Smith	SW Missouri, MES
Leslie J. Lyons	Missouri, ME

Some Highlights

As has already been observed, the Uniting Conference was devoted to writing the *Discipline* for the new church, and celebrating union. The developing of program and vision was left to the first General Conference of The Methodist Church, which was to meet in 1940. However, there were some interesting moments. Governor Alf Landon of Kansas was an at-large delegate of the Methodist Episcopal Church to the conference, and gave a special address to the body on the world outlook for peace and the foreign policy of the United States. It is important here to be reminded of two points. First, Governor Landon had been the unsuccessful Republican candidate for President in 1936. Second, the outlook for world peace was grim, even as he spoke. Germany had already occupied the Sudetenland and Czechoslovakia. Italy had invaded Ethiopia. And the armies of Japan were moving deeper into Mongolia and China. War was not just a possibility on the horizon; it was a present reality. In just a few short months Germany and Russia would invade Poland and divide it between themselves. United States foreign policy was divided on the question of world involvement/isolationism. The Journal of the Conference does not include the text of Governor Landon's address; it would be interesting to know what he said.

Related to the issue of world peace, Leslie J. Lyons of Missouri signed a statement of "patriotic devotion" which was adopted by the conference. Shortly after, the conference adopted a resolution for peace that:

1. resolved that the Methodist Church take a stand in opposition to the spirit of war;
2. pledged every influence to work for peace;
3. urged the President and the Congress to avoid entangling the United States in a world war "which we are convinced would bring our civilization into ruins"; and
4. committed to the Board of Education the responsibility of "laying the foundation of a system of Christian education which shall seek to eradicate the causes of war and train our children for Christian participation in the arts of peace."

One business item related directly to Missouri. The Missouri Corporation was an Endowment Fund which made payments (to the pension funds?) of the annual conferences in the Methodist Episcopal Church, South. Dr. Charles W. Tadlock, of St. Louis, was introduced to the conference to answer questions about the fund, which apparently would be folded into the pension funds of the new church. In 1939, the fund which had been raised as a special endowment for pensions totaled $6,000,000 (a neat sum at the end of the Great Depression), and was paying $2.13 per service year to annuitants for whom the board was responsible.

When the floor was opened for nominations to the Judicial Council, Martin E. Lawson of the Southwest Missouri Conference, Methodist Episcopal, South, was nominated. (He had been president of the Judicial Council of his denomination.) He was elected on the first ballot, along with Francis R. Bayley of the Baltimore Conference and J. Stewart French of the

Holston Conference. Judge Lawson was later elected vice-president of the Judicial Council, with Francis Bayley as president.

An unanswered question was "who assigns the bishops to their areas of responsibility?" Previously that had been the task of the General Conference, but at least some persons assumed that the Jurisdictional Conferences would now take on that responsibility. A motion was made to nominate a Committee on Episcopal Assignments. Dr. Edward Hislop of the Missouri Conference, M. E. Church, moved a substitute:

> Since it is stated in the Plan of Union, Article VI, Division Three, that "The effective Bishops shall be assigned for service to the various Jurisdictional Conferences by the Uniting Conference," and since there is no Standing Committee to which this responsibility has been committed, it is therefore moved, that a committee be raised by this Conference for this specific purpose, this committee to be created as follows: Five ministers and five laymen from each Jurisdiction, making sixty in all. The members of the committee are to be elected by the delegates of each Jurisdiction at the Jurisdictional Meetings to be hold on Monday evening, May 1. This committee, after making survey of the field, and verifying the number of effective Bishops available for service, shall report the assignments of Bishops to this Conference not later than Monday, May 8.[4]

This substitute called for a larger committee (sixty instead of thirty-six) and for elections by jurisdictional meetings, rather than by the conference. The Hislop substitute was adopted by the conference. After reconsideration the following day, it was defeated.

When the bishops were assigned, Charles L. Mead was assigned to Kansas City, and John C. Broomfield to St. Louis.

On a note familiar to United Methodists today, on almost every issue of organization, the first question raised was "would the new plan cost more or less than the previous combined costs?" If it cost more, there would be a major problem. Fortunately, almost everything cost less. One would, in fact, expect some savings through efficiencies in the new structure. The more things change, the more they stay the same!

Still on finances, the per diem for delegate expenses was $4. Remember that 1939 was the end of the Depression. The average income nationally was $1,731. A loaf of bread cost nine cents, and a new house $3,900. Gas was ten cents a gallon, and the Dow Jones average was one hundred thirty-two.

Conference boundaries were an important part of the work of the Uniting Conference. The resolution dealing with conference boundaries ordered three conferences for Missouri. The Missouri Conference, still bearing the proud name of that first conference of 1816, included Missouri north of the Missouri River (except the counties of Lincoln, Montgomery, St. Charles, and Warren) and North Kansas City. The St. Louis Conference included Lincoln, Montgomery, St. Charles, and Warren counties, and all of the state south of the Missouri River and east of a line beginning at the north point of Moniteau County and running west of south to the southeast corner of Cooper County, thence directly south to the northwest corner of Miller County, and thence southward following the west lines of Miller, Pulaski, Texas, and Howell Counties to the Missouri-Arkansas line. On the west line of Pulaski County, the boundary line deviated eastward to exclude the town of Richland and the Methodist congregation there. The Southwest Missouri Conference included all of Missouri south of the Missouri River not included in the St. Louis Conference. The northern boundary swung northward to include North Kansas City and the congregations there.

There is also one "lowlight" to report. The conference was so busy and the calendar so crowded that the special time for women's work was taken from the calendar. This was done "with the gracious consent of the presidents of the women's missionary societies, the local chair on women's work, the local program chair, and Dr. Georgia Harkness," who had planned a special trip to speak to the conference during this part of the agenda.

THE ACT OF UNION

Finally, the business was all done, the *Discipline* was written, bishops were assigned, and it was time to wind up and go home. On Wednesday evening, May 10, 1939, the Uniting Conference gathered for the last time. Bishop John M. Moore presided, and Bishop Ivan Lee Holt was one of the liturgists for the service. Bishop Edwin Holt Hughes preached.

Then came the great moment. Bishop Moore read the Declarations of Union, with the conference responding:

I

The Bishop: The Methodist Episcopal Church, the Methodist Episcopal Church, South, and the Methodist Protestant Church are and shall be one United Church.
The Delegates: We do so declare.

II

The Bishop: The Plan of Union as adopted is and shall be the Constitution of this United Church, and of its three constituent bodies.
The Delegates: We do so declare.

III

The Bishop: The Methodist Episcopal Church, the Methodist Episcopal Church, South, and the Methodist Protestant Church had their common origin in the organization of the Methodist Episcopal Church in America in 1784 A.D., and have ever held, adhered to, and preserved a common belief, spirit, and purpose, as expressed in their common Articles of Religion.

The Delegates: We do so declare.

IV

The Bishop: The Methodist Episcopal Church, the Methodist Episcopal Church, South, and the Methodist Protestant Church, in adopting the name "The Methodist Church," for the United Church, do not and will not surrender any right, interest, or title in and to these respective names which, by long and honored use and association, have become dear to the ministry and membership of the three uniting Churches and have become enshrined in their history and records.

The Delegates: We do so declare.

V

The Bishop: The Methodist Church is the ecclesiastical and lawful successor of the three uniting Churches, and through which the three Churches as one United Church shall continue to live and have their existence, continue their institutions, and hold and enjoy their property, exercise and perform their several trusts under and in accord with the Plan of Union and Disciple of the United Church; and such trusts or corporate bodies as exist in the constituent Churches shall be continued as long as legally necessary.

The Delegates: We do so declare.

VI

The Bishop and the Delegates: To The Methodist Church thus established we do solemnly declare our allegiance, and upon all its life and service we do reverently invoke the blessing of Almighty God. Amen.[5]

After a Prayer of Union, Bishop Moore recognized delegates to move the adoption of the Declaration. Earlier, the document had been adopted section by section. This motion was to adopt the whole, and was an important formality. One member of each of the constituent churches was recognized for movement and seconding the adoption. The movers from the Methodist Episcopal and Methodist Episcopal, South, churches had been members of the Joint Commission on Unification since 1916. The delegate from the Methodist Protestant Church was also a long-time supporter of union. The bishop then called for a standing vote, which was unanimous for the adoption of the Declaration.

Bishop Moore then uttered words that were at the same time a formal, legal declaration, a paean of joy, and a cry of hope: "The Declaration of Union has been adopted! The Methodist Church is! Long live The Methodist Church!"

The Greater Kansas City Messiah Chorus, Powell Weaver, conductor, then sang the "Hallelujah!" chorus from Handel's Messiah. One imagines that, as they sang, there was not a dry eye in the auditorium. There was rejoicing, hope, awe, and deep gratitude for what had been done.

REFLECTIONS

The new Methodist Church began life with 46,255 congregations, 21,687 ordained ministers and 15,969 local preachers, 7,856,060 members, and 5,926,155 enrolled in Sunday School. It held property with a net valuation of $656,474,867, and annual expenditures of $80,543,997. This was the largest Protestant denomination in America at the time of its birth (and for many years after). As Bishop McConnell pointed out in his devotional address to the Uniting Conference, the problems of the world were so large that they could be met only by a large organization.

The *Christian Century* noted, at the close of the conference, that the unity of the church was based on decentralization (because of the jurisdictional structure). Indeed, the *Century* reported, some delegates went home asking themselves, "Have we brought into being one Methodist church, or have we actually given birth to six churches?"[6] Subsequent history has proved that it was a thoughtful question, indeed, though it is one that is beyond the scope of this book.

The conference was aware that its business was unfinished. The General Conference would meet again in 1940 to develop programs and a direction for the new church. The call for a "Bishop's Crusade," announced at the end of the conference, pointed toward the future. There was great rejoicing in Kansas City, but also plenty of room for sober concern about the future.

In fact, there were several issues that would cause problems in the future. The jurisdictional system did, in fact, lead to decentralization, primarily because the election and assignment of bishops was given to the jurisdictional conferences. No matter that the language of the church is "general superintendency," and bishops are officially bishops of the entire church—in practice they are bishops of the jurisdiction in which they are elected and assigned.

The Uniting Conference stumbled on the question of full clergy rights for women. The final decision was to give women full rights of ordination and appointment, but not membership in the annual conference. Since it is conference membership that guarantees appointment, this meant effectively that women were denied clergy rights in the new church. Several more General Conferences would pass before women were admitted to full membership in the annual conferences.

The major issue for the future remained the question of theological standards. The Uniting Conference assumed there was general agreement on the Articles of Religion, the sermons of John Wesley, and his notes on the New Testament. The question, however, of what constitutes a "theological standard"—indeed, even what a theological standard is and how it is applied—continues to bedevil United Methodism and threaten what unity Methodists have achieved.

Chapter 9

MISSOURIANS WHO
BECAME BISHOP

This chapter raises an interesting question: who is a Missourian? For example, Bishop William Quayle was born in Missouri and later served here as bishop in the Methodist Episcopal Church. But he said frankly that he was glad his parents moved out of Missouri when he was still a baby, and he did not have to grow up here. He is not included in this chapter. On the other hand, Ivan Lee Holt and Monk Bryan, both of whom are closely identified with Missouri, were born in other states. They are included. There were other bishops who had some service in Missouri prior to their election, but were not primarily known as Missourians, who are also not included.

ENOCH MATHER MARVIN

Marvin was the first Missourian to be elected to the episcopacy—in a General Conference of which he was not a member, and where he was not present.

Enoch M. Marvin was born in Warren County, about two and one-half miles southwest of Wright City, on June 12, 1823. His mother, Catherine Mather, was related to Cotton Mather, the great New England Puritan preacher. His parents were married in New York in 1817, and immediately moved to Missouri to homestead. Both parents were schoolteachers and taught their children at home. Neither parent was associated with the church, and they had little use for the Methodist circuit riders who came through the area regularly.

Affectionately referred to as "Mather," Marvin worked on the farm but was always a sickly child compared to his sister and two brothers. Near the Mather homestead, the house of William McConnell was a preaching place for the

Methodists. McConnell himself became a kind of mentor for young Mather and helped him in his search for faith. After nearly three years of searching, Marvin was satisfied that his religion was real, and joined the church in December of 1840. Shortly after, he was made an exhorter. Then the Ebenezer Church near Marthasville recommended him for a license to preach. He was admitted on trial into the Missouri Conference at Palmyra in September 1841. He was not present at the conference, which may have helped his cause. He was tall and thin, with sharp features, and large hands and feet. He was a gangly, awkward teenager. He usually dressed in poor, worn clothes that did not fit him well. Later in life, he was noted for his long hair and beard, both of which also put off many who were concerned more with appearance than with reality.

Marvin's first appointment was the Grundy Mission, a newly organized circuit in north central Missouri. He borrowed one hundred fifty dollars to buy a horse, saddle, bridle, and saddlebags. Interest on the debt was 10 percent a year, or fifteen dollars, and that fifteen dollars was exactly his salary for that first year under appointment. He was able to survive physically only because church members fed him and his horse, and because women in the circuit sewed clothes for him. In spite of the poverty of his salary, there was a richness in his ministry—one hundred thirty-one new members joined the church during that year.

At the Conference of 1842, Marvin's appearance made a poor impression on the members of the conference. After conference, Marvin started for Wright City to visit his parents. Three older preachers caught up with him and advised him to drop out, since he was obviously not suited for the ministry. The three were Jacob Lanius, George Smith, and Samuel G. Patterson. Ten years later, the conference asked Marvin to preach Lanius's funeral sermon. Patterson later attended a funeral in Danville, where Marvin preached and was terribly embarrassed about his earlier statement after he heard the sermon. Later, after Marvin returned to Missouri as bishop, he made Smith's appointment. It was an ironic twist for one "not suited for ministry." Of course, the major issue was his appearance and awkwardness, not his qualifications for ministry.

In 1842, Marvin was appointed to another mission—this time the Oregon Circuit. He received one hundred fifty-seven new members, and was paid the princely sum of thirty dollars. Marvin was ordained deacon by Bishop James O. Andrew in 1843, and elder in 1845 by Bishop Joshua Soule. At the Conference of 1844, W. W. Redman, Marvin's presiding elder responded to the call for a passage on Marvin's character: "Bishop," Redman said, "he is a green-looking boy, but I tell you he can preach; and if he lives, he will be a star!" While junior preacher at Fourth Street Church in St. Louis, Marvin learned Latin and Greek, along with theology.

It is necessary to remember that even great preachers make human errors. Some errors are clear at the time; others are clear only in retrospect. Marvin's great error is one of the latter. He was not disturbed about slavery, even though his family had come from New England. He noted that the Bible did not condemn slavery, so he accepted it as a part of his society and culture. He believed that slavery was a political issue, not one for the church to decide.

Marvin married Harriet Brotherton Clark of Bridgeton in 1845. One week after the wedding, they took a steamboat to the annual conference. Marvin was appointed to Hannibal, one of the strongest churches in the conference in 1845, and re-appointed in 1846. In those days, two years was the maximum limit in any one charge, and Andrew Monroe (presiding in place of the bishop, who was late) assigned Marvin to Monticello circuit. By 1852, Marvin was presiding elder of the St. Charles District.

Marvin was elected a delegate to the General Conference of Methodist Episcopal Church, South, in 1854, and again in 1858 and 1862. He was only thirty-one at the time of his first election and was clearly a rising star in the West. At the 1858 General Conference, he worked for the election of his friend, William G. Caples, to the episcopacy. This attempt failed. The 1862 General Conference, scheduled for New Orleans, did not meet because of the war.

From 1855 to 1862, Marvin pastored Centenary and First Church, both in St. Louis. While in St. Louis, he became involved in a theological debate with a Catholic scholar. Father Smarius gave a series of lectures at St. Francis Xavier Church (St. Louis University) in which he attacked Protestantism. These lectures were printed in the newspaper and caused quite a stir in the city. Now St. Louis, because of its early years as a French and/or Spanish city, and because of the large numbers of European immigrants with Catholic backgrounds, has always been a "Catholic city." But Marvin stood tall for the cause of Protestantism. He gave a series of twenty-three lectures on Roman Catholicism, which were later printed in the newspaper and as a book.

The outbreak of the war and the quick occupation of Missouri by the Union Army made it difficult for the Methodist Episcopal Church, South, to continue its work. Marvin continued to preach at Centenary, but was increasingly uneasy. He knew the military authorities would compel him to take an oath of allegiance, which he did not want to do. So he made plans to leave Missouri secretly. He took his family to the old farm at Wright City and laid in enough supplies for three years, the length of time he thought the war would last. In February of 1862, he left for the South, and was soon safe within Confederate lines. At Memphis, he learned the General Conference had been canceled. Marvin went on to Woodville, Mississippi, where he supplied the Methodist church until December. After December, he moved to Grenada, Mississippi, and became a chaplain in General Sterling Price's army. There were many Missourians in this army, including members of churches Marvin had served, and he ministered with both zeal and effectiveness. He refused to take a military commission as a chaplain, which would have made him an officer in the army. But he did accept an appointment from Bishop Paine as Superintendent of Methodist Chaplains in the Western Department of the Army. The only battle at which he was present was at Helena, Arkansas, where he ministered to the wounded and dying. In addition to

Enoch Mather Marvin, the first Missourian to be elected a bishop. He was elected by the 1866 General Conference of the Methodist Episcopal Church, South, a conference of which he was not a member and did not attend.

being an army chaplain, he also was an itinerant evangelist in the areas where the army was camped.

In February 1865, Marvin was appointed pastor at Marshall, Texas. Someone in Missouri applied to President Lincoln for a pass that would allow Mrs. Marvin and their children to join him in Texas. When the war ended, Marvin could not return to Missouri because he could not afford to.

At the General Conference of 1866, there was an agreement that four new bishops should be elected. The bishops of the Southern church were old and ill, and the impetus given to the church by the Palmyra Manifesto called for new leadership. There was apparently an unspoken consensus that one of the new bishops should be from west of the Mississippi. W. E. Doty, of Greenwood, Louisiana, worked hard for Marvin's election as the "western" bishop. His support was important, because the two Missouri conferences were not unanimous in their support. Nevertheless, Marvin was elected on the first ballot. At the time of his election, he was on a steamboat on the way to New Orleans. He had a sudden conviction that he had been elected. Immediately, he asked for forgiveness for such presumption.

Bishop Paine was presiding when Marvin arrived at the church where General Conference was held. Paine called Doty to the chair and told him to take Bishop Marvin to the barber shop and clothing store and have him presentable for his ordination. Marvin agreed to the new suit, but not the barber. When he was told that the brethren did not like his full beard, Marvin replied that they had elected him with it and they would have to endure it. Bishop James O. Andrew, who had ordained Marvin a deacon twenty-three years before, ordained him a bishop. It is interesting that the language was "ordination," and not "consecration," as it is today. The Methodist Episcopal Church, South, held a "high" view of the episcopacy. Indeed, this was the constitutional reason for the separation in 1844. Marvin himself wrote:

> Thus the history of the office shows it not to be the creature of the General Conference at all, but to have sprung from another source. The written law makes it a part of the very organism of the church. Its existence and functions

are guarded with great jealousy by the Restrictive Rules. . . . The fact of their (bishops) solemn ordination, together with the character of the vows required of them, is inconsistent with the hypothesis that they are mere officers, removable at will. . . . The Bishops are the head of the executive administration of the Church; but they are not mere administrative officers. They have a pastoral function, the care of all the Churches. They are to promote, by all rightful means, the peace, purity, and growth of the Church. In the Annual Conferences they are not mere presiding officers, with power to station the preachers; they are also pastors, whose duty it is to promote all the interests of religion according to the wisdom that is in them.[1]

The first conference over which Marvin presided was the Indian Mission. They were discouraged and ready to disband because of all the losses they had suffered during the war. Marvin fired the preachers with new enthusiasm and sent them back to their circuits committed to rebuild the church. He personally pledged five thousand dollars for their salary support, and then traveled through the church the next year and raised the money.

In 1868, Marvin left his family in St. Louis and spent a year on the West Coast, encouraging and revitalizing Southern Methodist work there. He overcame defeatism, and help establish the Los Angeles Conference. Nearer to his home in St. Louis, he organized the Illinois Conference (made up of churches who left northern Methodism and requested affiliation with the Methodist Episcopal Church, South). He raised most of the one hundred thousand dollars needed to begin St. John's Church (St. Louis) in 1868.

Marvin was known across the church as a great preacher, yet during his time on the preaching circuit he never wrote a word of a sermon. He wrote sermons in his head and delivered them extemporaneously. (Travel on horseback is more conducive to this kind of sermon preparation!) Because he used a sermon many times on a circuit, his sermons were always perfected and polished. As he grew older—and busier—this kind of preparation became more of a handicap. It was difficult, not only to prepare polished new sermons, but also to remember all the old ones. (Think what he could have done with a computer!) He wrote often for newspapers. In addition, he wrote several books: *Lectures on Transsubstantiation and Other Errors of the Papacy* (1860); *The Work of Christ* (1867); *The Life of William G. Caples* (1870). A book of sermons appeared in 1876. These were the only sermons he ever committed to paper. Two books appeared posthumously: *The Doctrinal Integrity of Methodism* and *To the East by Way of the West*. The latter was a compilation of the letters written during his travels to the mission fields, and sold twenty thousand copies in six months.

The General Conference of 1874 voted to have a bishop visit the Orient and ordain any native preachers recommended by the missionaries. Marvin was given the assignment. He and E. R. Hendrix sailed from San Francisco in November 1876, and returned to New York in September 1877. This world tour was a great means of dramatizing the missionary movement and rallying the church to support it.

Unfortunately, the tour was also a tremendous drain on Marvin's strength and health. He became ill in November of 1877 and died on November 26.

EUGENE RUSSELL HENDRIX

Eugene Russell Hendrix was born in Fayette, Missouri, on May 17, 1847. He came of independent stock. His father, Adam Hendrix, had been a schoolteacher in Maryland, where he refused to trade at the store owned by the secretary of the school trustees. He was caught up in the spirit of westward expansion and came to Fayette in 1844. At first, Adam taught school, then became the banker for the community. He was one of the organizers of Central College and its treasurer for many years. Eugene Russell was the second of five children.

Eugene was sent to Wesleyan University at the age of seventeen (there being no Southern colleges open, because of the war). His journals from those student days show a young man bent on excelling in both his studies and in faith. He marks the date of his conversion as March 13, 1859 (when he was twelve). In 1866, while a student at Wesleyan, he received his license to preach. He returned to Fayette for the summer of 1866, and decided that Missouri would be the place of his labors. He graduated from Wesleyan in 1867 and entered Union Theological Seminary that fall.

After graduation from Union in 1869, Hendrix's first appointment was the Southern Methodist Church in Leavenworth, Kansas. In this setting hostile to Southern Methodism, he worked for reconciliation with the pastors of the two Northern churches in the city, and wrote a series of articles for the newspaper, trying to show that the term "South" in his church's name was not a political designation. His journal shows a deep commitment to working for a better understanding between the northern and southern branches of Methodism. In the fall of 1869 he was ordained a deacon by Bishop Lovick Pierce.

In 1870, Hendrix requested a transfer to the Missouri Conference, and was appointed to the church in Macon. In Macon, he focused on religious education and recreation ministries, as well as preaching. He was a "young Turk" bringing in new ideas of how the church should function in a community. During his two years at Macon, he was also involved in camp meetings, revivals, and addresses at Howard Female College and Central College. He also turned down the presidency of St. Charles College during this period. In 1871, he was admitted into full connection, and reassigned to Macon.

During trips to Kansas and western Missouri, he often stayed at the home of Nathan Scarritt in Kansas City. Once he even traveled from Gallatin to Macon by way of Kansas City, so he could spend some time at the Scarritts. Now, he had met Nathan Scarritt in Kansas, but the real reason for all these visits was his interest in Ann Eliza Scarritt, Nathan's daughter. The two were married June 20, 1872, and spent almost a month on a "bridal trip" to the East.

In the fall of 1872, Hendrix was appointed to Francis Street Church in St. Joseph, where he served for four years. In those four years, he baptized sixty-two adults, sixty children, and had two hundred twenty-three additions to the church. In 1876, he was appointed to Glasgow, where he served one year. At the end of that year, he went with Bishop Marvin on his trip around the world to strengthen the cause of missions. The two spent ten days in Japan, held a "Christmas Conference" in Shanghai, China, and visited Soochow, Hangchow, Hong Kong, and Canton. They were told there were twelve thousand Methodist converts in China. From China, they went on to Ceylon and India. In India, they discovered 311 ordained native preachers and 68,689 "communicants" in the churches. They landed in Palestine on Easter Sunday, and chose to walk from Emmaus into Jerusalem. From the Middle East, they went on to Europe, and were authorized by the College of Bishops as fraternal delegates to the British Methodist Conference in London. This was the longest overseas journey Hendrix would ever take, but it would by no means be the last.

On his return to Missouri, Hendrix assumed the presidency of Central College, the school his father had been so instrumental in beginning. Central College had been chartered in 1855 and opened in 1857, with Nathan Scarritt as its first president. The college was closed during the war, and did not reopen until 1867. Union troops occupied the college building and left it in poor condition. When Hendrix became president, there was one building, a debt of twelve thousand dollars and an endowment of forty-five thousand dollars. During his years, the debt was paid, three new buildings were built, and the endowment was increased to one hundred ten thousand dollars. Hendrix was able to interest influential laymen, such as Robert Barnes of St. Louis and Mr. Hoagland of St. Joseph, and raised a great deal of money for endowed professorships, student scholarships, and loans, as well as for the construction of new buildings. During his tenure, the gymnasium, Wills Hall, and a chapel were built, as well as a science building.

In addition to growth at the college, Hendrix continued to grow in his personal life. In 1880, he attended the Ecumenical Council in Cincinnati, and the Ecumenical Methodist Conference in London. As a result of those meetings, he predicted there would be only one episcopal Methodism by 1900. Already in 1881, he was being asked if he would give up the presidency of the college to become a bishop.

He did receive support at the 1882 General Conference in Nashville, but was most impressed by the fact that Atticus Haygood refused to accept election as a bishop. During the Centenary year of 1884, Hendrix was involved with the Church Extension Board of the Methodist Episcopal Church, South, as well as the Board of Missions. He spent seventeen days in Washington, D.C., and in Baltimore at the Centennial Conference. In 1885, he turned down offers to become dean of the theological faculty at Vanderbilt, and to become president of the University of

Missouri. He refused the latter on the grounds that he did not want to do anything that would hurt Central College.

Hendrix's journal entry for May 30, 1886, says, "Returned home on the 28th inst. [of this month] from the General Conference in Richmond, Virginia, where on the 18th inst. I was elected one of the Bishops of the Methodist Episcopal Church, South. . . . The belief that it was the will of God led me to accept despite my more congenial work at Central College."[2]

Bishop Hendrix was in charge, at various times, of mission conferences in the Orient, in Mexico, and in Brazil. He traveled in Mexico in 1893, 1912, and 1913. He was in Europe in 1900 and again in 1914. In 1895, he visited the Orient to study the work of the missionaries and explore opening new stations. In 1899, he was in Brazil as bishop in charge of the work. In addition to his work with the churches, he met with President Diaz in Mexico City in 1893. On his visit to the Orient, he carried credentials from President Grover Cleveland, asking the consulates to assist him in any way they could. He met with the King of Korea, Li Hsi, and visited widely in Japan, Korea, and China.

Hendrix' trip to Europe in 1900 was to visit the British Methodist Conference as a fraternal delegate. In 1912, he was again in Mexico, where he helped bring about an agreement with the Methodist Episcopal Church on whose missionaries would work where. He also met with President Madero on this trip. On a return trip to Mexico in 1913, his train was attacked by bandits! The trip to Europe in 1914 was to attend the Peace Conference at Constance. With all of Europe mobilizing for war, there was still an idealistic dream of peace. The dream was shattered, and Hendrix sailed for home on darkened ships to escape the German navy.

Hendrix also traveled widely in the United States. He was a bishop for the entire Southern Methodist connection, and preached widely in Arkansas, Louisiana, Missouri, Kansas, Tennessee, Virginia, Maryland, North Carolina, Montana, Washington, Oregon, California, Arizona, and Kentucky. In the first thirty-two years of his episcopacy, he preached an average of eighty-one sermons a year.

But he was more than a traveler. He was a great leader in the missionary movement, raising hundreds of thousands of dollars for the cause. In July of 1913, he raised $151,200 for missions at the Waynesville Assembly. He also recorded that there were many persons interested in volunteering for mission work, and that the laymen's movement for missions "came into its own."

During his term as bishop in Missouri, there came the 100th Anniversary of the founding of the Missouri Conference. Bishop Hendrix launched the "Go Forward" movement in Missouri. On October 14, 1916, Central College celebrated Benefactor's Day. Some three hundred thousand dollars was raised for the college endowment, making the total of the endowment five hundred thousand dollars. On November 5, Bishop Hendrix dedicated Barnes Hospital in St. Louis. The original gift of Mr. Robert A. Barnes had been held until it had grown enough to provide for both a building and an endowment. Certainly one of the great gifts of Methodism to the city of St. Louis and the areas surrounding it has been this great institution of healing and teaching.

Perhaps the most bitter controversy in the history of the Methodist Episcopal Church, South, was Vanderbilt University. In one form or another, it was an issue at the General Conferences of 1898, 1906, 1910, and 1914. From 1905 to 1914, it was the major issue before the church. Bishop Hendrix was in the heart of it, and was both severely criticized and highly praised for his role. The issue was, basically, the relationship of the University and the Church, and, more specifically, whether the bishops or the board appointed the trustees. Bishop Hendrix had become Chair of the Board of Trust of Vanderbilt in 1909. The General Conference claimed the right to appoint trustees—the board denied that right. When the Council of Bishops filed suit against the board, Bishop Hendrix both resigned as chair of the board and refused to participate in the bishops' suit. He tried to work as a reconciler in the church, but the General Conference session of 1914 proved to be a stormy one— and resulted in the university and the church going their separate ways.

Bishop Hendrix was also an early leader in the church union movement. There were still strong feelings of mistrust between the three branches of American Methodism, when in 1916, Bishop Hendrix publicly shook the hand of Bishop Earl Cranston of the Northern church and said he felt the Southern church was ready for union. Unfortunately, he was far ahead of his time, and was again criticized severely by Southern Methodists for daring to stand for union.

Bishop Hendrix was the first president of the Federal Council of Churches of Christ in America, elected to that office in 1908, and guided that organization through its turbulent early years.

Belle Bennett, the leader of Southern Methodist women, wrote to Bishop Hendrix: "You have done more to encourage and develop the growth of the Woman's Society than all the other members of the College of Bishops. The women know and appreciate this."

Bishop Hendrix was a liberal theologian, an advocate of church union, a progressive in matters of church administration, a deep thinker, and a deeply devout Christian. He died November 11, 1927, and is buried in Kansas City.

WILLIAM FLETCHER MCMURRY

William Fletcher McMurry was born near Shelbyville, Missouri, on June 29, 1864. He was the son of Rev. William Wesley McMurry and Mary Elizabeth McMurry. His mother was from the Colony area (Knox County) and his father had grown up in Shelby County. Like Bishops Marvin and Hendrix, McMurry's life was affected by the War between the States. Because of the unsettled conditions and the danger to many southern Methodist preachers, William Wesley McMurry left his appointment in Memphis and returned to Shelby County to farm, teach school, and preach occasionally. When the conference was able to meet again (1864) he was appointed to the Shelbyville Circuit.

So the future bishop grew up in rural Shelby County, attended the Shelbyville Church as a boy, then undoubtedly moved with his family as his father was named presiding elder of the Macon, St. Charles, and Hannibal Districts for a long period of years. He grew up in the church, knowing the importance of the church and the demands that the church makes on its clergy.

From 1880 to 1882, he attended St. Charles College (his father was then presiding elder of the St. Charles District), and Central College from 1882 to 1885. In spite of five years of attendance, he never completed a college degree. He did learn to study and to hunger for knowledge. Later, he would receive honorary degrees from Emory and Henry College (Virginia), Kentucky Wesleyan, Centenary College (Shreveport, Louisiana), and Central College in Fayette. The latter three honorary degrees were all awarded him in 1921.

In 1886, McMurry was ordained in the Methodist Episcopal Church, South. In 1888, he married Frances Byrd Davis of St. Joseph, Missouri. They had three children: Claudia, William Fletcher, and Frances. From 1886 to 1897, McMurry served various pastorates in Missouri. He was a presiding elder from 1897 to 1902, and then became pastor of Centenary Church in St. Louis, where he served from 1902 to 1906. The St. Louis World's Fair came during his appointment to Centenary. For that year, the eyes of the world were on St. Louis, and the excitement of a great World's Fair, the Olympic Games, and the hundreds of thousands of people crowding the city were a part of the background of his ministry. Some two thousand persons joined his church during this period.

From 1906 to 1918, McMurry was the corresponding secretary of the Board of Church Extension. This was the equivalent of a General Secretary, or Associate General Secretary of one of the boards of the church. In this position he oversaw both the church growth in the United States and on the mission fields. He made official visits to the mission fields in South America in 1910, and to the Orient in 1918. Under his leadership, the Church Extension Loan Fund was built up.

In 1918, at the General Conference in Atlanta, William Fletcher McMurry was elected a bishop in the church. In addition to his oversight of annual conferences and churches, Bishop McMurry was president of the Board of Finance of the Methodist Episcopal Church, South, member of the General Conference Commission to write the Constitution of the Methodist Episcopal Church, South, and member of the Joint Commission on Unification. In 1901 and 1921, he was a delegate to the Ecumenical Conference meeting in London. He was a director of the Methodist Publishing House in Shanghai, China. During his presidency of the Board of Finance, he worked hard to increase both interest and investment in pensions for retired ministers.

From 1924 to 1930, Bishop McMurry was also president of Central College in Fayette, Missouri. As president, he rebuilt the college, raised the endowment, enlarged the physical facilities, and increased the enrollment. But his greatest service to Methodist education in Missouri was the closing of all other educational institutions and focusing the attention, the effort, and the money of the conferences on Central College. One can be sure, given the realities of human nature, that there was disagreement and even anger over the loss of other educational institutions across the state. Yet history has shown the wisdom of consolidation, and committing both resources and excellence to one institution.

Pastor, preacher, presiding elder, church administrator, bishop, college president: any one of those would be career enough for any person. Bishop McMurry combined them all. His record shows his ability in financial matters and in enlisting others to follow enthusiastically where he wanted to lead them. Because of his strength and drive, he sometimes seemed overpowering to those who disagreed with him. Because he believed so strongly in what he was doing, he sometimes confused disagreement with personal opposition. He was said to have disliked those who disagreed with him as strongly as he disliked their opinions. But he also had a warm compassion and a sense of humor. He knew preachers and their situations, so he could be a counselor to them.

In early January 1934 (when the nation and the church were reeling from the effects of the Great Depression), he left St. Louis to tour his episcopal areas—Western Virginia, Baltimore, and Kentucky Conferences. When he returned home, he was ill with influenza and was immediately taken to Barnes Hospital. There he suffered a heart attack and died on January 17. His funeral services were held at Centenary Church, where Bishop Marvin's funeral had been held fifty years before. He was buried in the family plot in Shelbina, Missouri.

CHARLES C. SELECMAN

The first Missouri bishop to not be directly affected by the War Between the States was Charles C. Selecman, who was born October 13, 1874, on a farm near Savannah, in Andrew County. His parents were Isaac Henry and Josephine Selecman, both descendants of Virginia families. As in so many cases in the eighteenth and nineteenth centuries, their families had migrated from Virginia through Kentucky to Missouri.

In 1886, Rev. David F. Bone, of the Methodist Episcopal Church, South, conducted a revival at Bedford Chapel, located on the corner of Selecman's grandfather's farm. It was in that revival meeting that the future leader of Southern Methodism was converted. Charles and his siblings went to a one-room country school. When he was fourteen, Charles started high school in Savannah. He worked afternoons and evenings in a store to pay for his board and room. Two years later, he entered Central College as an academy student (similar to high school or college prep) and spent five years at the college. Because he had little money, he spent two years (between his second and third years at Central) teaching country school. In one school, he also preached every other Sunday and held a revival meeting. The result of the meeting was nearly sixty converts and the building of a new country church building.

Selecman returned to Central, where he won some oratorical contests. Once he represented Missouri in an Interstate Oratorical Contest in Topeka, Kansas. Between the results of his preaching and his work in oratory, it was clear the young man could preach!

Unfortunately, he never graduated from Central, primarily for financial reasons. Instead, he began serving churches in Missouri. He served for two years in Mexico, three years in Moberly, two years in Webb City, plus service in St. Joseph and St. Louis. A trip to England in 1907 to visit Wesleyan City Missions captured his imagination and commitment. So when Bishop Hendrix invited him to go to Melrose Church in Kansas City, he declined and went instead to Kingdom House in St. Louis. One result of his work at Kingdom House was an invitation to accept the appointment as Superintendent of Missions in New Orleans, Louisiana. After a few months in the Crescent City, he asked to be released because, in his opinion, the plan they had adopted would not work. It was from New Orleans that Selecman went to Webb City, Missouri.

After a short time in Webb City, Selecman was asked by Bishop Waterhouse in 1913 to become pastor of Trinity M. E. South, in Los Angeles, California. This was a small congregation, with a huge property and a huge debt. Business failures and the outbreak of World War I made the situation even worse. The church was made a mission charge, and several small, struggling congregations were added to the charge. The Women's Missionary Society of the Methodist Episcopal Church, South, provided money for an associate pastor, a social worker, a deaconess, and a director of religious education. For five years, pastor and people struggled to hold the church together.

The General Conference of 1918 set up the War Work Commission of the Church. Bishop W. R. Lambuth, the chair of the commission, asked Selecman and Grover C. Emmons (later the founder of *The Upper Room*) to go with him to Europe. So Selecman spent the summer and fall in Washington, New York, London, Paris, and at the front in eastern France. Then came a cable from Bishop DuBose, telling him to be back at Trinity on November 1. He arrived as a flu epidemic closed all public meetings in Los Angeles. So he visited annual conferences in Texas to promote interest in the soldiers' welfare. In 1919, Selecman was elected president of the California State Federation. At the General Conference of 1918, he was made a member of the Unification Commission. He also served on the Unification Commission that worked out the Plan of Union in 1928. These positions, plus his War Work Commission service, made him a national figure in the church.

In 1920, Bishop W. N. Ainsworth asked Selecman to become pastor of First Church, Dallas, Texas. A new church building was being planned for the congregation (surely Selecman must have asked, "Why me, Lord?" when he heard that!). Though he had some struggles trying to raise money to build the building, his service at First Church was relatively brief. In 1923, he became president of

Southern Methodist University, again at a time of controversy and turmoil. At that point, the university was only eight years old, and struggling to establish itself. When Selecman arrived, there were 2,011 students and seventy-five faculty. There were three permanent buildings, and four schools—Arts and Sciences, Graduate, Theology, and Music. Selecman remained as president of SMU until 1938, when he was elected a bishop in the Methodist Episcopal Church, South. During that time, he was a delegate to the Lausanne Faith and Order Conference in 1927, and to the Second Conference on Faith and Order at Edinburgh in 1937.

As a bishop, he served six years in Arkansas and Oklahoma, and four years in Texas. He retired in 1948, after a long and distinguished career. One of his continued legacies to Missouri Methodism was the establishment of the Charles C. Selecman Award for an outstanding senior student at Central College.

IVAN LEE HOLT

The giant of Methodism for many Missourians, Ivan Lee Holt was born January 9, 1886, in DeWitt, Arkansas. His father, a lawyer who traced his ancestry back to Jamestown, Virginia, died when Ivan Lee was only six. His mother took on the task of raising two small boys and gave her all to see them grown and educated. When Ivan Lee finished elementary school, they moved to Fordyce, Arkansas, so he could attend the Fordyce Training School. There, two accidents almost ruined Ivan Lee's career before it began. He fell between the joists of a new building and bit completely through his tongue. Four doctors agreed he would have a permanent speech impediment. One of the four decided he could save the tongue, and did. Another time, Ivan Lee stepped on a rusty nail and nearly died of blood poisoning. Just before graduation, Ivan Lee visited a young lady at a friend's house (much against the rules) and was nearly expelled from school. Punishment short of expulsion was finally agreed on, and he graduated with the highest grades in the school.

On July 4 in the year of his graduation, he won fifty dollars in gold as first prize in an oratorical contest. He was fifteen years old and ready for college. Mrs. Holt moved her boys to an apartment in Nashville, near the Vanderbilt campus. Because of family finances, Holt took his last two years in one. He graduated at age eighteen, earning Phi Beta Kappa honors.

After graduation, Holt turned down the offer of a job in Washington and a banking job in St. Louis to pursue an academic career. He became professor of Greek and Latin at the Stuttgart, Arkansas, Training School for Boys. There he also met Lela Burks, whom he married two years later. At Stuttgart, he also began the study of Sanskrit, and then turned to other ancient languages related to the Bible. (While teaching, courting, and being active in the Methodist Church!)

After three years in Stuttgart, Ivan Lee's younger brother graduated from the University of Arkansas, and his mother found some freedom from her financial worries. Holt moved with "divine recklessness," as he called it, to Chicago and entered the University of Chicago to study Semitic languages. His Ph.D. thesis was the translation of Babylonian tablets. He was offered a position as an assistant at Harvard, with the assurance he would become a professor within three years.

Then God intervened in his life. John M. Moore, one of the leading ministers of the Methodist Episcopal Church, South, came to see him in Chicago, and said to him:

> Holt, our church needs men like you. You are deeply rooted in religion and
> have a background which can make you a great preacher. We think God has
> chosen you for this work. Don't let it pass you by. You must consider a call
> to the ministry. Your friends feel you know that is your task.[3]

One wonders how many faithful servants of God have turned to ministry because someone else challenged them to consider the call of God. Ivan Lee Holt thought and prayed, then gave up Harvard and was ordained in the Methodist Episcopal Church, South. His first appointment was University Church in St. Louis, which he organized in January 1910. A wealthy Methodist bought the lot for the new church, but there was no organization when Holt came.

From that beginning, he faithfully served the church for forty-six years. Shortly after coming to St. Louis, his bishop asked him to go to Centenary Church in Cape Girardeau, a small, struggling church with a large debt and a salary of fifteen hundred dollars. He went. He soon had Centenary out of debt—then a fire destroyed the church and they had to start all over. At the same time, an offer came from First Church in Fort Worth, Texas, with an offer of the highest salary in southern Methodism—five thousand dollars, the same as St. John's in St. Louis. Holt turned it down and helped rebuild Centenary.

A year later, he did take the offer to become professor of Old Testament Literature, chairman of the theological faculty, and chaplain of the University at Southern Methodist University. He stayed at SMU from 1915 through 1918, teaching and ministering to college students. While there, Holt was a charter member of the Kiwanis Club of Dallas, and helped organize the Community Fund. When he left, he was honored at a lunch by fifty-six organizations in the city. It was said he knew more people in Dallas than any other person there.

In 1918, he was called to become pastor of St. John's Church in St. Louis. At this time, St. John's was known as the "Cathedral Church" of Southern Methodism. There he stayed for twenty years, as a leader in both church and city. Ten times during that period, he turned down offers to leave St. Louis—presidencies of colleges, university professorships, and pastorships of great churches across the nation. At the "Holy Corners," his leadership doubled the membership at St. John's. An education building and chapel were built. At the same time, Holt was writing books and articles, serving on general and conference boards and agencies, and providing leadership to the city. As in Dallas, he was a charter member of the Kiwanis Club of St. Louis, and a founder of the Community Fund. He helped raise funds for Jewish Charities and promoted fellowship between the different faiths.

While at St. John's Holt began his lifelong commitment to the cause of ecumenism. Twice he was president of the Metropolitan Church Federation of St. Louis. In 1935–36, he was president of the Federal Council of Churches. He began his term as president by visiting the National Councils of Churches in China, Japan, Australia, Hawaii, and the Philippines. (This was long before the organization of the World Council of Churches.) He closed his term by leading the National Preaching Mission, an ecumenical effort that saw 2.5 million worshipers in twenty-five cities across the nation. In addition, Holt was a member of the committee that drew up the charter for the National Council of Churches. He was a long-time member of the Commission on Church Union of the Methodist Church. He was vice-chairman of the American Section of the World Council during the process of forming that body (1937–1948). From 1948 to 1954, he was a member of the Central Committee of the World Council of Churches, and for twenty years was a member of the Commission on Faith and Order.

Within Methodism, Holt's contributions were equally important. He was Chair of the Commission on Worship, and helped create *The Methodist Hymnal* and *The Book of Worship*. He was chair of the Board of Pensions, and there oversaw the pension allowance for Methodist preachers going from two hundred or three hundred dollars a year to fifteen hundred to twenty-five hundred dollars a year.

At the General Conference of the Methodist Episcopal Church, South, in 1938, Holt was elected bishop on the first ballot. (This was also the General Conference at which Charles C. Selecman was elected bishop.) The announcement of his election came on a Friday. St. John's church did not have services until Sunday. But across the street at Temple Israel, Sabbath services were being held. The new bishop was invited to worship with the congregation and receive its blessing in his new work. This invitation was a symbol of all that Holt meant to the city of St. Louis and to the cause of inter-faith relations.

Holt's first episcopal appointment was to Dallas, where he served the Texas-New Mexico area until 1944, when he was transferred back to St. Louis. For the last twelve years of his active ministry, he was the bishop of the Missouri Area of the Methodist Church.

Holt was a tireless traveler, covering sixty thousand to seventy thousand miles a year in the air—long before business people were routinely flying those kinds of miles. This, in spite of the fact that he was not a good flier—he was often airsick and frightened. In spite of all the time he was gone from Missouri, he held services in every charge in the state, some seven hundred fifty places across Missouri. He was known and loved by Methodists in great city cathedrals and little churches among the fields and woods. He knew persons by name in every church he visited, and could call them by name if he met them out of context (away from their church).

ALONZO MONK BRYAN

Monk Bryan was the first Missourian to be elected to the episcopacy by a jurisdictional, rather than a general, conference. Like Bishop Holt, Bryan was not born in Missouri, but spent his entire ministry here and had a great impact on the life of the church and the state.

Monk Bryan was born July 25, 1914, in Blooming Grove, Texas, and was raised in Methodist parsonages in that state. His father, Gideon J. Bryan, was a minister in the Central Texas Conference for sixty-six years. His mother, Era Monk Bryan, was the daughter, granddaughter, and great-granddaughter of Methodist ministers.

Monk graduated from Baylor University in 1935, with majors in philosophy and psychology. He received the Master of Theology in 1938 from Perkins School of Theology, and did graduate work at Drew Theological Seminary. He was ordained a deacon in the St. Louis Conference in 1939, and an elder in 1941, with Bishop John Broomfield as the presiding bishop. His first appointment was the Boyce Circuit in the Central Texas Conference, which he served from 1939 to 1940. In 1940, Monk came to the St. Louis area and was the founding pastor of St. Luke's in St. Louis, where he served until 1947. Other pastorates included Centenary Church in Bonne Terre, Maryville (1949–57), and Missouri United Methodist Church in Columbia (1957–1976). As a pastor, his priorities were preaching, leadership in worship, and pastoral care. Worship is where the pastor has the most contact with his people and can have the widest influence, so it (and preaching) were always a high priority for Bryan. He was elected bishop at the Jurisdictional Conference in 1976 and assigned to the Nebraska area.

While a pastor, Monk served on the boards of Southern Methodist University, Saint Paul School of Theology, the Missouri School of Religion, the Protestant Radio Hour, the General Board of Social Concerns, and the General Board of Global Ministries. In addition to conference boards, he was president of the Missouri Council of Churches. He participated in every World Methodist Council/Conference from 1956 through 1996, and from 1981–84 was a member of the Executive Committee of the World Methodist Council. He was an elected member of seven General Conferences, and seven Jurisdictional Conferences. (Two of those General Conferences were special sessions.) He was a member of the General Conference Structure Study Commission from 1968 to 1972. He was an Exchange Minister in England in 1953 and has since preached in England some fourteen times over a period of twenty-seven years.

Monk was married to Corneille Downer. Her father was Professor of Latin and Roman Mythology at Baylor University. Her grandfather and uncle were executive secretaries of the Board of Foreign Missions of the Southern Baptist

Convention and the American Baptist Convention, respectively. Corneille adapted quickly to Methodism and was a full partner with Monk throughout his ministry. They had three children: Lucy, Robert, and James. Corneille died in July of 1989. In 1992, Monk married Twila Stowe, the widow of Bishop William McFerrin Stowe. They now live in Lake Junaluska, N.C., and Dallas, Texas.

In the episcopacy, Monk again set priorities. First, preaching and worship, then pastoral care, and then administrative duties, including making appointments. In his own words, he "tried to do the whole job and not be a conk-out in any area." In addition to trying to visit as many Nebraska churches as possible, Monk preached in twenty-five different annual conferences. His guidelines for choosing churches to visit were: 1) dedications, 2) consecrations, 3) centennials, and 4) churches where neither he nor his predecessors had been for years. He also worked hard to help with family or personal problems in parsonage families.

One surprise when he went to Nebraska was that the area did not feel a part of the South Central Jurisdiction, nor did the Jurisdiction feel Nebraska was a part of them. So a major emphasis in Monk's work was bringing the two together.

In addition to the boards of all the conference agencies and institutions on which a bishop sits, Monk was president of Lydia Patterson Institute Board of Trustees, from 1980 to 1985, and a member of the General Board of Higher Education and Ministry, the South Central Jurisdiction Council on Ministries, and the General Council on Ministries. He was actively involved with Education Opportunities and led some fifteen study tours to the Holy Land. He visited and studied widely around the world, on both episcopal visits and study leave.

LOUIS WESLEY SCHOWENGERDT

Lou Schowengerdt was born in a Methodist parsonage on April 27, 1926, the son of Charles Wesley and Ruth Schowengerdt. He graduated from high school in Raytown, Missouri, in 1944, just before the D-Day invasion of Europe. During those high school years, he felt and responded to a call to preach. As part of his preparation for ministry, he received a B.A. degree from Central Methodist College in 1947, and a B.D. from Perkins School of Theology in 1950.

In 1950, Schowengerdt received his first appointment as associate at Linwood Boulevard Church in Kansas City. After a few months, he was appointed to Trinity Methodist Church in St. Joseph. Under his pastoral leadership, Trinity merged with the Hundley church in 1953 to become Ashland Avenue Methodist Church. A new building was completed in 1954. With all the extra pastoral leadership required for merging churches and building a new building, Lou still found time to do clinical training at Osawatomie State Hospital in Kansas, and at Menningers. He also earned an M.A. degree from Southern Methodist University in 1956. A busy time!

Schowengerdt served the Ashland Avenue Church until 1966. His commitment to education also continued. He did summer studies at Garrett Biblical

Institute, the Institute of Advanced Studies, twenty-seven hours in clinical psychology at the University of Kansas City (now the University of Missouri at Kansas City), and clinical training at St. Joseph Hospital. In 1958 the St. Joseph Jaycees named Schowengerdt St. Joseph's "Outstanding Young Man of 1957." They noted "his boundless inspiration, devotion to his tasks, his progressive attitude, and foremost for his unselfish contributions to the people of his church and to the citizens of this community." Certainly Ashland Avenue grew and prospered under his leadership. During this time, he also served the community as a labor relations mediator. In addition, he was conference youth director (a "volunteer" position), on the Conference Board of Education, and chair of the Board of Ministry.

Family, however, was Schowengerdt's top priority. He was married to Ina Edmondson in 1951. She was a professional bassoonist who played with the Kansas City Philharmonic and the St. Louis Symphony. This may partly explain Schowengerdt's enjoyment of classical music. They were the parents of two sons, Allan Louis and Glenn Lee. On one occasion, the bishop was to attend a meeting at the Ashland church, where Schowengerdt was the pastor. Schowengerdt said, "I told him I was sorry I couldn't be there, but it was my wedding anniversary and I had a date with Ina that evening."

In 1966, Lou was appointed to University Methodist Church in the Missouri East Conference, where he served until 1973. This congregation, struggling with changing demographics and important decisions about the future, flourished under his leadership. During these years, Schowengerdt served as the chair of the Conference Board of Education, and of the Area Commission on Higher Education and Campus Ministries. He continued his education with management and human relations training.

The skills in management and human relations served him well during his tenure as superintendent of the Kansas City South District, from 1973 to 1979. In 1979, he became council director of the Missouri West Conference. He would have served in this post many years, but in 1980, he was elected a bishop in the United Methodist Church and assigned to the Northwest Texas-New Mexico Area. He served as their bishop until 1992, when he retired to Denison, Texas. Bishop Mutti, in a memorial tribute, said of Bishop Schowengerdt's leadership style: "He combined a fierce individualism with a passion for corporate excellence; a finely tuned intellectualism with deep personal compassion; a stubborn streak with a remarkable skill for settling conflict. His personal commitments and integrity sometimes left him standing strong against opponents. Occasionally, he stood alone against friends and colleagues as well."

In his retirement remarks to the 1992 South Central Jurisdictional Conference, Bishop Schowengerdt told a story about an annual meeting of United Methodist Women. A very gentle Navajo lady was making a presentation. She greeted the bishop and then said, "Now take that name of our bishop. They talk about Navajo words being hard to spell, but how do you spell his name? And then once you learn how to spell it, how do you pronounce it? You know, he must be an ethnic minority like us."

Schowengerdt's lifelong interests were opera, boating, and researching Mississippi River lore. He died August 10, 1998, on a day when he and his sons were preparing to launch his boat out into the lake.

ALBERT FREDERICK MUTTI, III

Albert Frederick (Fritz) Mutti III was born in Hopkins, Missouri, February 13, 1938, the son of Albert Frederick Mutti Jr. and Phyllis M. Turner Mutti. He graduated from high school in Hopkins. During his high school years, Fritz responded to God's call to ministry, and reaffirmed that response with a commitment to a lifetime of spiritual leadership in the church during his freshman year in college. This commitment led him to transfer from Iowa State University to Central Methodist College in the middle of his freshman year. He graduated from Central in 1960 with a B.A. in Philosophy and a wide range of awards and honors.

Just prior to his senior year in college, Fritz married his high school sweetheart, Etta Mae McClurg. They are the parents of three sons. Their two oldest sons, Tim and Fred, died of AIDS-related illnesses. A third son, Marty, is a radio broadcaster and salesperson in Winfield, Kansas.

The fall of 1960 found Fritz enrolled at Garrett Biblical Institute, where he received the M. Div. in 1963. He was admitted on trial in the former Missouri Conference in 1961, and full connection in the Missouri West Conference in 1963. His first full-time appointment was to Union Star-Star Chapel-Oak Grove in rural northwest Missouri. He served there two years. Moving to Savannah, Missouri, he became the founding pastor of the Crossroads Ecumenical Cooperative Parish. He served Savannah from 1965 to 1968, and the Crossroads Parish (including Savannah) from 1968 to 1974. Beginning with the annual conference of 1974, Fritz served eight years on the Missouri West Conference staff as director of Camping, director of Christian Education, director of Youth Ministries, and Conference Council Director. In 1982, he was appointed senior pastor of First United Methodist Church in Blue Springs, where the church grew rapidly under his leadership. In 1987, he became superintendent of the Central District, and moved to the Kansas City North District in 1989. During his years as pastor and administrator, Fritz was elected to every session of the South Central Jurisdictional Conference from 1976 to 1992, and every General Conference from 1980 to 1992. He led the Missouri West Delegation in 1984, 1988, and 1992.

Fritz Mutti was elected bishop by the South Central Jurisdictional Conference in 1992 and assigned to the Kansas Area. His priority as a bishop is spiritual leadership that is grounded in spiritual disciplines and pulled by a vision of the church faithfully alive in service to Jesus Christ. A pastor at heart, he regularly visits the churches in the Kansas area. Out of a deep concern for social justice, he helped to created the Rural, Religion, and Labor Forum of Kansas. In that forum, such important issues as health care, the North American Free Trade Agreement, and rural community development and the farm family crisis have been discussed. He chairs the Concern for Workers Task Force, established by the 1996 General Conference.

Out of the pain of the loss of two sons, Fritz and Etta Mae have given national leadership to HIV/AIDS education events and ministries. They have told their personal story in hundreds of settings, and helped countless persons deal with the pain and rejection related to HIV/AIDS. A book dealing with their experience is in the manuscript stage. In addition, both Fritz and Etta Mae have been active advocates for a church policy of openness and hospitality for all persons, but particularly gay and lesbian persons. Their stand has often aroused controversy, but they have been faithful to what they perceive God has called them to do in a church that is broken and divided on the issue of openness to gay and lesbian persons.

Bishop Mutti has always worked for ecumenical cooperation. In addition to his work in an ecumenical cooperative parish, he has been co-president of the Missouri Council of churches and the Kansas Christian Leaders Forum. He attended the World Council of Churches Assembly in Harare, Zimbabwe, in 1998.

Christian education has been another area of major emphasis. Fritz has served as a Laboratory Leader, helping church school leaders improve their teaching skills, and he was honored by the General Board of Discipleship with a permanent certification as a Laboratory Leader.

As part of his commitment to the global mission of the church, Bishop Mutti has traveled to Zimbabwe, South Africa, Zambia, Sierra Leone, Liberia, Indonesia, Australia, and New Zealand. Several partner relationships have been established after those visits. In addition, he has consulted in Mexico, Guatemala, China, Thailand, Israel, England, and Scotland.

Bishop Mutti has been a director of the General Board of Discipleship (1980–1988), The General Board of Global Ministries (1988–1996), and the General Commission on Christian Unity and Interreligious Concerns (1996–present). He represents the Council of Bishops on the National Youth Ministry Organization Steering Committee. He is author of *Faithful Members: Doctrines and Duties of the Christian Faith*; *The Acacia Tree: A Devotional on Mission in Southern Africa*; and *Breath of New Life: Eight Marks of the Spiritual Life,* which were the Willson Lectures of 1996.

Bishop Mutti continues to serve as episcopal leader of the Kansas Area at the time this book went to press.

Chapter 10

CRUSADE IN EUROPE TO CRUSADE FOR CHRIST 1939–1960

Missouri Methodism moved into the new united church with a sense of optimism and expansion, but also with a sense of unfinished business. As noted in chapter 8, The Methodist Church was the largest Protestant denomination in America. The Uniting Conference ended with a major question still unanswered: what was this new ecclesiastical giant going to do? How would mission and ministry continue in the new church? That was an important question for Missouri Methodism, as well as for the denomination. To fully appreciate the work of Methodism in Missouri in these "times of Crusade," one must see it in the context of global changes and how those changes impacted the life of this state.

The world in which Methodism would live was beginning to change rapidly. At home, the country was slowly fighting its way out of the Great Depression. Jobs were opening up, and there was hope that the new decade would bring relief to tired, broke, and hungry people. Overseas, there were war clouds on the horizon, but they still seemed far off. That, however, was about to change. On September 1, 1939, not long after the Uniting Conference had pledged itself to work for world peace, Germany and Russia invaded Poland, and war began in Europe. Middle America was still isolationist, and there was hope Americans could stay out of the Old World's troubles. Even with the isolationist spirit, cooperation with England meant that the industrial sector in the United States economy began building more ships, planes, trucks, and tanks. And the isolationist dream itself was shattered on December 7, 1941, when the Japanese attacked Pearl Harbor. The first Missourian to die in the war, Lieutenant George Whitman, was killed that Sunday morning in the skies over Pearl Harbor. Missouri and the rest of the nation would never be the same again. As the nation prepared for war, as thousands of young men left immediately for military service, and as young women went to work in offices, factories, and, finally, the military, American society entered a time of unprecedented change. Americans were united behind the war effort, but not always ready to deal with the changes that war would bring.

The General Conference of 1939 had focused on the organization of the united church and did not deal with program and mission, except in a cursory fashion. That was left for the General Conference of 1940, which also met in Kansas City. The Episcopal Address called for support of the Stewardship Movement, and direction of new funds to home mission and church extension. At the General Conference of 1939, there had been a vague commitment to something called "The Bishop's Crusade," which would have two goals. One was to have the bishops itinerate through the church. This would, it was hoped, overcome the sense of sectionalism growing out of the jurisdictions, and bishops being assigned to specific areas within specific jurisdictions. The second goal, also growing out of the itineration of the bishops, was a revival and renewal in the church. As it turned out, this crusade would be limited because of the disruption of the war. The Episcopal Address also showed a keen sense of awareness of the war in Europe and of the "winding down" of the Depression at home. In 1940, there was still hope that America could stay out of the war, but the more discerning among the delegates to the General Conference must have seen that would be impossible. One vote in the General Conference would have important implications for all the future life of the church. The conference adopted a resolution to have equal numbers of laity and clergy members on all committees, boards, and commissions in the church. Equal numbers of laity meant the infusion of new ideas, energy, and enthusiasm. It also meant larger boards and committees, and made for a more unwieldy decision-making process.

The immediate impact on both society and church, however, came as a result of the war. Young men enlisted by the hundreds of thousands. Missouri boys who had never expected to see much more than the back of the mule pulling their plow, signed up for the Navy and literally saw the world. Others signed up to become pilots, finding themselves doing things about which they had only fantasized a short time before. Young women flooded Washington to handle the clerical duties the war demanded. Others drove trucks, handled welding torches, became nurses (and helped organize what would later be known as M.A.S.H. units), or became pilots, and filled the ranks of the WACS and WAVES. At the time, their actions were seen as patriotic responses to the war effort. Little did anyone realize that they would bring about some of the greatest social changes in the history of our nation. On a more somber note, African-Americans who volunteered for military service were kept in segregated units, though this began to change slowly in combat. Japanese-Americans were forced into internment camps, in an expression of xenophobia that far exceeded what was done to German-Americans during World War I. The treatment of Japanese-Americans had no immediate impact on life in Missouri, but ultimately all Americans would feel the shame of that episode.

On the home front, defense contracts brought $4.2 billion to Missouri industries (at a time when the dollar bought a lot more than it does today). This meant hundreds of new jobs at places like McDonnell Aircraft, Ford, General Motors, Monsanto, Mallinckrodt, and even down to small plants in rural communities that hired only a dozen or so persons. Fire brick, plywood drums, and shipping materials were as much a part of the war effort as the building of planes and tanks. Missouri farmers raised more grain and meat for the war effort, and vacant lots and backyards were turned into "victory gardens." Rationing, war bond drives, and all kinds of collection drives marked the daily routine of Missourians. One of the author's most vivid childhood memories, for example, is receiving a quarter from his parents each Friday. He solemnly took it to the post office in the corner of the country store his parents owned (his father was also the postmaster) and bought a stamp to go in his little book that would become a savings bond. Even little children made their contribution to the war effort.

The attention of the nation—and the church—was on the war, so there were no great program emphases during the war years. General Eisenhower's "Crusade in Europe" took precedence over the Bishop's Crusade. Nevertheless, the church continued to grow, even with so many young men and women away from home. Table 1 shows membership statistics for the Missouri Conferences for the war years.

Table I
Membership Statistics, 1942–1946

Year	Conference	Membership	Sunday School Enrollment
1942	Central West	no statistics available	
	Missouri	61,582	22,846
	S. W. Missouri	69,035	27,169
	St. Louis	63,827	24,680
1943	Central West	10,779	2,302
	Missouri	60,130	19,067
	S. W. Missouri	69,195	23,484
	St. Louis	75,534	22,368
1944	Central West	13,389	3,430
	Missouri	58,130	19,236
	S. W. Missouri	69,086	23,414
	St. Louis	65,487	21,403
1945	Central West	13,389	3,043
	Missouri	60,473	19,221
	S. W. Missouri	67,491	23,521
	St. Louis	64,151	21,532

1946	Central West	9,810	3,077
	Missouri	62,894	21,550
	S. W. Missouri	70,757	26,478
	St. Louis	66,649	23,918

Two observations about the statistics are important. First, many church members were not able to attend worship or Sunday school, because they were either overseas, on a military base elsewhere in the country, or working a Sunday shift in a defense plant. Non-attendance did not change membership or Sunday school enrollment figures, but it undoubtedly changed the vitality of program and ministry. But even with the disruption of the war, church membership grew or held constant. Second, note that membership figures go up immediately after the end of the war when men and women began returning home. The church was important to these returning veterans (of both genders), and they gave it their full support.

THE POST-WAR WORLD

In the meantime, the state of Missouri was also preparing for massive changes in a post-war world. The old Constitution of 1875 was outdated and over-amended. The New Deal, President Roosevelt's attempt to bring the country out of the Depression and provide for a social safety net, did not do well in Missouri. An ultra-conservative administration in Jefferson City had resisted much of the New Deal, except when forced to accept parts of it by the federal government. Some elements of the safety net were adopted in the 1930s, notably in aid to the elderly and improvement of medical services. Aware of the need to adapt to a new world, a constitutional convention began meeting in 1943. By mutual consent, the delegates to the convention sought to avoid radical change, and any issue that might deepen divisions between St. Louis and Kansas City. The final document made few major changes (except for streamlining) from the Constitution of 1875, but the rural areas of the state still opposed it. One reason for the opposition was a proviso that allowed African-American children in areas where the black population was a small minority to go to white schools—if the community was willing. The proviso was far from mandatory and required community support, but even that was too much change for many people. Race relations continued to be a festering sore in the political and social life of the state for years to come.

Population shifts affected both the state and the church. Partly as a result of the war, people moved to the cities (or at least to county seats and large towns). In 1940, 51.8 percent of the population lived in urban areas (communities with a population of at least twenty-five hundred). By 1950, that had increased to 61.5 percent, which meant fewer people living on the land. The greatest loss of population was in the agricultural areas north of the Missouri River, which meant the churches of the Missouri Conference also suffered a major loss. Fewer farmers meant fewer customers for the agri-businesses, groceries, clothing stores, and other merchants in the villages, towns, and cities of north Missouri. It also meant fewer children for the schools and fewer members in the churches.

Fewer children for the schools led to one of the greatest shifts in rural communities in this century. In 1947, the Missouri General Assembly passed the District Reorganization Law, which called for the elimination of one-room country schools, and the consolidation of small high schools into larger ones. Between 1948 and 1964, the number of school districts in the state dropped from 8,422 to 1,028. In many areas, this meant an increased quality of education, better facilities, better-trained teachers, and more savings for the school districts. It also marked the beginning of bussing students to the larger schools, which changed the focus of school and social life for many communities. No longer did the youth in Granger, for example, go to Granger High School. Instead they rode buses into Memphis. This changed the focus of the village. People drove "into town" to attend basketball games or band concerts. They dealt with a larger community on school issues, which led to working together county-wide on other issues as well. On the other hand, school consolidation caused bitter resentment and left deep scars in many communities. As late as the early 1970s, people in dying rural churches refused to combine or go to the county seat church, even though their heads told them it was a smart move. The reason: "*They* took our school away from us; *they* aren't taking our church, too." What had been intended as a step toward better education for all children and youth became a festering sore of resentment in many areas. Where village and open-country churches were served by local pastors, many of whom were members of the community where they served, there was little help in working through the bitterness and seeing the potential of a wider base for community life. When those same churches were served by full members of the conference, there was a call for a wider under-standing, but often not an empathetic response to the hurts of the community. As a result, in some areas the church suffered a great deal because of the emotional responses to school consolidation and all the attendant changes.

The post-war world also brought the move from major cities to new suburbs. Young families bought homes in the suburbs, built businesses, schools, and churches. Both because of the nature of suburban communities and the need, in many cases, to commute back to the city to work, these moves led to increased automobile sales, better roads to allow them to get into the city to work, and, ulti-mately, the development of the interstate highway system. Public transportation systems (railroads, buses, and streetcars) suffered and all but disappeared. This is one post-war change that continues to haunt America even today, when ecological and financial crises almost demand efficient public transportation.

Women who had been used to working not only in offices, but also in facto-ries, were suddenly out of work, as men returning from the war were given priority for jobs. Women took their energies and organizational skills from the military and the factory into their homes, schools, churches, and communities. They shared with men a vision of a better world that had been put off while winning the war. The post-war era was the great period of Parent-Teacher Associations, community service, and, for Methodists, the growth of the Woman's Society of Christian Service and the Wesleyan Service Guild.

Tom Brokaw, in his best-selling book about the men and women who fought and won World War II, *The Greatest Generation*, makes several key points that relate not only to the post-war economic revival in America, but also the revival in the churches. First, he says, it was a generation that was used to action. Give them an objective and they were used to meeting it. Second, they were used to organizing, planning, and working together. Third, they had a larger vision of the world than any generation before them. They had seen the rest of the world, and their lives were changed by that. Finally, they felt they had lost five of the best years of their lives. They were committed to making up for the time lost, not only for themselves, but for the families and communities they had left behind them. These characteristics meant a great deal to a rebuilding nation, but were also incredibly important to the church. Action, organization, working together, a larger vision of what the world could be, and an almost obsessive desire to make up for lost time—these were passions and skills that the Methodist Church needed as desperately as did the general society and economy of the nation.

THE CRUSADE FOR CHRIST

The General Conference of 1944 met for a third time in Kansas City. The war was not over, but there was reason to believe it would not last much longer. There was a sense that the war was won, even though it was not over. The General Conference therefore began to look at what the world would look like after the war, and what new battles the church would have to fight. At the heart of the conference sessions was the presentation of the Crusade for Christ. The presentation pointed out two harsh realities. First, centers of Christian work throughout the world had been destroyed by the war, and the lives of thousands of Christians were still at risk. Somehow, the lives at risk would need to be saved, the societies in which those Christians lived would have to be rebuilt, and the centers of Christian work would have to be rebuilt and renewed. Second, "secular and pagan forces" trying to control the world were working with a speed, effectiveness, and power that needed to be matched by the church. In a spirit of compassion and hope, the conference adopted the Crusade for Christ, which had five major objectives:[1]

- a new world order
- post-war relief and reconstruction

- an evangelistic campaign
- stewardship cultivation
- an increase in church school enrollment and attendance

Included in the plan was a special effort to raise a minimum of $25 million for non-recurring and emergency items, in addition to the World Service Apportionment. It was understood by the framers of the plan that $25 million was only a small part of the money actually needed to rebuild and extend Methodist work in the world. In fact, the committee presenting the report expressed the hope that much more would be raised. The money was to be raised in a six-month period beginning December 1, 1944, with pledges payable on or before January 31, 1946. The time restrictions on the fundraising were so that the effort would not side track evangelism, stewardship, and church school attendance efforts. The Methodist Church's commitment to rebuilding the world in the name of Christ was as strong as the nation's commitment to winning the war had been. And the strategies set by the church were as far-reaching in scope and implication as the strategies developed by Eisenhower, MacArthur, Marshall, and their colleagues. With these marching orders, the church went forth to win victories for Christ, just as the military was winning victories for freedom around the world. The next section will look at how the Methodist Church in Missouri met those challenges and won victories for Christ.

Missouri Methodism and the Crusade for Christ

Some representative reports from the minutes of the Missouri conferences will illustrate how the church responded for the Crusade for Christ. The Missouri Conference, for example, moved quickly to implement the evangelism phase of the Crusade. The Board of Evangelism recommended:

1. Each pastor survey the charge immediately after conference to discover the members who have been lost sight of, and try to discover the "new material."
2. Attempt to re-enlist inactive members. There are over 1,000,000. (*Author's note:* this surely must mean in the denomination, and not in the Missouri Conference alone!)
3. Organize training classes to instruct workers to go out and do house to house evangelism.
4. Hold old-fashioned revivals.
5. Make evangelism the central theme of all your programs during the year.
6. Co-operate with the Board of Education in observing Religious Education Week.
7. Form new "G.I." classes in your church schools to assimilate the returning service men and women.

8. Finally, re-kindle the fires upon the home altars. Encourage all members to establish family altars.[2]

Both the Southwest Missouri and St. Louis conferences had similar plans. Note there is a blend of old (revivals) and new ("G.I." classes) strategies in the plan. There is a concern for reaching both inactive members and new prospects. The "home altars" is a reference to family times of devotion and prayer.

The plan worked. In 1946 (one year later), the Missouri Conference reported that 8,037 new members had been added, and seventeen new churches had been organized. There was a net gain of just over 2,400 members. Remember that the Missouri Conference was the agricultural area in north Missouri that showed the greatest population loss in the post-war period, so gains in membership would be offset by members moving away. But it was still a significant gain. The St. Louis Conference reported a net increase of some 2,500 members, and the Southwest Missouri Conference gained over 3,300. The Central West Conference (which included churches in Colorado as well as Missouri) showed a net loss from the membership peak of 1944. Taken together, the net gain for Missouri Methodism was still over 5,000 members in one year!

The Board of Evangelism of the Southwest Missouri Conference recommended in 1945 that all pastors follow the order of the Book of Worship by including an invitation to Christian discipleship in every worship service. In 1946, the Southwest Missouri Conference reported that two hundred seventeen of two hundred thirty-three (or 93 percent) ministers in the conference reported at least one person received on profession of faith. That report sounds like the circuit riders! Think of the celebration and rejoicing the report would have evoked from the members of the conference.

Religious education was also an important priority. The Board of Education of the St. Louis Conference heartily endorsed the Crusade for Christ, especially the part of the Crusade that emphasized church school attendance. Their report to the 1944 annual conference said, in part:

We feel the Church School is an agent to support the Crusade for Christ. It is the school of the Church and as such it should encourage loyalty to the whole Church. We should realize . . . that the Church School is not an organization separate from the Church. We believe that the matter of coordinating the Church School and the worship service of the Church is a problem that has to be dealt with in a particular way for each Church. However, it is a problem which we should not allow this Crusade for attendance to aggravate, but rather to solve.[3]

What did the reference to "coordinating the Church School and the worship service" mean? Was there a conflict in some churches over which part of the church got the prime time? Or was there already in the mid-40s a conflict over having worship and church school at the same time? That is not known at this remove, but these are questions that continue to plague the church even today. More importantly, the report recognized the importance of the church school as the place where children, youth, and adults learned the faith and the traditions of the church. The obvious implication was the importance of regular church school attendance. Indeed, later studies confirmed the wisdom of this statement, showing that there seems to be a direct correlation between Sunday school attendance and church membership. An increase in Sunday school attendance will be followed, about two years later, by a similar increase in church membership.

Having a plan worked! Working the plan meant great gains for the church. Even with the war and the gasoline shortage, there had been progress in youth work. John Ward Sr. was superintendent of the Maryville District (Missouri Conference) and organized a youth institute during the war for the youth of northwest Missouri and southwest Iowa. Called "Ia-Mo Institute," it was held at Tarkio College. When the war ended, the Missouri Conference began the "Cameron Institute" on the abandoned campus of a Methodist college at Cameron, Missouri. Some people brought tents and set them up on the campus to live in, since they couldn't afford the fees to stay in the old dormitories. Others lived in the dormitories. There were classes in Bible, Christian faith, missions, and evangelism—all for youth. There was also a strong emphasis on Christian vocation, and the call to serve in the ministry of the church. John Ward Jr. remembers receiving a call to ministry at the Cameron Institute. Monk Bryan was the speaker that evening, and Mary Longstreth was John's prayer partner. He recalls that it seemed like she prayed "all night." John also recalls being aware that his "call" was nothing like that of St. Paul on the road to Damascus, which was a concern to John.[4] This was true for many other youth in the post-war world as well. Was a call from God authentic if it was not bold and dramatic? What did it mean to say that God called one to ministry in the church?

The Cameron Institute was held only a few years when the Missouri Conference decided on one camp at Central College. But in those few years, it was a source of power, life, and joy for many youth in the Missouri Conference. Even today, one can find adults who remember feeling cheated because they had looked forward to being old enough to go to Cameron Institute, and then didn't get to go.

FOR CHRIST AND HIS CHURCH: 1948–1952

The General Conference of 1944 had challenged the church to raise $25 million for world rehabilitation and relief. The church actually raised $27 million—in addition to oversubscribing a $24 million World Service budget. Because the needs of the world continued to be so great, the World Service Commission recommended to the General Conference that the World Service

Apportionment be increased by one-third! Methodists were doing a great work and were eager to raise the money to make the work happen—to the extend of an $8 million increase in World Service giving!

Remember that this was 1948. American planes were flying almost non-stop into Berlin to carry food, fuel, and other basic supplies to a city blockaded by the Russians. Famine in other parts of the world was claiming the attention and resources of churches and relief agencies. Europe, Japan, China, and other parts of Asia were still struggling to rebuild their cities and their economies. The Marshall Plan was helping Europe turn the corner, and Japan was on its way to becoming a strong economy, but human need was as strong as ever. There were wars in Vietnam, Malaysia, and many other parts of Asia. The partition of India and Pakistan had occurred only the year before, and there were millions of persons who had fled from one country to the other. Refugees were still living in camps all over the world. The state of Israel came into being in 1948 and immediately began a desperate fight for basic existence.

The need of the world was, indeed, great. Because of the success of the special fund in the previous quadrennium, a special new fund called the Advance Fund was recommended. All Advance Special projects were to be "visualized and described." That is, they were personalized so Methodists could see the need to which they were asked to respond. Advance Specials were to be in shares of one hundred dollars each, and congregations could participate in as many "shares" as they chose. Methodists responded quickly to needs they could understand, and they gave generously. In the years since 1948, the Advance has been one of the great success stories of modern Methodism, and has changed the lives of persons all over the globe for the better.

The other part of "For Christ and His Church" was programmatic, rather than financial. It involved "a Teaching and Preaching Endeavor in which Methodists may achieve a deeper understanding of and commitment to *Our Faith, Our Church, Our Ministry, and Our Mission*." Each of the four years of the quadrennium was to have its own programmatic emphasis. The first year focused on "Our Faith." It involved a worldwide preaching mission, a series of study resources on key subjects of the faith, and an action project aimed at raising World Service giving. The second year's emphasis was "Our Church," and involved an understanding of the nature of the church and Methodism's unique contributions to worldwide Christianity. The action plan for the second year was an evangelistic outreach to the unchurched, and a program of church extension to build churches in new communities around the world. In the United States, the evangelistic outreach and church extension program was aimed primarily at the new suburbs springing up around older core cities.

The third year, "Our Ministry," was a look at Christian vocation and the meaning of the "priesthood of all believers." The action program was recruitment of top-quality youth for ministry and other Christian vocations. The fourth year, "Our Mission," was to be a study of mission. The action program was still to be determined, but would focus on the strengthening of the Christian home and the Christian community. Again, it is interesting to look at the responses of the Missouri conferences to these emphases.

During the first year with the evangelism emphasis, the Missouri Conference reported 2,020 new members on profession of faith and 3,367 by transfer "and otherwise." The St. Louis Conference reported 3,309 professions of faith and 3,236 new members by transfer. Their goal for the new year (1949–1950) was one new member for every 17 active members! The Southwest Missouri Conference reported 2,733 professions of faith (no statistics on transfers). That is a total of 8,062 professions of faith in one year, plus at least 6,603 by transfer, or over 14,000 new members in one year. Of course, at least some of the transfers were within the denomination and balanced each other out. There must also have been tremendous drains on the membership, since only the St. Louis Conference reported a net gain for the year.

What else happened in Missouri Methodism in those years? Church school attendance increased, as much as 19 percent in one year in the Missouri Conference. Vacation Bible Schools were held, with increasing numbers of both schools and children participating. Vacation Bible Schools were apparently a new thing in these postwar years, and they were accepted enthusiastically by the church. Laymen were active. In the St. Louis Conference, there was the beginning of the laymen's retreat at Arcadia, which became one of the great institutions for fellowship, service, and growth in faith for laymen in the St. Louis and Missouri East Conferences. The Board of Lay Activities of the St. Louis Conference developed a circulating library for pastors who could not afford to buy books. In 1947, they circulated seven hundred fifty-eight books to seventy-five pastors. Also in 1947, J. Clinton Hawkins was nominated as Conference Lay Leader for the coming year. He would continue in that role for many years. The Board of Lay Activities in the Missouri Conference had the upgrading of parsonages as a priority.

In 1950, the Woman's Society of Christian Service celebrated its 10th birthday (after union—there had been women's organizations in the churches for years before 1940). In the Southwest Missouri Conference, there had been two hundred ten charter societies and twenty-six Wesleyan Service Guilds in 1940. In 1950, that had grown to two hundred eighty-three societies and sixty-seven guilds, with a total membership of 16,000. Giving the previous year was $67,500. (Remember that, in 1950, a dollar went a long way. One could buy a hamburger, a sack of potato chips, and a soft drink, and have change out of a quarter!) There were deaconesses working in all three conferences. In the St. Louis Conference, one hundred eleven women attended the School of Missions in Fayette. The St. Louis Conference had two hundred forty societies and sixty-four Guilds, with a total membership of 14,027.

Youth work also grew. Caravans were popular and brought new enthusiasm and purpose to youth groups, particularly in smaller churches, all across the state.

A caravan was a group of older youth, primarily college students, who spent the summer traveling from church to church, leading a "Youth Activities Week" in each church. These were times of renewal for local MYFs. Subdistrict, district, and conference youth events flourished. In the Missouri Conference, the 1951 minutes record that in the previous year, two hundred seventy youth were enrolled in institutes, forty-eight went to the National Convocation at Purdue, and three hundred were reached by the caravan in the conference. In that same year, the St. Louis Conference hired its first full time Conference youth director—Gloria Hunt (Schlapbach)—at the princely sum of two thousand dollars a year. The youth of the conference were asked to increase their giving to help finance the Conference Director. (It seems youth are always asked to finance their own ministry.) Juanita Wood was hired as Conference director of Youth Work in the Southwest Missouri Conference.

The pioneer camp at the Missouri Conference campsite near Clarence (now Camp Jo-Ota) was held in 1952. Wilbur Longstreth was the director, and campers spent time working on the site.

In 1952, the last year of the quadrennium, membership figures were:

	Active Members	Professions of Faith	Sunday School Attendance
Central West	8,120	537	2,025
Missouri	66,170	3,381	26,403
S. W. Missouri	77,618	3,547	30,437
Saint Louis	69,983	4,049	26,994

There were a total of 221,891 active members on the rolls of the churches of the four conferences, and an average Sunday School attendance of 85,859.

1952–1956

Harry Truman left the White House for Independence, Missouri, and Dwight Eisenhower moved in. The Korean War wound down, and the nation settled into an uneasy time of "Cold War," dominated by the growing threat of nuclear weapons. A hot topic of discussion in many youth groups was, "would it be moral to shoot our neighbors trying to get into our fallout shelter? Letting them in would only mean we'd all starve." That seems strange in modern times, but the "lifeboat mentality" was very much a part of public life in the 1950s. Communism was a real enemy, one that Americans assumed was all around them. Senator Joe McCarthy held hearings about loyalty, accusing persons all over the political spectrum of being Communist and disloyal. The House Unamerican Activities Committee also tried to ferret out Communists in high places. Church leaders who were advocates for peace and social justice, such as Methodist Bishop G. Bromley Oxnam, were hailed before the committee, and their loyalty was questioned. Many writers in Hollywood were black listed and were out of work because they refused to cooperate with the Committee. All over the globe, the United States and the Soviet Union sought allies, spent huge sums on military preparedness, and tried to dominate the world at the other's expense. The world atmosphere was "us" and "them" written large across the globe. American foreign policy was based on containing Communism, and alliances were made with all sorts of oppressive governments, whose only virtue was that they were "on our side."

Civil rights became an important issue in this quadrennium. In 1948, President Truman had desegregated the armed forces by Executive Order. The most basic rights, however, were still denied to African-Americans. Public facilities, including transportation, restrooms, drinking fountains, and restaurants were still segregated. Signs that read "We reserve the right to refuse service to anyone" meant that only whites were welcome in that establishment. Public schools were segregated until 1954. In that year, the Supreme Court ruled, in *Brown vs. Board of Education,* that "separate but equal" schools were unequal by their very nature, and therefore unconstitutional. The clear legal implication was that segregated public schools were in violation of the law of the land. Many school districts in Missouri, including St. Louis and Kansas City, desegregated almost immediately. Residential patterns meant that many schools, particularly in the cities, were still *de facto* segregated, however, which led to bussing to integrate both white and black schools. The worship hour on Sunday, however, continued to be the most segregated part of the week. The church was following the courts, instead of leading the way for justice and equality.

The General Conference of 1952 had adopted youth ministry as a special emphasis for the quadrennium, even as the church continued to promote evangelism and spiritual growth. A Worldwide Mission of Evangelism called on each annual conference to reach at least a 10 percent *net gain* in membership during the quadrennium. It can be said immediately that, in spite of the best efforts of the churches, and large numbers of persons received on profession of faith, the Missouri conferences did not achieve this kind of membership gain. There was a gain in total membership from 1953 to 1956, but nowhere near 10 percent.

The figures given below include both active and inactive members (who were regarded as a primary mission field by the church).

1956	Active Members	Professions of Faith	Sunday School Attendance
Central West	14,012	213	2,410
Missouri	78,797	2,235	31,662
S. W. Missouri	91,999	2,562	36,022
St. Louis	83,564	2,833	30,590

The Missouri Conference lost nearly 3,000 members during the quadrennium; the other three conferences either held constant or showed minimal gains. Note, however, the totals: 268,372 members, and an average Sunday school attendance of 100,684. Even granted that the membership figures include inactive members, there were a lot of Methodists in Missouri in 1956.

But what about youth work, the primary emphasis for the quadrennium? It continued to flourish, with new opportunities being added all the time. In small towns, the MYF was often the focus of the social life of youth, as well as an opportunity for growth in Christian faith. Subdistrict, district, and conference events inspired youth with a vision of a church larger than themselves, helped them develop friendships with other youth in other communities, and inspired to find ways to work together to make a significant impact on the mission of the church and the needs of the world. Youth were raising dollars and canned goods for conference agencies, they were putting on plays and doing work days to raise money for missions overseas, and they were reaching out to other youth in the community and inviting them to become a part of the church.

Camping was an increasingly important part of youth ministry. In 1952, the Missouri Conference opened Camp Jo-Ota, using temporary equipment and housing. Some two hundred thirty youth participated in camps. Permanent improvements were underway. The camp was made possible because of the Barrow family of Clarence, for whom it was ultimately named. The first Missouri Conference Youth Convocation was held with three hundred eighty-three youth in attendance. The following year, the Maryville District had a new camp at Willow Row, which served one hundred thirty-four youth. There was a junior high camp at Crowder State Park each summer. Work continued on Camp Jo-Ota. There was a request for eight thousand dollars to construct a lake and other permanent improvements at Jo-Ota. Nearly nine thousand youth were enrolled in Sunday school. At the end of the quadrennium, the Board of Education of the St. Louis Conference reported that the need for camps/programs at Epworth Among the Hills, Arcadia, was so great that there were not enough weeks in the year.

The Woman's Society began the first missionary tour for young women in 1956. This was a significant project in mission education that would continue until sometime in the 1970s. One of the highlights of the quadrennium for youth was the National Youth Convocation at Purdue University in Indiana. The South Central Jurisdiction chartered a train which made its way through the jurisdiction, with Union Station in St. Louis the last stop before Purdue. Registration was limited because of space, and each district in the conference had a quota. Caravans also continued, as did Mid-Winter Institutes in the districts, monthly sub-district meetings, and Youth Activities Weeks in churches not reached by caravans.

In the Southwest Missouri Conference, a campsite at Eldorado Springs had been recommended for purchase in 1950. The site had ninety-three acres, including a three acre lake. The cost was not to exceed $9,750. The 1952 minutes reported that Dollar Day offerings had been large enough to employ a camp superintendent and begin development of the site. Additional land was given in 1952 and 1953. The plan was for a full year of youth camping in 1955. Camp Galilee was dedicated by Bishop Holt in 1955 and was indeed used for a full year of camping.

The significance of the camping program runs far beyond the dollars spent or the acres of land. Year after year, youth went to these conference camps, institutes, or convocations and returned to their churches full of enthusiasm for Christ and the church. Many of them learned the foundations of Christian doctrine, experienced the importance of missions, gave their lives to Christ, and responded to calls to full-time Christian service. It would be interesting to discover exactly how many clergy and lay leaders, both men and women, of the 1960s and 1970s made a serious commitment to Christ at these camps.

Finally, after a quadrennium of emphasizing youth work, the General Conference of 1956 set up a National Conference of Methodist Youth and provided for membership and financing for the organization. This was the predecessor of today's National Youth Ministry Organization. Youth ministry was written into the *Book of Discipline* as a key part of the ongoing life of the church.

Other things were happening around the conferences in the quadrennium. A part of the evangelism emphasis included, as it had in the previous quadrennium, the organizing of Fishermen's Clubs in local churches. These were groups of laymen and women who visited their unchurched or inactive neighbors in their homes and invited them to become followers of Jesus Christ. Fishermen's Clubs met monthly for fellowship and prayer, then fanned out across the community. Many professions of faith in this period can be credited to the faithfulness of these men and women, as well as youth. Juanita Wood, Conference youth director of the Southwest Missouri Conference, told the annual conference that "We've learned, and want to remind the conference that our youth are effective evangelists."

New experiments in cooperative ministry were taking shape. Larger parishes and group ministries combined the gifts and graces of several clergy and congregations to make significant differences in such places as Pemiscott County Larger Parish (in the Missouri Bootheel) and the Tri-County Group Ministry (in Montgomery and parts of Warren and Gasconade counties). Across the state, parsonages were being upgraded and improved. Pastors' salaries were increasing.

As early as 1953, the Missouri Conference Board of Education recommended that the three conferences set up a commission to study rearranging conference boundaries. That commission recommended to the 1955 conferences that conferences be held in the spring, beginning in 1956. The commission had studied the possibility of both one conference and two conferences in the state. Further study on the issue was recommended. If one quadrennium for study is good, then two or ever three quadrennia are better.

The Woman's Society of Christian Service continued to have strong Schools of Christian Mission. Laymen from the conferences attended the first National

Bishop Ivan Lee Holt, who led Missouri Methodism through the period of rebuilding and boom after the Second World War.

Conference of Methodist Men in 1953. There was a new emphasis on ministry in Town and Country. Conference commissions on Town and Country work were organized before 1952, but little work was done. In 1952, Bishop Holt appointed John Ward Sr. to be the area director of Town and Country work. His primary responsibility was promotion of the Lord's Acre, to improve rural church stewardship. Certainly the Lord's Acre program became a major part of the life of many churches. In the spring, individuals or families would pledge the produce from an acre of crop land, or a calf, lamb, or pig. Other families would pledge produce from gardens, woodworking, or crafts. In the fall, there would be a Lord's Acre Sale, with the crops, animals, and so on auctioned off. In addition, there would be sales of handwork, quilts, jelly, and apple butter. A dinner would be served. In many churches, the thousands of dollars raised through the Lord's Acre program would mean the difference between paying apportionments, improving the building, raising the pastor's salary, and not being able to do those things. In 1958, Dan Schores was appointed as Area Director. He led a new emphasis on lay speaker training, rural church extension, interdenominational cooperation, and research.

An era ended for Missouri Methodism in 1956, when Bishop Ivan Lee Holt retired. He had been the leader of Methodism in Missouri since 1944, and was greatly loved across the state. A new era began immediately with the assignment of Bishop Eugene M. Frank to the Missouri Area.

CENTRAL METHODIST COLLEGE

In 1939, Dr. Robert H. Ruff had been president of the college since 1930, and had guided the school toward recovery from the Great Depression. He initiated the first plan for retirement of faculty and staff on a limited pension. Because of the illness of Dr. Ruff, Dean E. P. Puckett took over many of the president's responsibilities on an interim basis. Dr. Harry S. Devore became president in 1941. His administration was a turbulent one, both because of his leadership philosophy and style, and because of the disruption brought about by the war. Company M of the Missouri National Guard, which was stationed in Fayette and contained many Central students, moved to another location and prepared for war.

On July 1, 1943, a U.S. Navy V-12 program arrived on campus. This greatly increased the number of male students. In 1947, a building which had been the Officers' Club at Camp Crowder, Missouri, was moved to the campus to serve as the student center. It was named The Eyrie, and has served the college for over fifty years.

Dr. Devore died in 1947, and Dean Puckett was elected acting president. Under his leadership, the Board of Curators authorized the construction of a field house, which was completed in 1950. It was later named the E. P. Puckett Field House.

Ralph L. Woodward was named president in 1950. In 1952, a ten year development program was begun. This resulted in a new women's residence hall (Holt Hall), a new science building (Stedman), and renovations of current buildings, as well as an increase in endowment. Among the renovations were Howard-Payne Hall. Also in 1952, an informal change in policy led to the admission of African-American students.

ST. PAUL SCHOOL OF THEOLOGY

Early in the 1950s, Methodists in Missouri began to express a need for a theological seminary in the area, and petitioned the General Conference to establish one. The 1956 General Conference did, in fact, agree to establish two new seminaries: one in Kansas City and one in Delaware, Ohio. Bishop Eugene Frank called together a provisional governing board for the seminary, when met in Kansas City on November 30, 1956. It adopted the following recommendations:

1. that the school be called "National Methodist Seminary"
2. that the seminary be a separate legal entity with its own board of trustees
3. that the board of trustees include one layman and one minister from each of the Central Kansas, Central West, Kansas, Missouri, Nebraska, St. Louis, and Southwest Missouri conferences, plus some ex-officio and at-large members

The provisional board also asked for moral and financial support from those conferences, and noted that the minimum annual budget of one hundred fifty thousand dollars would receive only about one-half that amount from general church funds. In 1957, a newly organized Area Commission on Christian Higher Education also affirmed the proposed seminary. In the summer of 1957, a search began for a president for the seminary, and Don W. Holter was selected in 1958.

The new National Seminary was scheduled to open in the fall of 1959, but there were no faculty members, no buildings, no library, and no students. Soon there were five faculty. The school then bought several libraries from retired professors in other seminaries, as well as new books in various fields, and began operation with thirty thousand volumes. But what about students? As Don Holter said, "What if we opened and no one came?" Ultimately, the school opened in the fall of 1959 with fifty Master of Divinity students.

What the seminary did have was a vision—it was clear from the beginning that the purpose of National Seminary was to train men (and, later, women) for pastoral ministry. Many other seminaries trained persons to be professors and scholars. National was designed to train pastors. Bishop Frank's first speech in Missouri asking support of the seminary had made this clear. "We know from experience," he said, "that if we are to have leadership for the local church in this region, we must have a strong and effective seminary here."

THE END OF THE FIFTIES

The 1950s were both a stormy time and a golden interlude between the storms of World War II and Korea on one hand, and the turbulence of the 1960s on the other. The progress America made as a nation also showed how far we had to go—in civil rights, for example. The church continued to grow in the 1950s. Many new buildings were built, persons were converted, lives were changed, ministries were enlarged, and Methodists continued to reach out to serve the world. World mission was a reality in homes and congregations as Methodists in Missouri (and elsewhere) responded to human need and to the demands of the gospel to reach out across the world.

Chapter 11

YEARS OF TURMOIL AND ANGST 1960–1979

FROM CAMELOT TO THE MOON

The 1960s were one of the most exciting and turbulent decades of the twentieth century. John F. Kennedy became the first Catholic to be elected to the presidency. His administration was a dynamo of energy and hope for the nation (even for many who voted against him), so much so that it evoked King Arthur and the Round Table, and became known as "Camelot." President Kennedy's call for service and sacrifice woke a response not only in his own generation of veterans, but in the younger generation as well. His statement, "Ask not what your country can do for you, but what you can do for your country," touched the deep patriotism and commitment of a nation. Thousands of people volunteered for service in the Peace Corps, and America set out to make the world a better place. The dream of Camelot may have ended in a hospital emergency room in Dallas, Texas, with Kennedy's assassination, but the ferment of idealism and service lingered on.

Let's remind ourselves of what happened in the 1960s. There was the failed invasion of Cuba at the Bay of Pigs, followed by the Cuban Missile Crisis, in which it seemed the U.S. stood on the brink of a nuclear world war. In 1963, the United States Supreme Court ruled that mandated prayer in the public schools was unconstitutional. Many Methodists defended that ruling and urged Congress not to pass new legislation or constitutional amendments requiring prayer in the schools. This was not an opposition to prayer, but to mandated prayer. (In the 1990s, the lack of prayer in the schools is named as the primary reason for the decay in the social fabric of our nation—it seems some issues never go away.) Early in the decade, the first sit-ins at drugstore lunch counters in the South sparked the resurgence of the Civil Rights Movement. "Freedom riders" appeared in the South, working to integrate buses and other public services. The Congress of Racial Equality and Student Nonviolent Coordinating Committee were among the leaders of the movement. In 1963, as part of a giant civil rights march and rally in Washington, D.C., Dr. Martin Luther King Jr. stood on the steps of the Lincoln Memorial and said to the world, "I have a dream. . . ." Millions of Americans identified with that dream of a day when all persons would truly be free and equal, both in the eyes of the law and in the practices of society. The dark side of that dream was the hatred in many whites, both north and south, which led to water cannons and police dogs being turned loose on peaceful demonstrators, a reign of terror in many black communities, and, ultimately, murders.

Lyndon B. Johnson became president after the assassination of John F. Kennedy and immediately began to use his vast experience and knowledge of the legislative process to pass laws that had been stalled earlier. The Civil Rights Act of 1964 banned discrimination in public places and led to voter registration drives for African Americans, particularly in the South. Several people working to register voters were murdered, which aroused a storm of protest nationwide, and ultimately helped the cause of registration. President Johnson had a dream of a "Great Society," in which discrimination, poverty, and illiteracy were eliminated. Under his leadership, Medicare was passed in 1965, the first environmental laws (the Water Quality Act) were passed, and Head Start became a reality, along with the Job Corps and VISTA (Volunteers in Service and Training for America), a sort of domestic Peace Corps. Johnson declared a war on poverty, and Methodists all over the country enlisted, giving many hours to help communities deal with issues such as poverty, unemployment, education, and medical care.

Unfortunately, the War on Poverty became entangled with the war in Vietnam, and the latter took priority. As the United States became more and more embroiled in Vietnam, and increasing numbers of Americans were killed, wounded, or captured in that tragic war, both supporters and opponents of the war became more vocal and rigid in their positions. United Methodists were found in the armed forces and in the peace movement. Annual conference sessions occupied many hours debating the war and what the church's response to it should be.

Even with a war, America continued to be a prosperous nation. Air-conditioning on a widespread scale changed the tempo of life, particularly in the South. More and more families added a second car as the move to the suburbs accelerated, and it was harder to walk to any activity. Churches moved with the people, and new churches were built in suburban communities. Older churches that had once been at the heart of sleepy villages now found themselves surrounded by thousands of new homes (Manchester is a prime example).

Nowhere was the turmoil of the 1960s more evident than on the social scene. In the last half of the decade, the inner cities of the nation exploded, with rioting in more than one hundred fifty cities. The first major riot was in the Watts neighborhood of Los Angeles in 1965, and the most devastating was in Detroit in 1967.

(The author was co-leader of the Missouri East Conference Missionary Tour in 1967. His busload of youth and adults left Detroit the day before the riots broke out.) Burned-out neighborhoods, patrolling National Guard troops, and fighting in the streets were symbols of the anger and frustration brought on by decades of poverty and racism in the central cities of the nation. The Black Panthers became a household name; U.S. athletes at the Olympic Games in Mexico City celebrated their victories with a Black Power salute. Women and minorities spoke out more and more, demanding equality and a "place at the table." Cesar Chavez organized Hispanic immigrant farm workers into a union. Betty Friedan wrote on *The Feminine Mystique.*

This was also the decade of alternative cultures. "Hippies" became both a household word and a sub-culture on the American scene. The drug culture (centered around marijuana, LSD, and heroin) gained a foothold in America, primarily among suburban white youth and young adults in the beginning stages. Campus riots protested everything from the war in Vietnam to the way college administrators worked, to the courses that were offered. "Love-ins" were a non-violent, anti-establishment form of protest against almost anything. Rock and roll still ruled the music scene, though folk music, particularly protest music, was also popular. Joan Baez, Bob Dylan, the Seegers, the Guthries, and Peter, Paul, and Mary expressed the restlessness and anger of a generation still searching for a focus and meaning. The culmination of the alternative cultures came at the great rally at Woodstock in 1969, where hundreds of thousands of youth tuned in, turned on, and dropped out. But Americans also listened to the Beatles, Julie Andrews in *The Sound of Music,* and the anti-war musical, *Hair.*

Politically, Richard Nixon appealed to the "silent majority" and was elected president in 1968, beginning a rightward swing in American government that continues until the present. In that same year of 1968, Robert F. Kennedy and Martin Luther King Jr. were assassinated, George Wallace was shot and left paralyzed, and the conflict between Chicago police and demonstrators erupted in riots at the Democratic National Convention. Violence had become a permanent part of American culture.

Not all was gloom and doom in the 1960s, however. Early in the decade, President Kennedy had challenged the nation to "put a man on the moon in this decade." On July 20, 1969, Neil Armstrong and "Buzz" Aldrin became the first humans to walk on the surface of the moon. One United Methodist preacher was driving to a village church to organize a youth group when he heard on his car radio that there had been "one giant leap for mankind." He says that he was so moved by the moment that he had to pull over to the side of the road and weep for sheer joy.

In the 1960s, children received oral polio vaccine and, for the first time, mothers in the United States did not dread the coming of summer. The first heart transplants occurred in the 1960s, as did the beginnings of the environmental movement.

THE METHODIST CHURCH

And what was happening in Methodism? Nationwide, there were three events that deeply affected Methodists, including those in Missouri. The General Conference of 1964 wrote the word "confirmation" into the *Book of Discipline* for the first time and turned the concept loose upon the church. Prior to 1964, there had been membership classes and pastor's classes for youth, but confirmation was a new concept. Confirmation was a name, a rite, and a concept in search of a theology. It recognized the importance of educating youth in the faith and preparing them for responsible membership in the church, but it lacked a clarity of purpose and a solid theological foundation. All over the country, laboratory schools were set up to teach Methodist pastors how to do confirmation. Resources were prepared to serve confirmation classes in local churches. United Methodists adopted a theology of confirmation that had first appeared in a National Council of Churches document. We said that we were:

1. baptized into Christ;
2. confirmed in the church universal; and
3. received into membership in the local church.

As confirmation matured in United Methodism, that theology would seem less and less adequate, and the 1988 General Conference would call for a new study on the theology of baptism, confirmation, and related rites.

The 1964 General Conference included sexuality in The Social Principles, also for the first time. One result was that resources were developed and leaders trained for Human Sexuality Seminars in local churches. The goal of the seminars was to help youth and their parents develop an understanding of the biological, social, and spiritual aspects of their sexuality. These seminars were welcomed eagerly in some United Methodist churches, and looked on with horror in others. The Missouri annual conferences developed teams of trained leaders who were available to lead seminars for youth and their parents. In the beginning, they were welcomed in local churches; then, as the country moved in a more conservative direction, the sexuality education movement became more controversial, and finally died out. Even today, at the start of a new century, there are many who would prefer the church have nothing at all to do with sexuality education.

The third national event that affected Missouri Methodists was the decision of the 1964 General Conference to abolish the Central Jurisdiction, which had been created as a non-geographic jurisdiction in 1939 for African-American Methodists. In Missouri, the Central Missouri Conference had been organized in 1887, taking in the African-American churches from the St. Louis and Missouri Conferences of the Methodist Episcopal Church. In 1929, the Central Missouri, Little Rock, and Lincoln conferences reorganized themselves into two conferences: the Central West and the Southwest. The Central West Conference had churches in Missouri,

Kansas, Nebraska, and Colorado. (In 1939, one of the General Conference delegates to the Uniting Conference was from Missouri, the other from Colorado.)

In 1964, following the action of the General Conference, the Central West conference voted to transfer out of its membership the churches in Kansas, Nebraska, and Colorado. Seventeen churches, with a total membership of approximately three thousand, were transferred out. The Missouri East and Missouri West annual conferences then invited the churches of the Central West Conference within their geographical boundaries to transfer to the geographic conferences. In 1965, the Central West conference voted 42 to 3 to transfer the conference to the South Central Jurisdiction and to merge with the conferences of the Missouri Area. In May of 1966, the Central West Conference ceased to exist and became part of the Missouri East and West Conferences. Nineteen stations and circuits were transferred to the Missouri East Conference; twenty-one to the Missouri West. In spite of a long history of separation, segregation, and racism in Missouri, there was little opposition to the merger.

Indeed, the most difficult part of the merger was not race. White church leaders were astounded, in Bishop Frank's words, at the closeness of pastors in the Central West Conference.[1] It was then, Bishop Frank said, that he finally understood the speech Joseph Lowery made at the 1964 General Conference. Lowery said, with tears in his eyes, that the jurisdiction was being dissolved. It was inevitable, he said, but he wanted people to understand the cost to the blacks. What the General Conference was doing was destroying the closeness that existed. When the merger was done, people who had been as close as brothers and sisters for years would be separated. Indeed, in Missouri, black pastors were assigned to this state who had lived most of their lives in Kansas.

Missouri Methodism

Across Missouri in the 1950s and 1960s, there were two great demographic shifts. In one, population moved from rural to urban areas. In 1950, 38.5 percent of the population lived in rural areas, primarily farms and small villages. By 1970, that had dropped to 29.8 percent. The number of farm families dropped, and the average size of the family farm increased, so that fewer people were working the same amount of land. With fewer people, there was less need for stores and businesses supplying farmers. Many villages ceased to exist, except for a few homes. County seat towns declined in population, and the average age of the population increased. Schools consolidated to make it possible to provide a quality education. Churches in rural areas suffered because of the population loss. Many closed. Others hung on with only a few members. Only those rural churches in the path of the growing suburban sprawl were able to grow.

The second demographic shift was the move from the central city to the suburbs. The post-war boom made it possible for workers to buy homes in the suburbs and, in many cases, to buy a car to commute back into the city to work.

The population that moved to the suburbs was primarily white, leaving the central cities to minority groups (who were not welcome in the suburbs) and those who were too poor to make the move. Methodist churches in the central cities also suffered from the population shifts, even while suburban churches were booming.

The loss of population in rural areas led to another merger in Missouri Methodism. By the early 1960s, the Missouri Conference was having a difficult time functioning as a conference because of the loss of population. It became clear that it was going to be increasingly difficult to make appointments and attract young preachers to come to that part of the state. This reality continued even after reorganization. The Missouri Conference had always been predominantly rural, with no large urban areas like St. Louis or Kansas City, and the decline in rural population hit it particularly hard. So, a movement began to reorganize Methodism in the state. Some members of the Missouri Conference were opposed to the reorganization plan (which was finally passed), and wanted the entire Missouri Conference to be merged with Southwest Missouri. There was, in fact, a real point to that feeling. The northern part of the state had always been linked to Kansas City because of the railroads. There were no real ties to St. Louis. In the final reorganization, the Missouri Conference was cut in half, and the eastern half was put in a conference where they had no relationships. Up to the end of the period covered in this book, the Hannibal-Kirksville District still did not feel at home in the Missouri East Conference.

The variety of cultures in Missouri made it hard to think about a logical way to organize the conferences. North Missouri, with its prairie agriculture, belongs more to Iowa, but its ties to Missouri cities have always been to Kansas City. Southeast Missouri is delta country, with more ties to Kentucky, Tennessee, and even Mississippi, than to north or southwest Missouri. Southwest Missouri is Ozark country with hills and shallow soil, and a strong base for evangelical and Pentecostal groups. St. Louis is a world of its own, isolated from the rest of the state, and oriented to the east. In 1961, there were Methodist preachers in St. Louis who didn't know for sure where Kansas City was, indeed had never been west of the Missouri River! One key question in the merger was Howard County, with Fayette as the county seat—where would it go? Bishop Frank asked Ralph Woodward, the president of Central College, which way he wanted to go. Dr. Woodward said he would go to the West conference because the college had lots of support from St. Louis, but not from the West, so he wanted to be over there.[2]

With all the differences across the state, the three conferences met in simultaneous sessions at Central College in 1961 and voted themselves out of existence. They then reorganized into two conferences, the Missouri East and Missouri West. In the East conference, the laity worked hard to get the laity merged. Clint Hawkins worked hard to get laity from the north to come to Arcadia for the lay retreat. The conference women's societies also worked hard to include women from the north.

Then, in 1968, came the merger with the Evangelical United Brethren. The instigator of the merger between Methodists and Evangelical United Brethren was Reuben Miller, who was a strong, aggressive leader and who pushed the EUB college of bishops to the merger. Why were the Evangelical United Brethren pushing so hard for a merger? Bishop Miller and Bishop Paul Washburn, who were the leaders in the movement, felt the future of the EUB was with a larger denomination. Since there were close historic ties to the Methodists, and since the theologies and politics were so similar, the Methodists were a logical choice. Bishop Frank says that he never sensed any great enthusiasm on the part of the Methodists for the merger. Certainly in Missouri, the merger went fairly well, though there was difficulty with some individual churches. There were twelve Evangelical United Brethren churches in the Missouri West Conference, and four in the Missouri East. There was some minor opposition from Methodist preachers, who felt that local preachers from the Evangelical United Brethren were being given membership rights in the annual conference that were still denied to Methodist local preachers.

Mission and Ministry

What about mission and ministry? All clergy, when they leave an appointment, can look back and say, "I did that," or "That happened under my leadership." When Bishop Frank was asked what he would say about his years in Missouri, he responded that there were three significant things that happened under his leadership in Missouri, and he would take credit for one of them. They were:

1. the founding of St. Paul School of Theology;
2. the organization of the Office of Creative Ministries; and
3. the organization of the Missouri Methodist Foundation.[3]

Something of the organization of St. Paul was noted in the previous chapter. The seminary continued to grow and provide significant leadership to the church throughout the sixties. It changed its name from "National Theological Seminary" to "St. Paul School of Theology, Methodist." Men and women graduated from St. Paul with a commitment to the local church and to being pastors to people. They made, and are still making, significant contributions to the life of Methodism in Missouri, as well as in other states. St. Paul also became a controversial leader in ministry through its involvement in the inner city parish in Kansas City.

The Office of Creative Ministries began when Melvin West was appointed to the Lake of the Ozarks area to start a new church. He reported back that the area did not need a new church, but needed a new ministry. So was born the Lake Ozark Parish, which focused on ministry to the resorts, the tourists who came to the Lake, and the people who worked in the tourist industry. From coffee houses, lakeside worship services, ministries to children, service personnel from Fort Leonard Wood, a gift shop, and other ministries at the lake came a new look at mission and ministry in Missouri. The Area Office of Creative Ministries was created and charged with doing ministry in areas where local churches were not reaching, and with discovering new ways for the church to be in mission. Following are some of the new ministries that came out of the office.

In 1966, there was a series of meetings on stewardship and on the Lord's Acre in local churches. A study of Missouri counties showing the percentage of Methodists was published. DeKalb County had the highest percentage, with 22.5; Ozark and St. Genevieve counties had 0.7 percent each. The Kansas City Young Adult Project offered a Kansas City Weekend for rural young adults. The focus was on adjustment to the city—how to find a job, how to find housing, and how to contact local churches. The Lake of the Ozarks Parish held worship services in Boy Scout and Girl Scout camps and had a vesper cruise, a boat-in worship service, and a drive-in worship service. In one week, eight hundred thirty-three persons attended worship services in Lake of the Ozarks programs, making the Lake Ozark Parish one of the largest churches in Missouri. Summer work camps were first announced in 1967. Given the emphasis on service among youth in the 1960s, work camps became the norm for youth and missions, quickly replacing the mission tours as "the" mission event. Also in 1967, the first booklets on "Church Office Standards" and "Parsonage Standards" were published. These soon became guidelines for church offices and parsonages all across the state. In 1968, the Mission '68 program was launched, using college students to assist in local churches. Many of these students made significant contributions to churches, providing leadership for youth ministries and other projects for a summer. This was particularly true for smaller churches in rural areas. All through its existence, the Office of Creative Ministries has had a concern for and an emphasis on the rural church. Larger parishes and other forms of cooperative ministries were lifted up as examples of creative ways for rural and village churches to work together in ministry. Workshops on cooperative parishes were held in many districts. In addition to the Lake of the Ozarks parish, significant work was done, for example, in Macon County Larger Parish, Custer Cooperative Parish, and Scotland County Larger Parish. Other exciting ministries in this decade included a Medical Mission Project in India, a barroom ministry in Kansas City, and the VIEW (Volunteers in Ecumenical Witness) program.

The United Methodist Foundation was begun in 1967 as a financial arm of the two conferences. It was to receive monies given to the church and invest the money. Interest on investments was to provide funds for grants and bequests. The mission of the Foundation was to respond to requests for funds from organizations associated with the United Methodist Church. Obviously, one of the most difficult questions for the board would be to define what was a valid request for funds. From the beginning, a priority was scholarships to seminary students. Early on, the Foundation agreed to provide thirty such scholarships, fifteen in each annual conference. In addition, a policy of providing ten thousand dollars to each new church was set up. This was money for program and mission, not bricks and mortar. Nor was money loaned to churches. Not only was there not enough money, but it was felt that the Church Extension Society was the proper body for making loans.

J. Clinton Hawkins, Oscar Cole, Harold Colbert, and Rogers Wohlberg were among those who helped organize the Foundation. Clint Hawkins was the executive director and ran the office out of his home. Clint did not take any salary for his work, and there was no rental expense. Finally, the Board prevailed upon him to take a salary in line with his Social Security payment. This continued well into the eighties. In the early years of the Foundation, many of the bequests were designated for specific causes or projects, and were in the form of Certificates of Deposit, or were managed by banks around the state. It was only when non-designated bequests came directly to the Foundation that there could be active management of funds and a significant increase in the value of the assets.

In the major cities of the state, new ministries were also taking shape. Metro Ministry was organized in St. Louis, with a charge to minister to those who were outside the churches and to assist the Methodist churches in the urban area in planning strategies for mission and ministry. Metro Ministry began to move in those areas of ministry, modeled for local churches how to minister to their own neighborhoods, and helped spark cooperative efforts in ministry to the urban poor. In Kansas City, the Inner City Parish was doing much the same kind of work, though perhaps with a bit more of an emphasis on justice issues. Both ministries were frequently criticized for the direction of their ministries.

At Central College, the 1960s began with a name change. The Board changed the name officially to Central Methodist College, to emphasize the close ties with the Methodist Church. Abel Muzorewa graduated in 1962 with a Bachelor of Arts. Abel would later become the bishop of the Methodist Church in Zimbabwe, and the first black prime minister of that country. New buildings went up, and old buildings were renovated. Stedman Hall, Burford Hall, Woodward Hall, and the Wayside Chapel all appeared on the campus. T. Berry Smith Hall (the old Science Hall) was completely renovated, and Cupples Hall was remodeled to house the Interactive-Television, the TeleCommunity Center, and some academic departments, as well as the college library. A Little Theater was also a part of the remodeling. Enrollment reached an all-time high in this decade.

The decade of the 1960s, with all its turbulence, ground slowly down. Bishop Frank recalls that he went away from the 1968 General Conference in a state of deep depression. He felt that "the dynamic and power of Methodism had been lost. From then on, it seemed to me that—though I can't tell you why—the life seemed to go out of us. Racial issues tore us apart. From 1968 on, we have the reputation of a declining denomination."[4]

In fact, Methodism in Missouri held fairly stable through the sixties. There were 273,548 members of the Central West, Missouri East and Missouri West conferences in 1961. In 1968, the combined membership of the Missouri East and Missouri West Conferences was 257,798, a loss of fewer than 16,000 members. But the signs of decline were already present. The Office of Creative Ministries reported in 1968 that during the last six years, 34,999 members were removed by quarterly conference action in Missouri—the equivalent to the loss of three rural districts. Unfortunately, that was only the beginning of a trend that would continue through the next two decades.

KENT STATE TO "STAR WARS"—THE SEVENTIES

The 1970s began with the same kind of turbulence that had marked the sixties. In 1970, the first Earth Day was held. This day became a symbol for the environmental movement, which has both helped to cleanse and renew the planet, and to infuriate those who see environmentalists always standing in the way of progress. Student protests over the war in Vietnam came to a tragic climax at Kent State University in Ohio on May 4, 1970, when National Guard troops shot and killed several students.

A clue that American society was continuing its rightward turn came in 1971, when the television show *All in the Family* debuted. Even though the premise of the show was the continual debate between a working class conservative and his liberal daughter and son-in-law, it was clear that the public's heart went out to Archie Bunker, and that many agreed with most, if not all, of what he was saying. Archie became a role model for many white conservatives, who shared his opinion that his liberal son-in-law was a "meathead."

The year 1972 brought an amalgam of news events. Richard Nixon visited China and opened the door to renewed relationships between the two countries. This was a shock to the right wing in American politics, since they had vowed never to have anything to do with the communist regime in China. And yet, Richard Nixon was their "darling." Just before the November elections, news stories began to appear about a break-in at Democratic headquarters in the Watergate Hotel in the heart of Washington. The news had no effect on the election, as Nixon trounced George McGovern soundly. The following year, however, the Congress began hearings on Watergate. Also in 1973, the Supreme Court ruled, in *Roe v. Wade,* that abortion was legal in the United States. This was perhaps the most controversial ruling of the decade by the court, and one that continues to be angrily debated to the present. The worst recession in forty years hit America in 1974, the same year that the House of Representatives voted to impeach Richard Nixon. Rather than face a trial in the Senate, President Nixon resigned his office, the first American President to do so. In 1975, South Vietnam fell to the North Vietnamese army, with the vivid scenes of people fighting their way onto rescue helicopters from the roof of the United States Embassy in Saigon. That same year, U.S. and Soviet astronauts worked together in a joint space mission.

Then came the Bicentennial—1976 was the two hundredth birthday of the United States, and it was celebrated in grand style. Tall ships crowded New York harbor, parading past the Statue of Liberty; speeches were made and bands played all across the country, while fireworks arced across the night skies. With all its faults and shortcomings, America said as a nation, "We are still Americans and proud of it!" Jimmy Carter, the governor of Georgia, was elected president of the United States that fall.

What about cultural events of the 1970s? This was the decade when the first *Star Wars* movie appeared, when Luke, Leiea and Han Solo fought against Darth Vader and the evil Empire. *Roots*, Alex Haley's powerful novel about slavery and African Americans finding their roots, appeared and was an instant best seller. A little company out in Silicon Valley, California, began to market a relatively inexpensive machine known as the Apple Computer. The personal computer probably did more to change life in America than anything else that came out of the seventies.

METHODISM IN MISSOURI AND BEYOND

And what of the church? The seventies, like the sixties before them, were a time of what we might call generic Christianity. The call was to transcend denominations and nurture persons to become Christians rather than Methodists or Catholics or Presbyterians. As far back as 1959, at the inauguration of Don Holter as president of National Seminary, Henry P. Van Dusen had struck this theme. In that address, he asked, "Should we not all *now* train men for the 'ministry of the Church of Christ,' and for no other?"[5] Insofar as this was an appeal for an ecumenical spirit in the church, as the author believes Dr. Van Dusen intended it to be, it was a positive note. But, many heard this question (and others even more pointed) as a call to abandon denominational loyalty and identity and become "just Christians." This loss of identity hurt the United Methodist Church, as a generation grew up without knowing its heritage, its unique theological contributions to the worldwide church, and particularly the call to holiness of heart and life.

The religious "boom" of the 1970s was a renewed interest in spirituality without religion. People looked for spiritual renewal without ever connecting spirituality to its roots in the church. The numbers of those who believed in God and prayed regularly soared, even while the number who attended worship regularly dropped like a stone. The seventies were also the height of "televangelism," and many persons connected with a remote figure on the television screen. Television religion was seductive. It was well done, packaged in a slick format, featuring a charismatic (and often physically attractive) preacher or preacher/spouse combination. It offered spiritual solace, sometimes attacked local churches as being out of touch, and asked nothing of its devotees, except a financial contribution "to keep this ministry going." The local church, with perhaps a fairly ordinary preacher and calls for service, mission, and commitment, could not compete with such a "free ride." Obviously, a national phenomenon like this meant the loss of membership, loss of financial support, and loss of vitality for the established churches.

The spirit was "going out of us." In Missouri, membership decline continued in rural areas and central cities, while suburban churches grew. The net result, however, was heavy loss. Between 1968 and 1978, the Missouri East Conference lost sixteen thousand members; the Missouri West lost over fifteen thousand. Membership decline was only a symptom of the loss of spirit within the church. Methodism was slowly being overwhelmed by the increasing secularization of the culture and the increasing turn away from the established churches. But the spirit was not completely gone. Even with the membership decline, mission and ministry were moving forward.

Another era ended for Missouri in 1972, when Bishop Eugene M. Frank left after sixteen years as our episcopal leader and Bishop Robert E. Goodrich Jr. was assigned to Missouri. Bishop Goodrich came to us from First United Methodist Church in Dallas, Texas, and brought with him a Texan's love for doing things in a big way.

Ralph Woodward retired as president of Central Methodist College and was replaced by Harold P. Hamilton. In 1972, Central joined the Allied Health Consortium. Programs in nursing and medical technology were offered on campus. Also that year, the college was chosen as one of thirty to participate in a Danforth Workshop on Liberal Arts Education. In 1976, President Hamilton resigned, and a search was launched for a new president. Dr. Joe A. Howell was installed as president of the college in 1977. In 1978, Dr. Howell began to advocate that Central expand its personal contact with students and establish the motto and reputation as "The College That Cares." He equated caring with Christian love and promoted that throughout his administration. The college also promoted a closer relationship with the Methodist Church in Missouri, and Rev. Ron Page was appointed as director of Church Relations. An endowment campaign called the "CMC 300" was launched with a goal of enrolling three hundred churches to endow twenty thousand dollars each to provide a scholarship for a student to attend Central Methodist. In 1978, the first Hall of Sponsors scholarship was established. These scholarships involved an endowment of twenty-five thousand dollars or more, in the name of the donor or a designated person or group. During the 1970s, the Mabee Foundation was hired to remodel the dining room in Holt Hall. Part of the remodeling was a private dining room, named the East-West Room to recognize the relationship of the two conferences with the college.

The Office of Creative Ministries continued to pioneer in outreach, often in areas where their ministry was too innovative and unpopular. One such area was the ministry in the Bootheel area. Teams of college students worked there during the summer in the DELMO villages. In 1972, Laura Wells, a Church and Community worker on the OCM staff, discovered a small group of women making quilts and crafts to help families in need. Working with those women out of the old horse barn in Hayti where they met, the Wardrobe ministry was established as a clothing thrift shop. Workcamp groups began to remodel the horse barn and lived there while they worked in the community. This ministry was seen as a threat to white churches in the area, and they ignored all the efforts of OCM. (The inner city parish in Kansas City, though not a part of the Office of Creative Ministries, was perceived as the same kind of threat to the established churches.) Summer ministries expanded, with a traveling Vacation Bible School led by college students that served children in communities where there was no church to offer Bible School. Film festivals were held across the state. Heifer Project was adopted as an ecumenical response to poverty and hunger around the world. A State Fair ministry began at Sedalia in 1971. "Through-the-week religious education" was a new model developed and promoted by the Office, and adopted in many local churches. In at least one church, the junior high youth attended a district youth rally at which Mel West spoke on through-the-week religious education, and came home demanding of their pastor that they have such a program. In 1973, there were twenty-one youth work camps scheduled through the office.

A key event for ministry in Missouri came in 1974. In that year, the first Festival of Sharing was held. It was called the Bishop's Convocation on Peace and the Self-Development of Peoples, and was held on December 2 in the livestock arena in Columbia. The value of gifts to that first Convocation was $194,338.02. Work camps were held on the Rosebud Sioux Reservation in South Dakota, and Heifer Project shipped animals to Haiti, Guatemala, Nepal, Kentucky, South Dakota, and Georgia.

Criminal justice and prisons became a priority in 1976, though Laura Wells and others had been working in that area for several years already. The United Methodist Rural Fellowship was chartered in the Missouri East Conference, and the West Conference began working toward a charter. The total value of gifts to

Youth help move food, kits, and other donations at the Festival of Sharing.

the Bishop's Convocation in 1977 was $393,255.95, almost twice the value of the gifts in 1975. The people of Missouri were responding to human need in a big way. The TRAG project was first announced in 1978. The TRAG, a light vehicle, was designed by Earl Miner of Marshfield. The value of gifts at the 1979 Bishop's Convocation was $538,973.25.

Larger parishes and group ministries were developed in the 1970s. They were designed to group together churches that were not strong enough to individually minister to their communities, but that together could provide trained pastoral leadership and creative ways of working together in ministry. In addition to the parishes mentioned in the section on the 1960s, at least the following are known:

Savannah–Amazonia Ecumenical Cooperative Parish
Sarcoxie Yoke Ministry with the Presbyterian Church
Bates County United Ministry
Missouri Delta Ecumenical Ministry
Kansas City Inner City Parish
Swope Park Mission Coalition (Kansas City)
Custer United Methodist Parish

In addition, in 1971, thirty staffers from fourteen cooperative parishes across Missouri gathered in Columbia to form a Fellowship of Cooperative Parish Staffs. Ministry and service were in the air that the Missouri Methodists breathed.

So, the decade of the 1970s remains hard to categorize. On one hand, there is Bishop Frank's concern that some of the spirit went out of Methodism and it became a declining church. In numerical terms, the church has continued to decline, and the decline began in earnest somewhere around 1970. In some ways, the church seemed to struggle against overwhelming pressures, and seemed to be beaten down by secularism, indifference, spirituality without religion, and a host of other worries. On the other hand, the seventies were also an exciting time for ministry in Missouri. Methodists tried out new ways of working, and opened up ministries in areas and "niches" where Methodists had not gone for many years. Missouri Methodists identified with the poor, and became more open and sensitive to the needs of racial-ethnic minorities and women. They reached out to the world in new ways through the Advance, Heifer Project, TRAG, and work camps. Although, in some ways, the spirit did go out of us, God was blowing the wind of His creative Spirit through Methodists in other ways.

THE EVANGELICAL UNITED BRETHREN CHURCH
THE MISSOURI CONFERENCE

The United Brethren Church was organized in 1800 by a group of German ministers led by Phillip William Otterbein, pastor of the Reformed Church in

Baltimore. Otterbein was born in Germany in 1726, and responded to a missionary call to America in 1752. He served first in Lancaster, Pennsylvania, where he went through a time of religious crisis that led to a new sense of peace and salvation. From that time on, his preaching emphasized grace and assurance. He gave up carefully prepared sermons and began speaking directly from the heart. He emphasized spiritual renewal in the church.

Martin Boehm was a Mennonite who had been chosen by lot in 1756 to be a minister to his congregation. Having to preach led him to a spiritual crisis. He describes how he was plowing one day, and stopped at the end of each furrow to kneel and pray. Finally, he cried, "Lord, save me. I am lost." He heard an inner voice say, "I come to seek and to save that which is lost."[6] This gave Boehm a sense of joy and assurance that he was, indeed, loved by God. He began preaching in German settlements in Pennsylvania and Maryland, and was made a bishop in the Mennonite church in 1759. Boehm was preaching in the barn at Isaac Long's farm on Pentecost in 1776. Phillip William Otterbein attended the service. After the benediction, he threw his arms around Boehm and cried, "Wir sind bruder." (We are brethren.)　From this moment eventually came the Church of the United Brethren in Christ.

The Evangelical Church grew out of the ministry of Jacob Albright, a German Lutheran. He was farming in Lancaster County, Pennsylvania, when several of his children died in an epidemic of dysentery. He saw this as an act of punishment from God, one which Albright could not understand. After listening to Otterbein and other German evangelicals preach, he finally met with Adam Riegel, a lay preacher of the United Brethren Church, for prayer and counsel, until he found spiritual victory. He then joined the Methodist class that met in the home of a neighbor, Isaac Davis. Albright soon became a Methodist lay preacher and began preaching to the German-speaking people. Three classes which he organized, with a total of twenty members, formed a separate organization in 1800, known as the Albright people. At first they called themselves Methodists, but later became known as the Evangelical Association.

United Brethren, Evangelicals, and Methodists all had a close working relationship. Otterbein and Asbury were close personal friends, and Otterbein laid his hand on Asbury in ordination. Together, they worked on a discipline for church members, which became the basis of the *Book of Discipline* for all three bodies. In fact, Lovely Lane Chapel, where the first Methodist conference was held and where Asbury was ordained, was organized in Otterbein's church in Baltimore. Asbury and Albright were also close friends, as were Asbury and Martin Boehm. In fact, Boehm's son, Henry, was a Methodist preacher who often traveled with Asbury.

Given the close relationships, why did the three groups go separate ways? One reason is language. Evangelical and United Brethren preachers felt called to preach to Germans in German. Asbury thought the German language would soon die out in America, and was not interested in setting up German-speaking congregations. A second reason was that the leaders all died too soon. Albright died in

1807, Boehm in 1812, Otterbein in 1813, and Asbury in 1816. Their followers were then caught up in following the frontier and establishing new congregations among those frontiersmen who spoke English (Methodists) or German (Evangelicals and United Brethren).

After a long and glorious history, the Evangelicals and United Brethren came together in 1946 to form the Evangelical United Brethren Church. Then, in 1968, they joined with the Methodist Church to become the present-day United Methodist Church.

The first United Brethren class known in Missouri was organized by John Everhart in Clark County in 1851. He was a member of the Iowa conference, and his work covered southern Iowa and northern Missouri. In that same year, the Sandusky Conference gave Bishop Glossbrenner one hundred twenty-six dollars to be used in Missouri, if he could find a suitable missionary. The first regular preaching in Missouri was in Jasper County, in the southwest corner of the state. Several United Brethren families, including some local preachers, had moved to this area and established a meeting in the home of John Harris.

In 1852, the Miami (Ohio) Conference elected Henry Kumler Jr. as the presiding elder for Missouri and sent him off to Jasper County. Kumler soon returned to the Miami Conference and raised money to buy materials to build a church building. Josiah Terrell, of the Illinois Conference, was appointed to Jasper County in 1853, and soon began preaching in that area and into "Indian Territory" near the present Fort Scott, Kansas. He reported to the Mission Board that being in a slave state was not a hindrance to the work, since very few of the people held slaves, and the majority were opposed to slavery. He also preached regularly to the Cherokee Indians and won several of them to the church.

On November 3, 1854, the Missouri Mission Conference was organized in Jasper County, with three ordained and two local preachers. The minutes of the Mission Board for 1856 say about Missouri:

> The Missouri Mission Conference consists of four ministers, exclusive of those connected with it who labor in Kansas. They have nobly maintained the doctrines and discipline of the church, upon the question of slavery not excepted. The "gold fever" carried off for a time a large number of the people from southwestern Missouri and Arkansas. This manipulated some-what against the work. But the greatest difficulties have arisen out of the violent and protracted agitation growing out of the repeal of the Missouri Compromise. . . . Our dear missionaries have been repeatedly threatened with violence if they did not desist from preaching.[7]

The effects of the Missouri Compromise repeal would continue to hinder the work of the United Brethren missionaries. They were staunchly opposed to slavery, which made them targets in a volatile society that was gearing up for a military defense of the institution.

The General Conference of 1857 set up a separate Missouri Conference, with the border between Missouri and Iowa also becoming the boundary line between the conferences. The Missouri Conference apparently covered only the territory from the Missouri River to Iowa, and did not include the missions in Jasper County. The work in Jasper County, the "Missouri Mission Conference," was put under the supervision of the Kansas Conference. The Missouri Conference (north of the river) was formally organized at Atlanta, in Macon County, in 1859. The conference grew. In 1861, there were eighty appointments (places for preaching), fifty-eight classes, and 1,001 members. In 1862, there was a net gain of 171 members. The preachers were sure that Missouri would be a free state, and needed a free church. The session of the Annual Conference in 1865 reported 1,337 members, and this grew to 2,382 in 1867.

In 1869, all of Missouri south of the Missouri River, plus three tiers of counties from southern Kansas were joined to become the Osage Conference. In that same year, the United Brethren began an academy at Avalon, Missouri, which became Avalon College in 1881. In 1890, the college moved to Trenton, where it continued until 1904. Later the buildings housed Trenton Junior College, now North Central Missouri Community College.

In 1881, the Missouri part of the Osage Conference was made the Southwest Missouri Mission Conference. By 1897, the conference had 1,450 members. That year it was united with the Missouri Conference, so that there was one United Brethren Conference for the entire state. At the end of 1966, the Missouri Conference had twenty-one charges, including one in Arkansas and two in Louisiana. There were seventeen preachers under appointment, and 2,787 members.

Chapter 12

PERSONAL
REFLECTIONS

The book is over, but the whole story has not been told. Every reader will see something that has been left out. The role of women in church leadership, for example, from the Women's Foreign Missionary Society to United Methodist Women, is not included. That story, in itself, could be an entire volume. There is little here about all the colleges that the various branches of Methodism founded, or about other institutions of ministry and service. This book has not told about the China mission of the Methodist Episcopal Church, South, or about all the dedicated men and women who went from Missouri to the mission field. There is material in plenty for at least another volume in this series. But this volume has come to an end. It has been a delight to research and write, and I am indebted to the Commissions on Archives and History of the two conferences for the opportunity.

One question still haunts me as I write these final words: What happened? How was it that such a strong church declined so quickly? In the late twentieth century, even as we began all kinds of new ministries, reaching out to people who had not known the ministry of God's Church for a long time, we lost members. And we lost them not by the handful, but by the hundreds. Year after year. What happened?

Part of the reason is demographic. People move and do not always connect with a church after their move. But that very statement suggests a mission and a strategy for keeping persons in the church. Part of the reason for the decline is death. Our members have died at a faster rate than we have replaced them. Part of the reason is cultural. The revival of the seventies, with its focus on spirituality without religion, meant that the energies of a generation were not offered to the service of the church. Part of the reason is what Bishop Frank called "the life going out of us." How and where did we lose our power?

We lost members when the population of the country was growing. The ministries of service and advocacy we developed were important ministries, but they seemed to take us away from the quest for souls. Perhaps there was not enough energy for both. And yet, John Wesley was able to spend his life preaching the gospel, winning souls for Christ, building up a church—and fighting against slavery, establishing schools and medical clinics, raising money for the poor, and working for child labor laws. Even when both Northern and Southern Methodists were caught up in the pre-war struggle over property rights, both churches continued to grow rapidly. What has happened to us?

So, were the old days better? I doubt it. In fact, John Wesley, Jacob Lanius, and Andrew Monroe might well wonder at, and be envious of, the mission and ministry of today's United Methodist Church. But the fire seems to be gone. The life has gone out of us, in part, because our spirit and energy have been sapped by all the demands and frustrations of our society. We are tired of fighting the good fight, of opening doors only to have them slammed in our faces. We are, indeed, weary in well-doing.

What haunts me, still, is the issue of the passion for souls. I believe that numbers are important—that's why you've seen so many of them throughout these essays. Numbers are important because each number represents another person won to faith in Jesus Christ and commitment to the church. It is said that in 1816, Bishop McKendree changed the mission of the Methodist Church, putting evangelism ahead of reform (where they had been equal before). That change apparently "lit the fire" for Methodism's phenomenal growth in the nineteenth century. I sometimes think that, today, we have put reform (and service) far ahead of evangelism. The Christmas Conference—and Bishop Asbury—certainly intended for reform and evangelism to be of equal importance to the church.

As I researched and wrote this book, I learned one lesson, above all others. In the period from 1844 to 1870, the northern and southern branches of the church demonized each other. Each side saw the other as the source of the problems in church and society. Each side used carefully selected proof texts to make their case and to hurl at the other side. The result was anguish, separation, and wounds that took generations to heal. I grieve that we still have not learned that painful lesson, that we continue to hurl Scripture at each other, and that we try to exclude those who disagree with us. If we learn only one thing from our history, may this be the lesson: we are brothers and sisters in Christ and in the United Methodist Church, no matter how much we may disagree with each other.

Having said that, I want to close with words of hope. "The Order for Confirmation and Reception Into the Church" in the 1964 hymnal began with these words:

Dearly beloved, the Church is of God, and will be preserved to the end of time, for the conduct of worship and the due administration of his Word and

Sacraments, the maintenance of Christian fellowship and discipline, the edification of believers, and the conversion of the world. All, of every age and station, stand in need of the means of grace which it alone supplies.[1]

God is not yet through with the United Methodist Church. We will continue in existence so long as God has a purpose for us. May we always be faithful in those things to which God has called us.

ENDNOTES

Chapter 1

The primary sources for this chapter are: Woodall, *Annals of Methodism in Missouri*; Godbey, *Pioneer Methodism in Missouri*; Tucker, *A Sketch of the Life of the Reverend John Clark*; and the conference journals.

1. Quoted in Norwood, *Sourcebook of American Methodism*, 195–96.
2. Elmer T. Clark, "Early Methodism in Missouri," *Journal of the St. Louis Annual Conference* (1960): 105–7.
3. W. A. Woodard, *Annals of Methodism in Missouri*, 30.
4. Ibid., 32.
5. Ibid., 32.
6. *The United Methodist Hymnal*, #553.

Chapter 2

The primary source for this chapter is Gooch, "Black Methodism in Missouri," and the conference journals.

1. *Minutes of the Annual Conference* (1780): 12.
2. W. W. Wrightman in the *Southern Quarterly Review*, cited by Dwight W. Culver, *Negro Segregation in the Methodist Church* (New Haven: Yale University Press, 1953): 44.
3. David Rice McAnally, *A History of Methodism in Missouri, Volume I*. (St. Louis: Advocate Publishing House, 1881): 147–48.
4. John Scripps, *Western Christian Advocate* (January 20, 1843).
5. Ibid.
6. Jacob Lanius, *The Journal of the Reverend Jacob Lanius*, ed. Elmer T. Clark, (April 1834): 21.
7. Jacob Lanius, *The Journal of the Reverend Jacob Lanius*, ed. Elmer T. Clark, (March 6, 1836): 47.
8. Ibid., 48.

9. *Minutes of the Missouri Annual Conference*, 1821. Hand-written manuscript in the manuscript collection of the Methodist Episcopal Church, Collection #2039, Missouri State Historical Society Archives, Columbia, Mo. The reliability of early records begins to appear in question here. The printed *General Minutes* show considerably fewer black members than does Scripps's hand-written copy. I have chosen to follow the manuscript copy. It must be pointed out that, at least until after 1830, one cannot be certain as to the exact figures for any given circuit in any given year. Conclusions drawn from these reports will have to remain tentative, although the data are probably sufficiently accurate to justify the conclusions.

Chapter 3

The primary sources for this chapter include: Anson, "Variations on the Indian Conflict"; Caldwell, *Annals of the Shawnee Methodist Mission and Indian Manual Labor School*; Woodard, *Annals of Methodism in Missouri*; Greene, *Life of the Reverend Jesse Greene*; and Sweet, *Religion on the American Frontier, Volume IV: The Methodists.*

1. For the story of these early missions to American Indians, see Holland N. McTyeire, *A History of Methodism* (Nashville: Publishing House of the Methodist Episcopal Church, South, 1910), 577–81.
2. The story of Indian emigration is told by Anson, "Variations on the Indian Conflict: The Effects of the Emigrant Indian Removal Policy, 1830-1854," *Missouri Historical Review, Vol. LVIV:1* (October 1964): 64–89.
3. Mary Greene, *Life, Three Sermons, and Some Miscellaneous Writings of the Reverend Jesse Greene* (Lexington, Missouri: Patterson and Julian, 1852): 61–62.
4. Ibid., 47.
5. Ibid., 45.
6. Ibid., 60.
7. Ibid., 62.
8. Ibid., 62.
9. Ibid., 63.
10. Ibid., 69.
11. William Warren Sweet, *Religion on the American Frontier, 1783–1840, IV: The Methodists* (Chicago: University of Chicago Press, 1946), 501.
12. Ibid., 507.
13. Jerome C. Berryman, *A Circuit Rider's Frontier Experience.*
14. Sweet, 536–37.
15. *Western Christian Advocate*, 1835.
16. Sweet, 516.

Chapter 4

Primary sources for this chapter include: Burnett and Leubbering, *German Settlement in Missouri*; Douglass, *The Story of German Methodism*; Fabre, *Souvenir of the West German Conference*; Kettelcamp, "German Methodism in Missouri"; and Wolff, "A History of Central Wesleyan College."

1. Robyn Burnett and Ken Luebbering, *German Settlement in Missouri: New Land, Old Ways* (Columbia: University of Missouri Press, 1996), 6–7.
2. For a detailed account of Bethel, see Gooch, "William Keil, A Strange Communal Leader," *Methodist History, Vol. V:4* (July 1967): 36–41.

3. Paul F. Douglass, *The Story of German Methodism* (New York: The Methodist Book Concern, 1939), 48–49.
4. Ibid., 54–55.
5. Ibid., 215.

Chapter 5

Primary sources for this chapter include: Sweet, *Methodism in American History*; Elliott, *Southwestern Methodism*; Redford, *History of the Organization of the Methodist Episcopal Church, South*; Baldwin, "The Methodist Episcopal Church and the Great Schism"; Winter, "The Division in Missouri Methodism in 1845"; McAnally, *History of Methodism in Missouri*; West, *Report of Debates in the General Conference of 1844*; the General Conference journals, and the conference minutes.

1. Redford, *History of the Organization of the Methodist Episcopal Church, South* (St. Louis: Advocate Publishing House, 1880), 108.
2. Ibid., x.
3. Robert A. West, *A Report of the Debates in the General Conference of the Methodist Episcopal Church, 1844* (New York: Carlton and Phillips, 1856).
4. Redford, *History*, 155.
5. Ibid., 322.
6. Ibid., 175–79.
7. Ibid.
8. Hauser Winter, "The Division in Missouri Methodism in 1845," *Missouri Historical Review* (October 1942): 9.
9. "Letters to Jacob Lanius," file in the Missouri East Conference Archives.
10. Winter, "Division," 17.
11. Andrew Monroe, *Recollections of the Reverend Andrew Monroe covering his ministry for the years of 1819 to 1870*. Original manuscript in the Clark Collection, General Commission on Archives and History, 167.
12. J. N. Norwood, *Schism in the Methodist Church, 1844: A Study of Slavery and Ecclesiastical Politics* (New York: Alfred University Press, 1928), 124–25.

Chapter 6

Primary sources for this chapter include: Parrish, Jones, and Christensen, *Missouri, The Heart of the Nation*; Stowell, *Rebuilding Zion*; Leftwich, *Martyrdom in Missouri*; Elliott, *Southwestern Methodism*; Harris, "A Remnant Shall Remain"; Sweet, *Methodism in American History; The St. Louis Christian Advocate*; Lewis, *The History of Methodism in Missouri, 1860–1870*; conference journals.

1. J. E. Godbey, *Lights and Shadows of Seventy Years* (St. Louis: St. Louis Christian Advocate Co., 1913).
2. W. M. Leftwich, *Martyrdom in Missouri, Volume I* (St. Louis: Southwestern Book and Publishing Company, 1870).
3. Ibid.
4. Godbey, *Lights and Shadows*, 51.
5. Leftwich, *Martyrdom in Missouri, Vol. II* (St. Louis: Southwestern Book and Publishing Company, 1870), 62f.
6. David W. Stowell, *Rebuilding Zion: The Religious Reconstruction of the South, 1863–1877* (New York: Oxford University Press, 1998), 29.

7. W. H. Lewis, *The History of Methodism in Missouri for a Decade of Years from 1860 to 1870* (Nashville: Publishing House of the Methodist Episcopal Church, South, 1890), 175–178.

8. *St. Louis Christian Advocate,* December 7, 1865.

9. "One Who Was There," quoted in Brunner, *The Union of the Churches,* 67–68.

Chapter 7

1. "Things As They Were," *St. Louis Christian Advocate* 2:28 (March 17, 1853).

2. *St. Louis Christian Advocate* (March 31, 1853).

3. J. E. Godbey, *Pioneer Methodism in Missouri* (Kirkwood: William P. Mason, 1929), 47–48.

4. *The Journal of the Reverend Jacob Lanius,* 21.

5. *The St. Louis Christian Advocate* (October 28, 1852), 4.

6. *The St. Louis Christian Advocate* (December 23, 1852), 74.

7. Charles F. Deems, ed. *Annals of Southern Methodism for 1855* (New York: J. A. Gray's Fire-Proof Printing Office, 1856), 263.

8. Walter N. Vernon, *Methodism in Arkansas, 1816–1976* (Little Rock: Joint Committee for the History of Arkansas Methodism, 1976), 12.

9. J. C. Simmons, *The History of Southern Methodism on the Pacific Coast* (Nashville: Southern Methodist Publishing House, 1886), 15.

10. Albea Godbold, "Table of Methodist Annual Conferences, USA," *Methodist History* 3:1 (October 1969): 25–26.

Chapter 8

Primary sources for this chapter include: Hudzinki, "Missouri Methodists and the Uniting Conference"; *Journal of the Uniting Conference of the Methodist Episcopal Church, Methodist Episcopal Church, South, and Methodist Protestant Church*; Maser, "The Story of Unification, 1874–1939"; *The Christian Century; The Christian Advocate;* and Moore, *The Long Road to Methodist Union.*

1. Frederick E. Maser, "The Story of Unification, 1874-1939," in *The History of American Methodism, Volume 3* (New York and Nashville: Abingdon Press, 1964), 441.

2. Ibid., 455.

3. *Minutes of the Missouri Annual Conference, Methodist Episcopal Church,* 1938 (New York: Carlton and Porter, n.d.)

4. *Journal of the Uniting Conference of the Methodist Episcopal Church, Methodist Episcopal Church, South, and Methodist Protestant Church* (New York and Nashville: The Methodist Publishing House, 1939), 205.

5. Ibid., 399–400.

6. *The Christian Century* (May 24, 1938), 662–64.

Chapter 9

Primary sources for this chapter include: Holt, *The Missouri Bishops; Biographical Directory of United Methodist Bishops, Spouses, and Widows;* Leete, *Methodist Bishops, Personal Notes and Biography;* Biographical materials from Monk Bryan, A. F. Mutti, and Mrs. Ina Schowengerdt.

1. Ivan Lee Holt, *The Missouri Bishops* (Nashville: The Parthenon Press, 1953), 3–39.

2. ———— . *Eugene Russell Hendrix: Servant of the Kingdom* (Nashville: The Parthenon Press, 1950), 59.

3. "The Story of the Ministry of Bishop Ivan Lee Holt," 6.

Chapter 10

Primary sources for this chapter include: Parrish, Jones, and Christensen, *Missouri: The Heart of a Nation;* Nagel, *Missouri: A History;* Brokaw, *The Greatest Generation;* the *Journals* of the General Conferences, and the *Minutes* of the annual conferences.

1. For the full report on the Crusade for Christ, see *Journal of the 1944 General Conference of the Methodist Church* (Nashville: The Methodist Publishing House, 1944), 775f.
2. *Minutes of the Missouri Annual Conference,* 1944.
3. *Minutes of the Saint Louis Annual Conference,* 1944.
4. Interview with John W. Ward Jr. (June 1999).

Chapter 11

Primary sources for this chapter include: the *Journals* of the General Conferences; the *Minutes* of the Annual Conferences; interview with Bishop Eugene M. Frank; source documents provided by Central Methodist College, St. Paul School of Theology, the Missouri United Methodist Foundation, and the Area Office of Creative Ministries; for the Evangelical United Brethren, Milhouse, "The Historical Background of Evangelical United Brethren-Methodist Union," and Newland, "History of the Missouri Conference."

1. Interview with Bishop Eugene M. Frank (May 1998).
2. Ibid.
3. Ibid.
4. Ibid
5. "Service of Inauguration of Don W. Holter as President, National Methodist Theological Seminary," contains addresses by Dr. Henry Pitney Van Dusen, Bishop Donald H. Tippett, and President Don W. Holter. (n.p.: 1959).
6. Paul W. Milhouse, "The Historical Background of Evangelical United Brethen-Methodist Union," *Journal of the Missouri West Conference* (1965): 113–17.
7. Lowell, Newland, "History of the Missouri Conference," in Marvin M. Polson and William J. Dale, eds. *A Summary of the Histories of the Annual Conferences of the former Evangelical United Brethren Church within the Bounds of the South Central Jurisdiction, The United Methodist Church.* Paper presented at the Historical Workshop of the South Central Jurisdiction, (June 17–18, 1968): 2.

Chapter 12

1. *The United Methodist Hymnal,* 1964, # 829.

BIBLIOGRAPHY

A History of the Methodist Church in Southeast Missouri. Unpublished manuscript in the Missouri East Conference Archives.

Agnew, Theodore L. "Methodism on the Frontier." In *The History of American Methodism.* Vol. 1. New York and Nashville: Abingdon Press, 1964. 488–545.

Ahlstrom, Sidney. *A Religious History of the American People.* New Haven: Yale University Press, 1972.

Anderson, James W. and Samuel Warner. *The Methodist Episcopal Church in Missouri: Its Heroes, Its Struggles, and Its Victories.* Kirksville, Mo.: Journal Printing Company, 1935.

"Another Church Wanted." *St. Louis Christian Advocate* 2:10 (28 October 1852).

Anson, Bert. "Variations of the Indian Conflict: The Effects of the Emigrant Indian Removal Policy, 1830–1854." *Missouri Historical Review.* Vol. 59:1 (October 1964): 64–89.

Bagnall, Norma Hayes. *On Shaky Ground: The New Madrid Earthquakes of 1811–1812.* Columbia: University of Missouri Press, 1996.

Bailey, Louis C. "The Clint Hawkins Years—The Foundation's Beginnings, Mission, and Church Relationship." Missouri United Methodist Foundation, 1997. Mimeographed.

Baldwin, Glenn. "The Methodist Episcopal Church and the Great Schism." *Journal of the Missouri Annual Conference* (1958): 156–63.

Bawley, James P. *Two Centuries of Methodist Concern: Bondage, Freedom, and Education of Black People.* New York: Vantage Press, 1974. 35.

Behney, J. Bruce and Paul H. Eller, *The History of the Evangelical United Brethren Church.* Nashville: Abingdon Press, 1979.

Benjamin, Walter W. "The Methodist Episcopal Church in the Postwar Era." *The History of American Methodism*, ed. Emory Stevens Bucke. Vol. 2. Nashville: Abingdon Press, 1964. 315–80.

Biographical Directory of United Methodist Bishops, Spouses, and Widows. Office of the Secretary, Council of Bishops, November 1981.

Boogher, Sophia Hogan. *Recollections of John Hogan.* St. Louis: Mound City Press, 1927.

Brokaw, Tom. *The Greatest Generation.* New York: Random House, 1998.

Bruce, Dickson, Jr. "Christianity on the Early American Frontier." *Christian History* (February 1995). Online document.

Brunner, John H. *The Union of the Churches.* New York: Phillips and Hunt, 1886.

Bucke, Emory Stevens, ed. *The History of American Methodism.* 3 vols. New York and Nashville: Abingdon Press, 1964.

Burnett, Robyn and Ken Luebbering. *German Settlement in Missouri: New Land, Old Ways.* Columbia: University of Missouri Press, 1996.

Caldwell, Martha B. *Annals of Shawnee Methodist Mission and Indian Manual Labor School.* Topeka, Kansas: Kansas State Historical Society, 1939.

Cameron, Richard M. "The Church Divides, 1844, Sections 1–4." In *The History of American Methodism.* Vol. 2. New York and Nashville: Abingdon Press, 1964. 11–47.

Candler, Warren A. *Great Revivals and the Great Republic.* Nashville: Publishing House of the Methodist Episcopal Church, South, 1904.

Clark, Elmer T. "Early Methodism in Missouri." *Journal of the St. Louis Annual Conference* (1960).

Crenshaw, Floyd. "Methodist Thought in Missouri in the Nineteenth Century." *Toward the Setting Sun* Vol. 2:2 (Spring 1984): 1–17.

Culbreth, J. M. *Studies in Methodist History.* Nashville: Cokesbury Press, 1925.

Culver, Dwight W. *Negro Segregation in the Methodist Church.* New Haven: Yale University Press, 1953.

Daily Christian Advocate, the Uniting Conference of 1939. The Methodist Book Concern, Publisher, Punton Bros. Publishing Co., Printers, 1939.

DeArmond, Fred. "Reconstruction in Missouri." *Missouri Historical Review* 61:3 (April 1967): 364–77.

Deems, Charles F., ed. *Annals of Southern Methodism for 1855.* New York: J. A. Gray's Fire-Proof Printing Office, 1856.

Douglass, Paul F. *The Story of German Methodism.* New York: The Methodist Book Concern, 1939.

Elliott, Charles. *Southwestern Methodism: A History of the M. E. Church in the South-West from 1844 to 1864.* Cincinnati: Poe and Hitchcock, 1868.

Erwin, James Otis, ed. *The Final Journal of the Central West Conference, the Methodist Church.* Little Rock, Arkansas: n.p., 1966.

Fabre, Irene, trans. *Souvenir of the West German Conference.* Typescript by Theodore H. Wolff, n. d., n. p.

Faherty, Justin L. "The Story of the Ministry of Bishop Ivan Lee Holt." *The Saint Louis Globe-Democrat Magazine* (19 February 1956).

Ferguson, Charles W. *Organizing to Beat the Devil: Methodism and the Making of America.* Garden City, New York: Doubleday and Company, 1971.

Finney, T. M. *Life and Labors of Bishop Marvin.* n.p., n.d.

Foley, William E. *A History of Missouri. Volume I: 1673–1820.* Columbia: University of Missouri Press, 1971.

Fortieth Anniversary and Patriotic Number: Official Minutes of the St. Louis German Conference. Cincinnati: The Methodist Book Concern Press, 1918.

Frank, Eugene M. "Making History." *Toward the Setting Sun* 8:1 (Fall 1989): 1–9.

Frank, Eugene M., conversation with author, Kansas City, Mo., 27 May 1998.

Frank, Eugene M. and Don W. Holter. *A History of the Beginnings of Saint Paul School of Theology.* Introduction by Lovett H. Weems Jr. Produced by Saint Paul School of Theology, n.d. Videocassette.

Fuller, Erasmus Q. *An Appeal to the Records: a Vindication of the Methodist Episcopal Church in its Policy and Proceedings Toward the South.* Cincinnati: Hitchcock and Walden, 1876.

Garber, Paul Neff. *The Legal and Historical Aspects of the Plan of Union.* Greensboro, N.C.: Piedmont Press, 1938.

Gewehr, Wesley M. "Some Factors in the Expansion of Frontier Methodism, 1800–1811." *Journal of Religion* 8 (1928): 98–120.

Gladwell, Penelope. "The Beginnings of Methodism in St. Louis, 1798–1822." *Toward the Setting Sun* 1:1 (October 1982).

Glazier, Robert C. "Methodism in Springfield." *Toward the Setting Sun* 2:2 (Spring 1984): 23–33.

Godbey, J. E. *Pioneer Methodism in Missouri.* Kirkwood: William P. Mason, 1929.

———. *Lights and Shadows of Seventy Years.* St. Louis: St. Louis Christian Advocate Co., 1913.

Godbold, Albea. "Bishop Ivan Lee Holt, World Traveler and Devotee of Church Cooperation." *Toward the Setting Sun* 7:1 (Fall 1988): 1–8.

———. "Enoch Mather Marvin—Dedicated Genius." *Journal of the Missouri East Annual Conference* (1963): 151–61.

————. "Table of Methodist Annual Conferences, USA." *Methodist History* 3:1 (October 1969): 25–26.

Gooch, John O. "Black Methodism in Missouri, 1807–1844." *Toward the Setting Sun* 1:1 (October 1982): 7–31.

————. "Missouri—Mother of Conferences." *Toward the Setting Sun* 4:1 (October 1985): 1–22.

————. "Pioneer Circuits in Missouri." *Toward the Setting Sun* 1:2 (Spring 1983): 22–26.

————. "William Keil, A Strange Communal Leader." *Methodist History* 5:4 (July 1967): 36–41.

Gray, Marcus L. *The Centennial Volume of Missouri Methodism: Methodist Episcopal Church, South.* Kansas City: Burd and Fletcher Printing Co., 1906.

Greene, Mary. *Life, Three Sermons, and some of the miscellaneous writings of Rev. Jesse Greene.* Lexington, Missouri: Patterson and Julian, 1852.

Greene, Lorenzo J., Gary F. Kremer, and Antonio F. Holland. *Missouri's Black Heritage.* St. Louis: Forum Press, 1963.

Harmon, Nolan B. "The Organization of the Methodist Episcopal Church, South." In *The History of American Methodism, Volume 2.* New York and Nashville: Abingdon Press, 1964. 86–143.

Harris, G. Gay. "A Remnant Shall Remain." *Toward the Setting Sun* 4:1 (October 1985): 23–49.

Harrison, Wm. P. *The Gospel Among the Slaves.* Nashville: Publishing House of the Methodist Episcopal Church, South, 1848.

Hartzell, Joseph C. "Methodism and the Negro in the United States." *Journal of Negro History* 8 (July 1923): 310–15.

History of the Organization of the Methodist Episcopal Church, South, with the Journal of Its First General Conference. Nashville: Publishing House, Methodist Episcopal Church, South, 1925.

"History of Town and Country in Missouri, 1952–1963." Mimeograph. n.a., n.d.

Holt, Ivan Lee. *Eugene Russell Hendrix: Servant of the Kingdom.* Nashville: The Parthenon Press, 1950.

————. "Glimpses of Missouri Methodism—Divided and United." *Journal of the St. Louis Annual Conference* (1955): 104–11.

————. *The History and Mission of Kingdom House.* Kingdom House: 1953.

————. *The Missouri Bishops.* Nashville: The Parthenon Press, 1953.

Hudzinski, Nancy R. "Missouri Methodists and the Uniting Conference: Kansas City, Mo: April 26–May 10, 1939." *Toward the Setting Sun* 3:1 (September 1984): 23–47.

Johnson, Charles A. *The Frontier Camp Meeting: Religion's Harvest Time.* Dallas: Southern Methodist University Press, 1984.

Jones, Arthur E. Jr. "The Years of Disagreement, 1844–61." In *The History of American Methodism Volume 2.* New York and Nashville: 1964. 144–205.

Jones, Preston C., Sr. *The Ethnic Minority Local Church: The United Methodist Church, the Missouri West Conference.* Kansas City, Mo.: n.d., n.p.

Journal of the First General Conference of the Methodist Church, 1940. Nashville: The Methodist Publishing House, 1940.

Journal of the 1944 General Conference of the Methodist Church. Nashville: The Methodist Publishing House, 1944.

Journal of the 1948 General Conference of the Methodist Church. Nashville: The Methodist Publishing House, 1948.

Journal of the Uniting Conference of the Methodist Episcopal Church, Methodist Episcopal Church, South, and Methodist Protestant Church. New York and Nashville: The Methodist Publishing House, 1939.

Kettelkamp, Oscar F. "German Methodism in Missouri." *Minutes of the Missouri Annual Conference,* 1957.

King, Willis J. "The Negro Membership of the (Former) Methodist Church in the (New) United Methodist Church." *Methodist History* 7:3 (April 1969): 32–43.

Kingdom House, 80th Anniversary, 1902–1982. Kingdom House, 1982. Mimeograph.

Lane, Martha. "Ozark Summer Ministry." *Together* (June 1968): 33–40.

Lanius, Jacob. *The Journal of the Reverend Jacob Lanius.* ed. Elmer T. Clark, 1918. Transcribed and re-edited Theodore H. Wolff, 1963. Mimeograph.

Leete, Frederick DeLand. *Methodist Bishops: Personal Notes and Bibliography.* Nashville: The Parthenon Press, 1948.

Leftwich, W. M. *Martyrdom in Missouri, Volume I.* Saint Louis: Southwestern Book and Publishing Company, 1870.

———. *Martyrdom in Missouri, Volume II.* Saint Louis: Southwestern Book and Publishing Company, 1870.

Leiffer, Murray H., *The Methodist Churches of St. Louis: Central West Conference.* Evanston, Ill.: Bureau of Social and Religious Research, 1956.

Lewis, W. H. *The History of Methodism in Missouri for A Decade of Years From 1860 to 1870.* Nashville: Publishing House of the Methodist Episcopal Church, South, 1890.

Lionberger, I. H. *The Annals of St. Louis, 1764–1928.* n.p., 1929.

Lippy, Charles H. "The Camp Meeting in Transition: The Character and Legacy of the Late Nineteenth Century." *Methodist History* 34:1 (October 1995): 3–17.

Longstreth, Mary K. "Camp Jo-Ota: A History." *Toward the Setting Sun* 1:2 (May 1983): 1–17.

Luccock, Halford E. and Paul Hutchinson. *The Story of Methodism*. New York: The Methodist Book Concern, 1926.

March, David D. *The History of Missouri, Volume I*. New York: Lewis Historical Publishing Co., 1967.

Margaret, E. C., Friedrich Munz, and George B. Uddicks. *Jubilaumsbuch der St. Louis Deutschen Konferenz*. Cincinnati: Jennings and Graham, n.d.

Martin, Sandy Dwayne. "Black Churches and the Civil War: Theological and Ecclesiastical Significance of Black Methodist Involvement, 1861–1865." *Methodist History* Vol. 32:3 (April 1994): 174–86.

Maser, Frederick E. "The Story of Unification, 1874–1939." In *The History of American Methodism, Volume 3*. New York and Nashville: Abingdon Press, 1964. 407–78.

Maurer-Batjer, Christiane. "The United Brethren in Christ: North Missouri Conference. Fifty Years of Service." *Toward the Setting Sun* 3:1 (September 1984): 1–19.

May, James W. "The War Years." In *The History of American Methodism*. 206–256. New York and Nashville: Abingdon Press, 1964.

McAnally, David Rice. *History of Methodism in Missouri, Volume I*. Saint Louis: Advocate Publishing House, 1881.

McCandless, Perry. *A History of Missouri*. Vol. 2: 1820–1860. Columbia: University of Missouri Press, 1972.

———. *The Missouri Experience*. Davenport, Iowa: Bowden Brothers, Inc., 1978.

McDowell, Gary. *Mistakes in Frank C. Tucker's Old McKendree Chapel and The Methodist Church in Missouri, 1789–1939*. Mimeograph.

McGettigan, James W. Jr. "Boone Co. Slaves: Sales, Estate Divisions, and Families, 1829–1865, Part I." *Missouri Historical Review* 72:2 (January 1978).

McReynolds, Edwin C. *Missouri: A History of the Crossroads State*. Norman: University of Oklahoma Press, 1962.

McTyeire, Holland N. *A History of Methodism*. Nashville: Publishing House of the Methodist Episcopal Church, South, 1910.

"Methodists Open Uniting Session." *The Christian Century* (10 May 1939): 615–16.

"Methodist Reunion." *The Christian Century* (26 April 1939): 534–535.

"Methodists Rush New Legislation." *The Christian Century* (17 May 1939): 648.

Milhouse, Paul W. "The Historical Background of Evangelical United Brethren-Methodist Union." *Journal of the Missouri West Conference, 1965*. 113–17.

Minutes and Historical Review of the St. Louis German Conference of the Methodist Episcopal Church. Warrenton, Mo: Banner Publishing Co., 1925.

Minutes of the Annual Conferences of the Methodist Episcopal Church, 1852–1855. New York: Carlton and Porter, n.d.

Minutes of the Annual Conferences of the Methodist Episcopal Church, 1856–1857. New York: Carlton and Porter, n.d.

Minutes of the Annual Conferences of the Methodist Episcopal Church, 1858–1859. New York: Carlton and Porter, n.d.

Minutes of the Annual Conferences of the Methodist Episcopal Church for 1860. New York: Carlton and Porter, 1860.

Minutes of the Annual Conferences of the Methodist Episcopal Church for 1865. New York: Carlton and Porter, 1865.

Minutes of the Annual Conferences of the Methodist Episcopal Church for 1874. New York: Nelson and Phillips, 1874.

Minutes of the Annual Conferences of the Methodist Episcopal Church, 1885. New York: Phillips and Hunt, 1885.

Minutes of the Annual Conferences of the Methodist Episcopal Church, 1894. New York: Hunt and Eaton, 1894.

Minutes of the Annual Conferences of the Methodist Episcopal Church, Volume I, 1773–1828. New York: T. Mason and G. Lane, 1840.

Minutes of the Annual Conferences of the Methodist Episcopal Church, South, 1858–1865. Nashville: Southern Methodist Publishing House, 1866.

Minutes of the Annual Conferences of the Methodist Episcopal Church, South, for the Year 1845–1846. Nashville: Southern Methodist Publishing House, 1847.

Minutes of the Annual Conferences of the Methodist Episcopal Church, South, 1866–1873. Nashville: Southern Methodist Publishing House, 1873.

Minutes of the Annual Conferences of the Methodist Episcopal Church, South, 1874–1878. Nashville: Southern Methodist Publishing House, 1879.

Minutes of the Annual Conferences of the Methodist Episcopal Church, South, 1885–1889. Nashville: Southern Methodist Publishing House, 1890.

Minutes of the Annual Conferences of the Methodist Episcopal Church, South, 1894. Nashville: Publishing House of the Methodist Episcopal Church, South, 1894.

Minutes of the Council of Bishops, The Methodist Church. H. Lester Smith, Secretary. Kansas City, (April 1939).

Minutes of the Missouri Annual Conference, 1821. Handwritten manuscript in the manuscript collection of the Methodist Episcopal Church, Collection #2039, Missouri State Historical Society Archives, Columbia, Mo.

Minutes of the St. Louis Annual Conference, 1940–1961.

Minutes of the Missouri Annual Conference, 1940–1961.

Minutes of the Southwest Missouri Annual Conference, 1940–1961.

Minutes of the Missouri East Annual Conference, 1961–1989.

Minutes of the Missouri West Annual Conference, 1961–1989.

"Missouri United Methodist Foundation, Statement of Mission"

Mitchell, Joseph. "Southern Methodist Newspapers during the Civil War." *Methodist History* 11 (January 1973): 20–39.

Monroe, Andrew. *Recollections of the Reverend Andrew Monroe covering his ministry for the years 1819 to 1870.* Original manuscript in the Clark Collection, General Commission on Archives and History.

Montgomery, J. C., Jr. "Ivan Lee Holt, Evangelist." *Toward the Setting Sun* 7:1 (Fall 1988): 26–28.

Moore, John M. *The Long Road to Methodist Union.* New York and Nashville: Abingdon-Cokesbury, 1943.

Nagel, Paul C. *Missouri: A History.* Reprint of *Missouri: A Bicentennial History.* University of Kansas Press, 1977.

Neely, Thomas B. *American Methodism: Its Divisions and Unification.* New York: Fleming H. Revell, Co., 1915.

Newland, Lowell. "History of the Missouri Conference," in *A Summary of the Histories of the Annual Conferences of the former Evangelical United Brethren Church within the Bounds of the South Central Jurisdiction, The United Methodist Church,* eds. Marvin M. Polson and William J. Dale (Paper presented at the Historical Workshop of the South Central Jurisdiction, June 17–18, 1968). Manuscript in the Missouri West Conference Archives, Central Methodist College, Fayette, Mo.

Norton, Wesley. "The Central Christian Advocate of the Methodist Episcopal Church in St. Louis." *Methodist History* 3:2 (January 1965): 39–49.

Norwood, Frederick A., ed. *Sourcebook of American Methodism.* Nashville: Abingdon Press, 1982.

———. *The Story of American Methodism.* Nashville: Abingdon Press, 1974.

Norwood, J. N. *Schism in the Methodist Church, 1844: A Study of Slavery and Ecclesiastical Politics.* New York: Alfred University Press, 1928.

Paine, Robert. *Life and Times of William McKendree.* Nashville: Southern Methodist Publishing House, 1922.

Parrish, William E. *A History of Missouri, Volume III: 1860–1875.* Columbia: University of Missouri Press, 1973.

————. *Missouri Under Radical Rule, 1865–1870.* Columbia: University of Missouri Press.

————. Charles T. Jones Jr., and Lawrence O. Christensen. *Missouri: The Heart of a Nation,* 2nd ed. Wheeling, Illinois: Harlan Davidson, Inc., 1992.

Posey, Walter Brownlow. *The Development of Methodism in the Old Southwest, 1783–1824.* Tuscaloosa, Alabama: Weatherford Printing Company, 1933.

————. "The Earthquake of 1811 and Its Influence on Evangelistic Methods in the Churches of the Old South." *Tennessee Historical Magazine.* (Spring 1952): 107–114.

Ransford, Charles Orrin. *John Scripps: Methodist Preacher—Newspaperman.* Shelbina, Mo., n.p., 1960.

Redford, A. H. *History of the Organization of the Methodist Episcopal Church, South.* St Louis: Advocate Publishing House, 1880.

St. Louis Christian Advocate, 1852 following. Collection in the Library of Central Methodist College, Fayette, Mo.

Seaton, Richard A. and Dorothy A. Bass. *Hallelujah in the Forest.* Acton, Mass.: Tapestry Press, Ltd., 1993.

Seaton, Richard. *History of the United Methodist Churches of Missouri.* Missouri Methodist Historical Society, 1984.

"Service of Inauguration of Don W. Holter as President, National Methodist Theological Seminary." Contains addresses by Dr. Henry Pitney Van Dusen, Bishop Donald H. Tippett, and President Don W. Holter. n.p., 1959.

Shippey, Frederick A. *Saint Louis Methodism, 1900–1951.* New York: Board of Missions and Church Extension, The Methodist Church, 1952.

Simmons, J. C. *The History of Southern Methodism on the Pacific Coast.* Nashville: Southern Methodist Publishing House, 1886.

Sites, John. "Church Extension Efforts of the Methodist Episcopal Church, South, in Missouri from 1865 to 1900." Unpublished manuscript.

Smith, Ellwood K. "Background and Consequences of Methodist Union." *Methodist History* New Series, 2:2 (January 1964): 1–30.

Spellman, Norman W. "The Church Divides, 1844, Sections 5–7." In *The History of American Methodism, Volume 2.* 47–85. New York and Nashville: Abingdon Press, 1964.

Spencer, Claudius B. *"That They May Be One:" in Behalf of the Organic Union of American Methodism.* New York: The Methodist Book Concern, 1915.

Stowell, Daniel W. *Rebuilding Zion: The Religious Reconstruction of the South, 1863–1877.* New York: Oxford University Press, 1998.

Sweet, William Warren. *Methodism in American History.* New York: The Methodist Book Concern, 1933.

————. *The Methodist Episcopal Church and the Civil War.* Cincinnati: The Methodist Book Concern, 1912.

————. "The Methodist Episcopal Church and Reconstruction." *Journal of the Illinois State Historical Society* VII: 147–165.

————. *Religion on the American Frontier, 1783–1840. Volume IV: The Methodists.* Chicago: The University of Chicago Press, 1946.

————. *The Rise of Methodism in the West. Being the Journal of the Western Conference 1800–1811.* New York and Cincinnati: n.p., 1919.

————. *The Story of Religion in America.* New York: Harper & Row, 1950.

"The Methodist Church." *The Christian Century* (24 May 1938): 662–64.

"Things as They Were." *St. Louis Christian Advocate* 2:28 (24 February 1853): 109.

"Things as They Were." *St. Louis Christian Advocate* 2:31 (17 March 1853).

Thogmorton, James C. "Highlights from the History of Central Methodist College (Central College) from 1939 to 1989." n.p., 1999.

Thrift, Charles T. "Rebuilding the Southern Church." In *The History of American Methodism, Volume 2.* 257–314. New York and Nashville: Abingdon Press, 1964.

Tigert, John J. *Constitutional History of American Episcopal Methodism, Revised and Enlarged.* Nashville: Publishing House of the Methodist Episcopal Church, South. 1911.

Towne, Ruth Warner. "Abram Still: Missionary to the West." *Toward the Setting Sun* 2:1 (November 1983): 26–41.

Tucker, Frank C. *The Methodist Church in Missouri, 1798–1939.* Nashville: The Parthenon Press, 1966.

————. *A Sketch of the Life of The Reverend John Clark.* Pamphlet published by the Historical Societies of the Missouri East and Missouri West Annual Conferences, 1969.

VandeVenter, C. I. *Sketches of Methodism in Northwest Missouri.* St. Joseph: Combe Printing Co., 1894.

Vernon, Walter N. *Methodism Moves Across North Texas.* Historical Society, North Texas Conference, 1967.

————. *William Stevenson: Riding Preacher.* Dallas: Southern Methodist University Press, 1964.

————. *Methodism in Arkansas, 1816–1976.* Little Rock: Joint Committee for the History of Arkansas Methodism, 1976.

Wamble, G. Hugh. "Negroes and Missouri Protestant Churches." *Missouri Historical Review* 61:3 (April 1967): 321–347.

Ward, A. Sterling. "Early Methodism in Northeast Missouri." *Minutes of the St. Louis Annual Conference* (1964): 184–190.

————. "Glimpses of Our History Found in the St. Louis Christian Advocate of 1851–1854." *Methodist History, New Series* 2:2 (January 1964): 37–50.

Ward, John W. Jr., conversation with author, Ballwin, Mo., June 1999.

Waltz, Alan K. *Characteristics of Methodist Ministers and Churches in Missouri—1961.* Philadelphia: Department of Research and Survey, Division of National Missions of the Board of Missions of The Methodist Church, 1961.

Weems, Lovett H. Jr., Eugene M. Frank, and Don W. Holter. *A History of the Beginnings of Saint Paul School of Theology.* St. Paul School of Theology. Videocassette.

Wendell, Marie G. "The Camp Meeting in Missouri." *Missouri Historical Review* Vol. 37 (1943): 253–70.

West, Melvin. *Creative Ministries Is . . .* 1984. Mimeograph.

————. "Brief Chronological Review of the History of the Office of Creative Ministries." 1985. Mimeograph.

West, Robert A. *A Report of Debates in the General Conference of the Methodist Episcopal Church, 1844.* New York: Carlton and Phillips, 1856.

Western Christian Advocate. Copies from 1838–1848. Archival Collection of the St. Louis Public Library, St. Louis, Mo.

Whaley, Ennis, compiler. *In Those Days . . . A Historical Review of the Central West Conference.* n.p., n.d.

Wigger, John H. "Circuit Rider Ministry." *Christian History* (February 1995): www.christianityon-line.com/christianhistory/.

Winter, Anna. *Across the Wide Missouri. A Citation Saga of Missouri Methodism.* n.p., n.d.

Winter, Hauser. "The Division in Missouri Methodism in 1845." *Missouri Historical Review* (October 1942): 1–18.

————. *A History of Schism in the Methodist Episcopal Church in Missouri.* Unpublished thesis, University of Missouri, 1942.

Wolferman, Kristie C. *The Osage in Missouri.* Columbia, Mo.: University of Missouri Press, 1997.

Wolff, Theodore H. "A History of Central Wesleyan College." *Minutes of the St. Louis Annual Conference,* 1957.

————. *A Narrative of the St. Louis Annual Conference, the Methodist Church.* Unpublished manuscript in the archival collection at Central Methodist College, Fayette, Mo.

Woodard, W. S. *Annals of Methodism in Missouri.* Columbia, Mo.: E. W. Stephens, 1893.

Woodson, Carter G. *The History of the Negro Church.* 2nd ed. Washington, D. C.: Associated Publishers, 1945.

INDEX